# WOOD FURNITURE
## FINISHING
## REFINISHING
## REPAIRING

by James E. Brumbaugh

THEODORE AUDEL & CO.
a division of
HOWARD W. SAMS & CO., INC.
4300 West 62nd Street
Indianapolis, Indiana 46268

FIRST EDITION

FIRST PRINTING—1974

International Standard Book Number: 0-672-23216-2
Library of Congress Catalog Card Number: 73-91640

# Foreword

The purpose of this book is to supply the practical information needed to repair furniture and refinish wood surfaces. This book provides the reader with the knowledge he needs to accomplish these repairs and refinishing with minimum of effort and without resorting to time-consuming guesswork.

The text is arranged in a logical sequence, with an introduction to types of wood; wood finishing, with the various tools and supplies required; furniture repair, both structural and surface; veneering; inlaying; decorating furniture; and antiquing or glazing.

Each chapter is also divided into logical sections that deals with the preparation of various woods for different types of finishes; the types of stain to use and their reactions to various kinds of wood; and the selection of a finish coat. Complete chapters are presented on the step-by-step operation of antiquing, glazing, gilding, bronzing, and decorating furniture—including the process of flocking, decorating with fabric or wallpaper, and decoupage.

With the aid of this book, the reader will be able to successfully finish or refinish furniture by following the simple finish schedules listed for the particular wood finish desired.

The author is indebted to the many companies for their permission to *use* the information contained in this book. Thanks is given to the *Fine Hardwoods Association* for the many photographs they furnished of wood grain and texture.

JAMES E. BRUMBAUGH

# Contents

# Chapter 1

# Introduction to Wood Finishing

Furniture is a cultural by-product and its quality and design have long been related to the ascendency or decline of a civilization (Figs. 1 and 2). In this respect, it is similar to styles of dress, types of pottery, architecture, and other elements of the material world with which man surrounds himself. To an archaeologist or historian, these are clear indicators of cultural change and serve to supplement and verify historical data. In the absence of historical data, these cultural by-products may be the only means by which the development of a civilization can be charted.

There are many very excellent examples of furniture that date from the earliest historical periods. Some pieces have been obtained intact from tombs or have been reconstructed from remains discovered at archaeological sites. Other designs are known to us because some unknown artist saw fit to include them in a fresco, painting or in the design on a piece of pottery. All of our records, whether historical or archaeological, indicate that the development of furniture designs has been uneven, and is closely related to the level of civilization. A high level of civilization is often paralleled by innovation and experimentation in furniture design. This is particularly true during periods of economic affluence. The histories of the Roman, Chinese, and Egyptian civilizations provide us with ample evidence of the periodic fluctuations in the quality of furniture design. Western civilization presents us with more recent examples of this close parallel between the quality of furniture craftsmanship and the ascendency of a civilization. The peri-

9

od lasting from the seventeenth to the nineteenth centuries in England, France, and other countries of Europe witnessed not only the development of vast colonial empires and rapid economic growth, but also a tremendously varied development in furniture design. Some of our finest furniture styles are traced to this period in European history.

Along with the developments in the structural design of furniture, one can also trace changes in the way furniture has been finished and decorated. Some times the finish and structural design will complement one another; at other times they will strongly conflict and produce a piece of furniture that is absolutely abominable.

An example of the way structural design, the finish, and decorative effect can complement one another and result in an especially fine piece of furniture is a well-executed chair of the Regency style (1793-1830) (Fig. 3). Much of this furniture was lacquered, frequently in black, and trimmed with gilding. Unfortunately, this

Courtesy Reliance Universal, Inc.

**Fig. 1. Furniture from a contemporary dining room.**

black and gold combination became so popular with the public that it was used too extensively. The result was that it spoiled the overall appearance of furniture that was otherwise well designed.

It is always essential that a proper balance be maintained between the finish (including any decorative effect) and the structural design. One should not overwhelm the other. This is an important point to remember, because there is a strong tendency for the beginner to become overly enthusiastic particularly when decorating a piece of furniture. Too much gilding, striping, or the use of stencils that are too large or elaborate will ruin the effect one is trying to create.

## WOOD FINISHING

Wood finishing can be either the most satisfying or the most frustrating of experiences for the beginner. It is both an art and a

Courtesy Reliance Universal, Inc.

Fig. 2. Furniture in a contemporary living room.

11

skill, with the latter being acquired largely through experience and practice. However, with careful attention to detail and an understanding of the basic fundamentals of wood finishing, the beginner will achieve considerable success.

Placing some sort of finish on the wood surfaces of furniture dates from the earliest periods of history. Whether or not these first wood finishes were intended primarily as decoration or as a means of preserving the wood is unknown. The early Egyptian varnishes and Oriental lacquers probably combined both these purposes. On the other hand, the hand-rubbed sweat finishes prevalent in Europe prior to the seventeenth century provided little more than a decorative effect for the wood.

Modern wood finishes are designed to be both protective and and decorative. The nature or extent of the protection provided by the finish depends upon the type used, which in most cases is usually (but not always) determined by the intended service usage of the piece of furniture. A shellac finish, for example, does not provide the toughness and durability of varnish, enamel, or lacquer. It is therefore not advisable to use shellac on table and

**Fig. 3. Regency chair (1793-1830).**

Courtesy Reliance Universal, Inc.

desk tops, children's furniture, chair arms, and other surfaces subject to hard wear. On the other hand, shellac finishes are much easier to apply by the beginner, and are often used for this reason. It should be apparent at this point that the selection of a finish is determined by a number of interrelated factors. Since some of these factors, such as ease of application and the degree of toughness, may be conflicting in nature, the worker must choose among the best possible combinations when making the selection of the most suitable finish to use.

Some of the factors used in selecting a wood finish include the following:

1. Ease of application,
2. Cost,
3. Intended service conditions,
4. Appearance desired.

## Ease of Application

This factor is generally of primary consideration to the beginner. The experienced worker will be familiar with the problems involved when working with various finishes and will approach each accordingly. The beginner should be cautioned against placing too much importance on the ease of application. Although much is said about the difficulty of working with such finishes as varnish or lacquer, these techniques can be learned after a relatively short practice period.

## Cost

Although better quality finishing materials arc not always equated on a one-to-one basis with higher prices, you will generally discover that the better ones cost more. It is quite discouraging to find that the bargain priced finish you acquired has resulted in a curiosity you prefer to keep hidden in the attic. On the other hand, do not rush to your nearest retail supplier and purchase the most expensive item in stock. If you are acquainted with the people working there, ask their advice. They will usually be quite honest with you and will try to supply you with finishing materials that will best fulfill your needs.

## Intended Service Conditions

How is the piece of furniture to be used? In other words, to what specific service conditions will the wood surface be subjected? These are very important questions for they bear rather heavily upon your ultimate selection. Furniture that will be subjected to rough usage should be well protected by a tough finish.

13

## Appearance Desired

As a general rule, clear finishes (e.g. lacquer, varnish, shellac, etc.) are used over wood surfaces that have a particularly attractive grain pattern and/or color. The finish is designed not only to protect and to preserve the wood, but also to enhance it. The opaque and semi-opaque finishes are usually applied to surfaces with unattractive grain patterns, poor colors, or various defects that would detract from the overall appearance. Their purpose is to obscure or hide these surfaces.

Sometimes another more expensive type of wood can be imitated by applying a finish that will give this appearance. For example, white pine can be finished to imitate walnut; basswood or gum to imitate cherry; and so on. Special decorative effects can be obtained through antiquing, gilding, inlaying, and other special finishing and decorating techniques. Determine the type of appearance you desire within the limitations of the wood with which you are working, and proceed from there.

## FURNITURE KITS, PLANS, AND CABINET WOODS

Furniture kits are available from a number of different mail-order houses whose advertisements are regularly found and periodicals devoted to the homecraftsman and homeworkshop. These furniture kits are primarily reproductions of pieces from the American Colonial Period. Examples range in complexity from the rather simple canopied cradle to the more complex corner chair, drop leaf table, or settee. These furniture kits consist of parts made from higher quality woods (that is to say: cabinet woods) than the common variety of assembled unfinished furniture sold in many retail outlets. They assemble without great difficulty and present an excellent appearance when finished.

Furniture plans are also available at a modest price from the same mail-order houses. Many times these are full-size plans that do not require enlargement from a smaller size. As a result, the possibility of making an error in the pattern is practically eliminated. The better plans will include a perspective sketch indicat-

CHIPPENDALE BAIL PULL

BAIL PULL

FRENCH GILT PULL

BAIL PULL

CONCEALED TABLE HINGE

PIVOT HINGE
FOR DROP LIDS

DROP LEAF TABLE LAZY TONG HINGE

**Fig. 4. Various types of furniture hardware.**

ing how the parts are assembled as well as a complete list of materials and hardware.

Constructing a piece of furniture from a plan not only requires considerable woodworking skill, but also a source for fine cabinet woods. Once again, many of the same mail-order houses that sell furniture kits and plans also offer a wide variety of cabinet woods and veneers. Moreover, a complete line of furniture hardware and

EARLY AMERICAN        SPANISH        TRADITIONAL

Fig. 5. Examples of furniture legs available from mail-order houses.

16

trim in both contemporary and period styles can also be purchased (Fig. 4). Finally, a number of different styles of furniture legs are available to the homecraftsman. These are generally made from fine hardwoods in sizes ranging from 4 to 28 inches. Most are mounted by means of top plates or hanger bolts (Fig. 5).

As was mentioned previously, pieces of furniture assembled from kits are generally made from fine hardwoods. The quality of

Fig. 6. Examples of unfinished furniture.

the wood is such that knots and other surface imperfections are relatively rare when compared to the woods used in the cheaper pieces of assembled unfinished furniture. This results in a much better appearance when a finish is applied. Furthermore, the opportunity to use transparent finishes is both increased and encouraged.

## ASSEMBLED UNFINISHED FURNITURE

There are two general categories of assembled unfinished furniture. One category consists of pieces that are usually made from pine (Fig. 6). The wood is cheap, commonly contains knot holes and other surface imperfections, and finishing nails are used in the construction. It is this type of assembled unfinished furniture that is so easily obtainable in paint stores, hobby stores, and other retail outlets that are geared to the needs of the homecraftsman. The second category of assembled unfinished furniture is obtained from individual cabinetmakers and small furniture factories that specialize in a specific period or piece of furniture (e.g. Windsor chairs). These are of a higher quality than the cheaper pine furniture, and will be somewhat more expensive. The higher expense is generally offset by the fact that applying a finish is easier in the long run because the wood will have far fewer surface imperfections to correct. The major problem in obtaining these better quality pieces is locating a cabinetmaker or some other source that produces them. These sources usually do not advertise and will require some effort to locate. Generally, inquiries can be made at furniture stores that sell the better quality lines and at local cabinet shops.

## ANTIQUES AND REPRODUCTIONS

It is probably the dream of many amateurs to eventually obtain and refinish a genuine antique. If you *are* fortunate enough to obtain one of them, I would strongly recommend placing it in the hands of a professional finisher. A furniture store or department store that handles the higher quality, more expensive furniture lines generally sends any pieces it wants finished to a professional who specializes in this kind of work. Since these men are independent craftsmen who are employed on a contractual basis, the store will usually give their names and addresses.

Actually, finding an antique that needs refinishing is a lot more difficult than one would imagine. Antique dealers frequently do their own refinishing, so this is not a very promising source, and it certainly will not be a bargain. It would probably be more profitable to look for antiques at used furniture stores, Goodwill Stores, Salvation Army Stores, or junk dealers. Auctions and tax sales occasionally provide good antique pieces.

Locating antiques that require refinishing is difficult not only due to their scarcity, but also to the problem encountered in identifying them. The word "antique" can mean many different things to different people. For example, the average person who does not possess an extensive knowledge of furniture is quite willing to use the term very loosely, and to identify any old piece of furniture as an antique. The antique dealer, on the other hand, is more selective in the application of the term. Moreover, the dealer recognizes that antiques will vary in quality and value even though they may come from the same period. A good genuine antique is a period piece that dates from about the middle of the nineteenth century or before, and is generally an original made by a noted cabinetmaker of a particular period. In addition it will be somewhat rare, well built (though it may be in a state of disrepair when you obtain it) and aesthetically pleasing. This is an admittedly very loose definition for the word "antique", and I have no doubt that there are those who will take issue with one or more aspects of it. In any event, it will have to serve our purpose here.

Unless the buyer has a fairly extensive knowledge of antiques, he will be confronted with the problem of distinguishing them from restorations, imitations, and reproductions. A genuine antique should have all, or nearly all, of its original parts. This includes not only the wood portions but also the hardware. A missing leg, a chair slat, a drawer knob or other items may be replaced without the particular piece of furniture losing its status as an antique (*if* the replacements are kept to a minimum and are of the same material and style as the original). Extensive restoration results in a piece of furniture that becomes greatly reduced in monetary value, because the extent of its restoration has resulted in producing a copy or reproduction of the original. In other words, not enough of the original antique remains to justify identifying it as such.

Age is frequently accepted as a basic criterion for identifying a piece of furniture as an antique. However, this is only one of several factors used to make this identification. Being recognized as an original of a particular cabinetmaker is also extremely important. Every furniture style has had its imitators, many of them contemporaries of the better known cabinetmakers. Sometimes their imitations were of much poorer quality; sometimes quite excellent.

The fact that a piece of furniture is an imitation, even a poor one, does not necessarily mean that it is not an antique. It is certainly not as valuable as an original, nor is it particularly sought after by the sophisticated collector. However, the older the imitation, the greater the possibility that it is a handcrafted item. This in itself lends some value to it, and distinguishes the piece from later factory produced furniture.

Reproduction and imitations are not exactly the same thing although they may result in two pieces of furniture that are exactly identical. It is probably a question of ethics. An imitation is an attempt to copy another cabinetmaker's work and to pass it off as his own (and thereby gain financial reward if the deception is successful). A reproduction, on the other hand, is a reproduced copy of an original. No attempt is made to conceal this fact from the buyer. In fact, a reproduction is almost always advertised as such.

## SECOND-HAND FURNITURE

There is a lot of good second-hand furniture that make excellent subjects for refinishing. These are not antiques and are not especially valuable, but many second-hand pieces of furniture are well constructed and are made from good hardwoods. A few minor repairs and a new finish will often work wonders, and you will have added an interesting piece of furniture to your home. However, the value of such furniture is erratic and not easily predictable. The market value for certain pieces may increase with the passage of time. Predicting which ones will increase in value requires a good knowledge of furniture and the ability to foresee future demand.

## FINISHING SCHEDULE

All through this book you will encounter the term "finishing schedule." Each schedule is a collection of instructions given in the form of an ordered listing of the steps to be followed in applying a specific finish.

Follow these steps in the order established by the schedule. As you gain experience, you will probably change certain portions of a schedule you are using, because you will find that some things work better than others. This is a perfectly acceptable practice. Never feel bound by a finishing schedule to a form of blind obedience. Learn through experimentation. Alter your finishing schedules in accordance with what you learn.

There are hundreds of finishing schedules available to the wood finisher. Entire books have been written on the subject. Those finishing schedules included in this book are offered simply as examples for the beginner. As you gain experience in wood finishing, I would suggest keeping a card file of those finishing schedules that have proven most successful.

## TYPES OF FINISHES

All wood finishes can be grouped within one of three major categories:
1. Transparent finishes,
2. Opaque finishes,
3. Semi-opaque finishes.

A *transparent finish* (also referred to as a *clear* or *natural finish*) is one that reveals the grain and usually is the natural color

21

of the wood. It is added to the surface to protect and enhance the beauty of the wood, not obscure or hide it. Examples of transparent finishes include: (1) shellac, (2) varnish, (3) lacquer, (4) wax, (5) penetrating oil stain, and (6) boiled linseed oil.

An *opaque finish* is designed to completely obscure the wood surface. This is usually because the wood is particularly unattractive. Examples of opaque finishes include: (1) pigmented shellac, (2) pigmented lacquer, (3) enamel, and (4) paint.

A *semi-opaque finish* gives the appearance of being transparent, but really is not. In almost every case, the wood surface is either partially or completely obscured. Examples include: (1) a clear finish mixed with pigment, or (2) a pigmented wiping stain.

# Chapter 2

# Finishing Tools and Supplies

The tools and materials used in wood finishing can be as limited in scope as a retail finishing kit purchased for a specific job, or as varied in number as a completely equipped shop will require to satisfactorily do any number of different jobs. The purpose of this chapter is to give as complete a description as possible of the many different types of tools and materials available to the wood finisher. It will be your task to select among them those items required for your specific needs. Only you can properly make this selection.

## THE WORK AREA

Ideally, the work area should be free from dust, low in humidity, and have a room temperature ranging from 65°F to 75°F. Temperatures extending beyond this range tend to adversely affect the application of the finish. Basements often provide the best work areas in houses. Garages, on the other hand, frequently suffer from varying humidity, temperature and dust in the air.

The work area should always be kept well ventilated. Many finishing materials and supplies give off strong fumes that can be quite unpleasant and which can even be harmful if inhaled too long.

You should also provide yourself with enough space to work comfortably. The work area should be sufficiently isolated from other areas to prevent activities from interfering with your project.

At best, a finishing work area will constitute a separate room. The door to the room can then be shut and wet finishes allowed to dry for the required period of time without the fear of accidental marring. This is particularly true where children are present.

If it is impossible for you to locate your work area in a separate room, try to separate it from other areas either by partitions or about three to four feet of space. Once again the prime consideration is to establish a work area that will remain undisturbed by other activities. The worst situation, of course, is one in which you must constantly put away your tools, materials, and the piece you are working on.

Some finishing books recommend applying certain types of finishes, bleaches, and other coatings outdoors. The principal concern here, of course, is adequate ventilation for materials that are quite harmful when inhaled. However, you should take into consideration the fact that you will run the risk of dust and dirt blowing onto the wet surface before it has had a chance to dry. The one factor should be weighed against the other. If your indoors work area has adequate ventilation, then I would recommend working there.

Adequate storage facilities for the finishing tools, materials, and supplies are also extremely important. These storage facilities should be within easy reach of the work area. They should also be a safe distance from heat sources. Remember that many finishing materials and supplies are extremely flammable.

## PROTECTIVE CLOTHING

Always wear protective clothing when stripping or applying finishes. Old clothing is a must. No matter how careful you try to be, you will eventually, perhaps inevitably, spill or drop something on your clothes, or carelessly wipe a sleeve or another part of your clothing across a wet surface.

Some people have skin that is extremely sensitive to the various finishing supplies. Selecting a comfortable pair of rubber gloves (Fig. 1) will often eliminate skin irritations and discomfort. These can be purchased in most hardware or paint supply stores.

VINYL-COATED GLOVES

DISPOSABLE POLYETHYLENE
GLOVE

*Courtesy Singer Safety Products*

Fig. 1. Examples of protective gloves.

Filter masks (Figs. 2 and 3) are strongly recommended for use especially when spraying surfaces with paint or other finishes. Inhaling these fumes can make a person ill. In some cases, the

Fig. 2. Respirator-type mask recommended for spraying.

*Courtesy Dockson Company*

fumes are so toxic they can prove extremely dangerous. This is particularly true in the case of oxalic acid (used in bleaching wood).

## HEALTH AND SAFETY MEASURES

As was already mentioned, many finishing materials are potentially dangerous to the user's health or safety. This is attributed to the fact that they contain substances that are flammable and which can cause severe irritation or even damage to the

25

Fig. 3. A protective face mask equipped with cotton pad filters.

*Courtesy Dockson Company*

skin, eyes, and lung tissues. It is therefore necessary to take every precaution to protect yourself from these harmful effects when using. *Always* read the manufacturer's health and safety warnings on the container and *follow them to the letter*.

Bleaches can be particularly dangerous to use when not used correctly. Bleach in an undiluted solution will not only attack and destroy clothing fibers, it will also severely irritate the skin. Wearing old clothing and gloves is therefore especially important when working with a bleach. Some kind of eye protection should also be considered, because bleaches sometimes splatter. If the bleach comes in contact with the skin, wash it off *immediately* with water. Finally, bleach should be applied to bare wood *only*. When a bleach is applied over a finish (especially shellac, varnish, or lacquer), a chemical reaction resulting in spontaneous combustion may occur.

From time to time you will find it necessary to heat a finishing solution in order to prepare it for use. An example of this would be boiled linseed oil. This is usually mixed on a one-to-one basis with a flammable solvent (e.g. turpentine) and then heated to a predetermined temperature. *Always* do any of this type of heating in a container of boiling water. *Never* attempt to heat a finishing solution over an open flame or electric heating coil. The can containing the finishing material should be inserted into the

26

container containing the boiling water (Fig. 4). In this manner, any spatter from the heated finishing material will drop into the boiling water and not onto the heating coils or flame.

FINISHING MATERIAL

WATER

HEAT SOURCE

Fig. 4. Heating finishing materials.

## TACK RAGS, CLOTHS, AND PADS

Soft, clean, lint-free cloths are used at every stage in the finishing schedule to lightly dust the surface after each coat has thoroughly dried. Cheesecloth, muslin, and lint-free cotton cloths find the widest use in finishing.

Cheesecloth is frequently used to make tack rags, although other types of cloth can be substituted. The purpose of a tack rag is to pick up any dust or sanding particles that might fall on the surface. Dust, lint, and other particles trapped in a finish will result in a very unsightly and unprofessional appearance. This is a major problem encountered by the finisher, especially when working with varnish. If the problem becomes too severe, the surface will have to be stripped and refinished. As a result, the tack rag serves as a very useful tool to the finisher.

Tack rags can be purchased in most paint and hardware stores, or can be easily made from a piece of cheesecloth (Fig. 5). If you decide to make your own tack rags, be sure that the cloth is clean. Store your rags in a tightly closed glass jar. The lid of the storage container must be tight enough to keep the tack rag moist. Never allow the tack rag to dry out or it will be useless. When it appears to be drying, use the steps illustrated in Fig. 5 to

27

re-moisten it. Tack rags purchased from paint and hardware stores (or mail-order houses such as *Minnesota Woodworkers of Minneapolis*) are chemically treated so that they will always re-

Fig. 5. A process used in making a tack rag.

main soft and tacky. At least this is the manufacturer's claim.

Burlap is frequently used to remove excess filler by rubbing across the grain of the wood (Fig. 6). The burlap should be

Fig. 6. Removing excess filler with burlap.

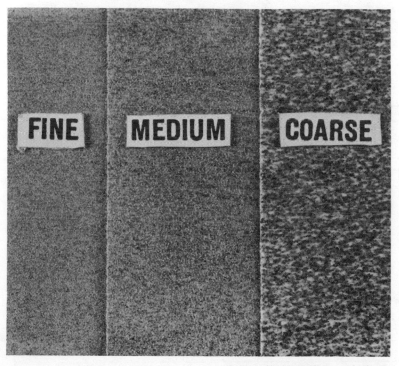

Courtesy Minnesota Mining and Mfg. Co.

Fig. 7. Examples of three grades of sandpaper.

clean, dry, and folded into a pad about the size of the hand.

## SANDPAPER

Sandpaper is a coated abrasive available in a number of different types, sizes, and grits (Fig. 7). This great variety results in there being a sandpaper to meet the requirements of almost every type of sanding application.

A coated abrasive such as sandpaper consists of three principal parts:

1. The abrasive mineral,
2. The adhesive (bonding agent),
3. The backing.

The abrasive mineral functions as the cutting agent. It may be of natural origin (flint, garnet, or emery) or artificially produced (aluminum oxide or silicon carbide). Garnet paper is recommended for use in furniture finishing, although other types may also be used. Table 1 lists the various abrasive minerals and gives some of their major characteristics.

The mineral grains used in the manufacture of sandpaper are obtained by reducing rock-size chunks under great pressure to

### Table 1. Comparative Qualities of Different Types of Abrasive Minerals

| TYPE OF MINERAL | COLOR | CUTTING POWER | DURABILITY | USES |
|---|---|---|---|---|
| Flint | Grayish-White to Tan | Poor to Fair | Short | Removing Paint, Minor Sanding Operations |
| Garnet | Red to Reddish-Brown | Good | Long | All Types of Woodworking and Wood Finishing |
| Emery | Black | Poor | Short | Woodworking, Wood Finishing, Metal Finishing |
| Aluminum Oxide | Reddish-Brown or White | Good to Excellent | Long | Woodworking, Metal Finishing |
| Silicon Carbide | Bluish-Black | Good to Excellent | Long | Woodworking, Metal Finishing |

the small particles that are bonded to the backing. Most mineral grains are separated according to size by passing them over a series of silk screens, each having different sized holes. This process produces the very coarse to very fine grades. A water sedimentation or air-flotation process is used to produce the extra fine and super fine grades. The *grit size* of each grade of sandpaper is the basis for its identification.

Grit sizes can be expressed by the older arbitrarily assigned numbering system (0, 2/0, 3/0, 4/0, etc.), by the modern two and three digit system based on the mesh number (60, 80, 100, etc.), or by descriptive terms (fine, very fine, extra fine, etc.). A comparison of these three systems is shown in Table 2.

Paper or cloth are the two most common types of backing used for sandpaper. Fiber backing and two types of combination

### Table 2. Comparison of Sandpaper Grit Sizes

| GRIT SIZES | | | GENERAL USE |
|---|---|---|---|
| | 600 | | |
| | 500 | | |
| Extra Fine | 400 | 10/0 | |
| | 360 | | |
| | 320 | 9/0 | |
| | 280 | 8/0 | Sanding Finishes |
| Very Fine | 240 | 7/0 | Sanding Finishes |
| | 220 | 6/0 | Sanding Finishes |
| | 180 | 5/0 | Sanding Finishes |
| Fine | 150 | 4/0 | Sanding Finishes, Intermediate Coats |
| | 120 | 3/0 | Sanding Finishes, Intermediate Coats |
| | 100 | 2/0 | Sanding Finishes, Intermediate Coats |
| Medium | 80 | 1/0 | Intermediate Coats, Rough Sanding |
| | 60 | ½ | Intermediate Coats, Rough Sanding |
| Coarse | 50 | 1 | Rough Sanding |
| | 40 | 1½ | Rough Sanding |
| | 36 | 2 | Rough Sanding |
| Very Coarse | 30 | 2½ | Rough Sanding |
| | 24 | 3 | |
| | 20 | 3½ | |
| Extra Coarse | 16 | 4 | |
| | 12 | 4½ | |

31

backings (paper and cloth, fiber and cloth) are also used. Paper backing is available in four different weights: A-weight, C-weight, D-weight, and E-weight. A-weight backing paper is used to make fine grade grit sandpaper. It is also the lightest and most pliable grade of sandpaper.

Cloth backing is available in two weights: J-weight and X-weight with the former having a lightness and flexibility similar to A-weight paper backing.

Some backings are waterproof so that the paper can be used in either dry or wet (with an oil, water, etc.) sanding operation. These will be so marked by the manufacturer.

## SANDING BLOCKS

Sanding blocks are used to hold the sandpaper so that it can be applied uniformly to a flat surface. They are available commercially or can be made in the home workshop. The commercial variety (Fig. 8) are usually made of hard rubber, plastic, or metal. However, it is often preferable to make your own sanding block, because you can design it to fit your specific needs.

Fig. 8. Examples of commercially available sanding blocks.

A sanding block can be made from a piece of hardwood cut to the size you require, a piece of rubber, or a felt pad. The last two are excellent backings for sanding curved surfaces because they are flexible and will bend to conform to the surface curvature. If hardwood is used for the sanding block, a piece of felt should be inserted between the sandpaper and the wood block (Fig. 9). Otherwise, you will run the risk of scratching and marring the wood surface with the hard edge of the sanding block.

Fig. 9. Sanding block with felt insert.

## ELECTRIC SANDERS

A portable electric sander (Fig. 10) can be very useful for sanding long frame pieces and for removing paint or other finishes. These machine sanders are available in a number of sizes ranging up to 4 inches in width and slightly over two feet in length. The heaviest machines will weigh about 22 to 23 pounds. The smaller size machines are recommended for finishing work.

Sanders can also be classified according to their method of operation. The principal methods of operation are:
1. Rotating band or belt,
2. A rotating disk,
3. An oscillating surface which may be either orbital or in-line.

The in-line oscillating motion is the most desirable for finishing work because it seldom leaves marks on the surface.

33

(A) Belt.

*Courtesy Stanley Tools*

(B) Vibrator.

*Courtesy Black and Decker*

(C) Orbital.

**Fig. 10. Portable electric sanders.**

## STEEL WOOL

Steel wool is available in seven different grades ranging from coarse to super fine (Table 3). As an abrasive, it offers certain advantages over sandpaper. For example, it has much less tendency to scratch the surface, it is easier to clean, it can always be used wet, it will produce a finer and smoother surface, and it is so flexible that it can reach into corners, cracks, and carvings where sandpaper cannot. A principal disadvantage of using steel wool is that it sheds fine metal particles during the rubbing operation. These particles must be completely removed before preceding with the next step in the finishing schedule. They are unfortunately harder to detect than the wood particles left by sanding.

### Table 3. Steel Wool Grades

| GRADE | QUALITY | APPROXIMATE STRAND SIZE |
| --- | --- | --- |
| No. 3 | Coarse | .003" |
| No. 2 | Medium Coarse | .0015" |
| No. 1 | Medium | .001" |
| No. 0 | Fine | .0008" |
| No. 00 | Very Fine | .0005" |
| No. 000 | Extra Fine | .0003" |
| No. 0000 | Super Fine | .0002" |

Steel wool can be used either wet or dry, although the latter is presently the most common form of usage. The No. 3, No. 0, No. 000, and No. 0000 grades are used for dry rubbing in wood finishing. Both the No. 3 and No. 0 grades are used for preliminary smoothing operations in which the wood surface is prepared for the finishes. The No. 000 grade is commonly used between the various steps in the finishing schedule. No. 0000 (super fine) is used in the last step in the finishing schedule *before* the final finishing coat is applied. It also has other special uses such as producing a dull sheen on a lacquer finish or buffing a waxed surface.

No. 0 grade steel wool can be used wet (soaked in paint remover) to remove paint or varnish. The No. 0000 (super fine)

35

grade is excellent with linseed oil or mineral spirits for adding special touches to finishes.

## CABINET SCRAPERS, HAND SCRAPERS, AND SPOKESHAVES

Some finishes use a cabinet scraper and hand scraper to prepare a flat wood surface *prior* to the sanding operation. Scrapers are planelike tools used in wood preparation when large amounts of material have to be removed from the surface, particularly when this cannot be accomplished satisfactorily with a plane (e.g. on a hard, cross-grained wood). The cabinet scraper (Fig. 11) is used initially for the coarser work, and is followed by the hand scraper which is designed to produce an even smoother surface. The

Fig. 11. A cabinet scraper.

spokeshave provides the same smoothing operation for curved surfaces (e.g. legs, arms, spindles, etc.) (Fig. 12).

Fig. 12. A spokeshave.

The hand scrapers illustrated in Fig. 13 are designed to provide a number of different blade adjustments for cutting. Some cabinet scrapers are provided with reversible blades, one end for

**Fig. 13: Commercially available hand scrapers.**

fast scraping and the other for smooth finishing. Fig. 14 illustrates a very simple but effective hand scraping method. Note that the hand scraping movement is toward the body of the worker. Because there are a number of different designs on the market, you will have to base your selection on your own particular needs. Remember: the cabinet scraper will not work well on soft woods, because it will shave the wood too deeply. Both cabinet scrapers and hand scrapers work most effectively on the moderately hard to hard woods (do not confuse the term "hard wood" with "hardwood". They do not mean the same thing. (See Chapter 3, TYPES OF WOOD).

Fig. 14. The hand scraper is a rectangular piece of steel with a gauge or thickness of .035 and used for fine smoothing operations.

## PUMICE STONE

Pumice stone is a white powder used for polishing and buffing a surface after the last sanding of the final finishing coat. The grades are based on the size of the particles and range from a No. 7 which is extremely coarse to the super fine No. FFFF grade. Grade No. FF (fine) and grade No. FFF (very fine) are generally used for operations that require fine rubbing. Sometimes coarser grades (e.g. No. 1 or 1½) are used for work that requires coarser rubbing.

Powdered abrasives such as pumice stone and rottenstone are more difficult to use than other types of abrasives. It is often recommended that pumice be sifted through some sort of screening

38

device before use in order to remove lumps and impurities. The screen must be of a design that will allow the fine pumice powder to penetrate into a pan below while at the same time blocking the passage of lumps and other impurities. Cheesecloth is frequently recommended for this purpose.

Pumice stone is coarser than rottenstone and therefore faster cutting. It should only be used on surfaces that are absolutely flat or the powder will fall away from the surface and reduce the overall efficiency of the rubbing operation.

A felt pad or a clean lint-free cloth is recommended when rubbing with pumice stone. Paraffin oil, a light motor oil, sewing machine oil, raw linseed oil, boiled linseed oil, and others have all been used with varying degrees of success as the lubricant with pumice stone. Paraffin oil and the two types of linseed oil are recommended over the others. Mail-order houses sell a rubbing oil especially designed for use with both pumice stone and rottenstone.

## ROTTENSTONE

Rottenstone is another powdered abrasive similar to pumice stone but its particles are much finer. As a result, rottenstone is commonly used after the pumice stone to obtain an extra high polish. It is used with many of the same lubricants used with pumice stone.

## BRUSHES AND BRUSH CARE

Brushes should be selected with as much care as the finish. It is to your advantage to purchase the most expensive brush that you can afford. It will last longer (if it is properly cleaned and stored), and it will produce a better finish.

A typical brush with the basic parts labelled is illustrated in Fig. 15. The *ferrule* is a metal (sometimes leather) band wrapped around the brush and fastened to the handle. A good brush will have a tightly fastened ferrule. In a cheaper brush, the ferrule will not be as tight and the bristles can be easily pulled out. This frequently occurs as you are applying a finish, and is true even with brand new brushes. For this reason, I do not recommend purchasing a cheap brush with the idea of using it only one time.

FERRULE

BRISTLE

FILLER

Fig. 15. Brush components.

Brush bristles are made either from natural animal hair (usually hog bristle) or a synthetic material (e.g. nylon), and are available with flat, round, or oval shapes. Open any mail-order catalog from a firm that sells finishing supplies or go to any local retail outlet that stocks them and you will find that there are many different kinds of brushes available for this type of work (Fig. 16). Among those available you will find artists brushes, fitch brushes, glue brushes, oxhair brushes, varnish brushes, and filler brushes. Some are named according to their composition (e.g. oxhair, red sable brushes, etc.), others receive their name from the function they perform (e.g. varnish brushes, glue brushes, etc.). You will have to determine your brush selection on the basis of

CAMEL HAIR
BRUSH

RED SABLE
ART BRUSH

RED SABLE
LINER

RED SABLE
ONE STROKE

FITCH
FLOWING
BRUSH

STENCIL
BRUSH

Fig. 16. Examples of brushes used in finishing.

what works best for you. My recommendation is that you purchase a suitable brush for each type of finishing operation and *label* it as such. Your work area might have a collection of brushes as extensive as the following:

1. Scrub brush,
2. Dusting brush,
3. Varnish brush,
4. Enamel brush,
5. Lacquer brush,
6. Shellac brush,
7. Stain brush,
8. Paint brush,
9. Paint and varnish remover brush,
10. Striping brush,
11. Filler brush,
12. Picking brush,
13. Glue brush.

Your own experience and the advice you receive from store clerks will help you in matching the most suitable brush with each of the above finishing operations.

A good quality brush will have the following characteristics:

1. The tip-edge of the bristles will be cut to form a wedge or chisel shape. A blunt edge is usually an indication of a cheap brush.
2. The tip of the bristles will taper to a fine, narrow, almost invisible edge.
3. The bristles will be securely fastened to the handle, and will not come loose while the finish is being applied.
4. The bristles will have a good flex to them (that is, they will be firm without being stiff, and they will be flexible without being excessively loose or floppy).

Carefully clean your brushes after you use them. Clean them in the solvent recommended for the finish or a commercial brush cleaner and then wash them in soap and water.

Brushes should be stored so that the bristles retain a flat, tapered shape. This can be accomplished by wrapping them in paper and laying them flat, or by hanging the brush by the handle so that the bristles do not touch any surface (Fig. 17). Brush storage containers can be purchased in paint or hardware stores.

Most professional finishers recommend preconditioning the brush before using it. The most common technique is to wrap the brush in paper and suspend it in a container of linseed oil for 18 to 20 hours. The brush is then removed and the linseed oil is pressed out of the bristles. Clean the bristles with turpentine and press it dry a second time. Shape the bristles with a comb and hang it up to dry. Before using it on a surface, dip it in the finish and brush

Fig. 17. Brush storage methods.

it across a piece of scrap wood several times. This method of conditioning will soften the bristles and lessen their tendency to stiffen after frequent use.

## SPRAY GUNS AND COMPRESSORS

Spraying a finish onto a surface has a number of advantages over brushing. Not only is spraying much faster, it dries more quickly and generally produces a more uniform coat. Moreover, spraying a finish will enable the worker to reach areas that are difficult to cover with a brush.

A portable spraying outfit generally consists of a spray gun, a compressor, and air hoses (Fig. 18). The compressor supplies air to the spray gun at approximately 30 lbs. or more of pressure.

### PIPE SIZE

| VOLUME AIR C.F.M. | LENGTH OF PIPE IN FEET | | | |
|---|---|---|---|---|
| | 50 | 100 | 150 | 200 |
| 10 | 1/2" | 3/4" | 3/4" | 3/4" |
| 20 | 3/4" | 3/4" | 3/4" | 3/4" |
| 30 | 3/4" | 3/4" | 1" | 1" |
| 40 | 1" | 1" | 1" | 1" |
| 50 | 1" | 1" | 1" | 1" |
| 70 | 1" | 1" | 1-1/4" | 1-1/4" |

*Courtesy Reliance Universal, Inc.*

**Fig. 18. Compressor with pressure-feed hookup.**

Spray guns are available in a number of different types and designs. However, it should be pointed out that not every spray gun is suitable for every type of compressor. The CFM rating (cubic feet per minute) of the spray gun should match the CFM rating of the compressor. Otherwise you may find that your compressor is supplying more air to the spray gun than it can adequately handle.

There are basically two types of compressors:

1. The diaphragm-type compressors,
2. The piston-type compressors.

Fig. 19. Spray gun used in spraying finishing materials.

The diaphragm-type compressors are less expensive, and cannot supply as much air pressure (only about 30-45 psi) as the piston-type compressors. The diaphragm-type compressor consists of an electric motor with an eccentric drive crankshaft. The latter moves a connecting rod against the center of a flexible diaphragm. The diaphragm moves up and down in an enclosed space compressing the air above it.

The piston-type compressor is also driven by an electric motor, but in this case the motor drives a piston within a cylinder. Because the compressed air is produced within the cylinder, special precautions must be taken to prevent the oil required to lubricate the piston from mixing with the compressed air. A filter system is necessary for this purpose. Diaphragm-type compressors do not have this problem because the chamber in which the compressed air is formed is separated from the motor and connecting rod by the diaphragm. Piston-type compressors are capable of producing air pressure in excess of 40 psi.

Spray guns (Fig. 19) can be classified into two basic types depending on how the finishing liquid is fed to the nozzle. These two types are:

1. The pressure-feed type,
2. The suction-feed type.

The *pressure-feed type* gun (Fig. 20) uses a portion of the air pressure to force the finishing liquid from its container up into the nozzle. Because the pressure is so strong in this type of gun, faster spraying with heavier liquids is possible.

The *suction-feed* type gun (Fig. 21) uses a vacuum and the siphon principle to bring the finishing liquid to the nozzle. The vacuum is created by passing the air over the feeder tube at a high rate of speed. The vacuum causes the finishing liquid to be sucked up into the nozzle.

Spray guns can also be classified as bleeder-type or non-bleeder type guns. Bleeder-type spray guns allow the air to pass through continuously. There is no device on the gun to shut off or control the air pressure. The finishing liquid however is controlled by the gun trigger. The finishing liquid flows through the gun only as long as the trigger remains in the pulled position. Bleeder-type spray guns can only be used with compressors, because they would soon exhaust a limited air supply.

COMPRESSED AIR

**Fig. 20. The pressure-feed spray gun.**

Non-bleeder type spray guns control both the finishing liquid and the air supply with the trigger mechanism. As a result, they can be used with limited air supplies such as tanks or other types of containers.

Spray guns can also be equipped with either internal-mix or external-mix nozzles. Internal-mix nozzles (Fig. 22) mix the finishing liquids and compressed air before they leave the opening.

47

AIR PRESSURE

COMPRESSED AIR

FINISHING MATERIAL

FINISHING MATERIAL

**Fig. 21. The suction-feed spray gun.**

These are found only on pressure-feed spray guns. External-mix nozzles (Fig. 23) are found on both pressure-feed and suction-feed spray guns. In this type of nozzle, the air is mixed with the finishing liquid after the latter leaves the opening.

The controls illustrated in Fig. 24 adjust the spray width and the rate of fluid flow. Spray width is adjustable to a variety of patterns ranging from round to flat (Fig. 25). Fig. 26 illustrates a number of faulty spraying patterns and the methods used in correcting them. Poor spraying results can also be caused by not holding or moving the spray gun correctly (Fig. 27).

## AEROSOL SPRAY CANS

A number of finishes (stains, enamels, lacquers, paints, etc.) are available in throw away aerosol spray cans. These cans usually contain about 16 ounces of fluid. They are inexpensive, easy to use, and require no thinning. Aerosol spray cans are very convenient for spraying small areas or small pieces of furniture (e.g. stools, end tables, or book cases). For larger pieces, spray guns and compressors are recommended.

Always shake the can well before using. As you shake it you will hear what appears to be the sound of small steel balls rattling in the can. This is exacty what they are. They are inserted in the can to aid in stirring the fluid. Test the spray on a piece of cardboard or a piece of paper. If it appears too thin, it probably needs more shaking.

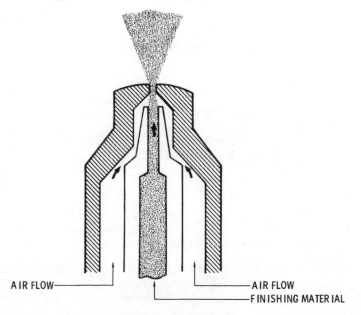

AIR FLOW

AIR FLOW

FINISHING MATERIAL

**Fig. 22. Internal mix nozzle.**

49

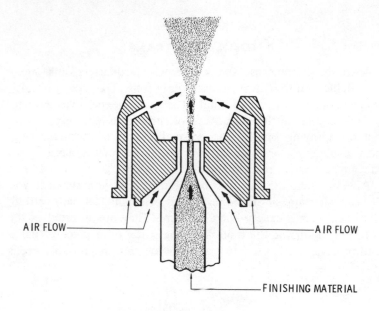

Fig. 23. External mix nozzle.

Courtesy Reliance Universal, Inc.

Fig. 24. Spray gun adjustment controls.

Spray cans are also manufactured with different types of nozzles. Some produce a conical spray, others a fan spray. Some nozzles are fixed, whereas others rotate. No spray can nozzle will give a spray as wide as that produced by a spray gun, and this is a major limitation.

Some spray cans are of the refillable type. The compressed air propellants are replaceable, and the finishing material must be thinned for effective use.

MATERIAL CONTROL SCREW

SPRAY WIDTH ADJUSTMENT

The spray pattern of the gun is variable from round to flat with all patterns in between.

In normal operation, the wings on the nozzle are horizontal as illustrated here. This provides a vertical fan-shaped pattern which gives maximum coverage as the gun is moved back and forth parallel to the surface being finished.

SPRAY WIDTH ADJUSTMENT

MATERIAL CONTROL SCREW

*Courtesy Reliance Universal, Inc.*

**Fig. 25. Gun with adjustments.**

Correct and incorrect techniques for using aerosol spray cans are shown in Fig. 28. *Read* the manufacturer's instructions on the can before using it. Never store these cans near a heat source or use them near a flame. Proper ventilation is just as important when using spray cans as with finishes in any other form.

## TOOLS FOR VENEERING AND INLAYING

The tools for veneering and inlaying are largely specific to those two methods of decorating the wood surface. Consequently, they are described in detail in Chapter 4, VENEERING and Chapter 5, INLAYING. For purposes of reference, veneering and inlaying tools include the following:

1. Veneer saw,
2. Veneer roller,

51

| PATTERN | CAUSE | CORRECTION |
|---|---|---|
| | Dried material in side-port "A" restricts passage of air through it. Results: Full pressure of air from clean side-port forces fan pattern in direction of clogged side. | Dissolve material in side-port with thinner. Do not poke in any of the openings with metal instruments. |
| | Dried material around the outside of the fluid nozzle tip at position "B" restricts the passage of atomizing air at one point through the center opening of air nozzle and results in pattern shown. This pattern can also be caused by loose air nozzle. | If dried material is causing the trouble, remove air nozzle and wipe off fluid tip, using rag wet with thinner. Tighten air nozzle. |
| | A split spray or one that is heavy on each end of a fan pattern and weak in the middle is usually caused by (1) too high an atomization air pressure, or (2) by attempting to get too wide of a spray with thin material. | Reducing air pressure will correct cause (1) To correct cause (2) open material control to full position by turning to left. At the same time turn spray width adjustment to right. This will reduce width of spray but will correct split spray pattern. |
| SPITTING | (1) Dried out packing around material needle valve permits air to get into fluid passageway. This results in spitting.<br>(2) Dirt between fluid nozzle seat and body or a loosely installed fluid nozzle will make gun spit.<br>(3) A loose or defective swivel nut on siphon cup or material hose can cause spitting. | To correct cause (1) back up knurled nut (E), place two drops of machine oil on packing, replace nut and tighten with fingers only. In aggravated cases, replace packing.<br>To correct cause (2), remove fluid nozzle (F), clean back of nozzle and nozzle seat in gun body using rag wet with thinner, replace nozzle and draw up tightly against body.<br>To correct cause (3) tighten or replace swivel nut (G). |

*Courtesy Reliance Universal, Inc.*

**Fig. 26. Faulty spray patterns and methods used in correcting them.**

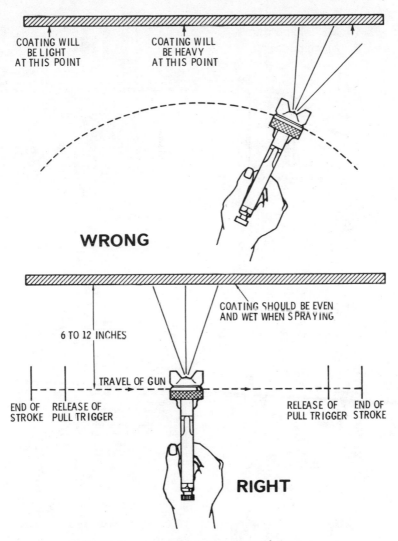

COATING WILL
BE LIGHT
AT THIS POINT

COATING WILL
BE HEAVY
AT THIS POINT

**WRONG**

COATING SHOULD BE EVEN
AND WET WHEN SPRAYING

6 TO 12 INCHES

TRAVEL OF GUN

END OF     RELEASE OF
STROKE    PULL TRIGGER

RELEASE OF     END OF
PULL TRIGGER   STROKE

**RIGHT**

Fig. 27. Correct and incorrect spraying techniques.

3. Veneer edge trimmer,
4. Veneer groove cutter,
5. Veneer strip and border cutter,

6.  Veneer press frame,
7.  Small hand router,
8.  Machine router,

TOO CLOSE - RUNS AND SAGS

TOO FAR - DUST CLOUDS AND GRITTY FINISH

CORRECT

INCORRECT

CORRECT

INCORRECT

FAN SPRAY

CONE SPRAY

SPRAY OVERLAP SEQUENCE

**Fig. 28. Correct and incorrect techniques for using aerosol spray cans.**

54

9. Veneer repair tool,
10. Veneer tape.

## PAINT AND FINISH LIFTERS

Lifters are tools used to scrape off paint or finishing material once it has been softened by a solvent. Typical examples of paint and finish lifters are:

1. Putty knives,
2. Scrapers,
3. Picking sticks,
4. Steel brushes,
5. Tooth brushes,
6. Pocket knives.

For large surfaces, a scraper made from a piece of hard wood is recommended. Metal scrapers (as well as putty knives and pocket knives) tend to scratch the surface unless their edges (corners) are rounded.

A picking stick can be made from a sharpened dowel. With its tip wrapped in cloth, a picking stick can probe into the recesses of carvings and other difficult to reach areas. Toothbrushes are also useful for this purpose. Steel brushes, on the other hand, are useful for removing paint and other finishes from large surfaces. Once again, you run the risk of scratching the surface because the "bristles" are made of steel.

**Fig. 29. Striping tool capable of making two parallel lines, evenly spaced.**

There are a number of other finishing tools and materials that are very useful, and which should be mentioned before concluding this chapter.

Masking tape (or a masking liquid) is used when spraying furniture or when any decorative painting is being done in which two or more colors are used. It is placed as protection over those areas you do not intend to paint at the moment.

*Albert Constantine and Son* sells a striping tool (Fig. 29) that paints stripes on a surface. The tool comes with interchangeable tips, and can be used with a number of different finishing materials (enamel, lacquer, etc.).

*Mason* jars with screw on lids make very good storage containers for finishing materials. Old drinking glasses can be used for mixing finishes or solvents.

# Chapter 3

# Types of Wood

The ability to identify the different types of wood used in furniture construction is very important in wood finishing. This knowledge should include not only the ability to recognize a particular wood, but also an understanding of how it reacts to different types of finishes. This requires a more sophisticated knowledge than simple recognition. For example, the worker must be able to distinguish between an open-grained and a close-grained wood, because the former requires a filler in order to create a smooth surface for finishing. He should have some knowledge of grain and texture, as these characteristics of the wood are important considerations in veneering, inlaying, and other aspects of wood finishing. As you can see, wood finishing requires a certain basic knowledge of the various types of wood used in furniture construction. It is the purpose of this chapter to identify some of these woods and their characteristics.

## HARDWOOD AND SOFTWOOD

Hardwood and softwood are the two most common terms of reference and the two which probably produce the most confusion. The term *hardwood* does not necessarily mean that the surface of the wood is hard. Although it is true that many hardwoods do have surfaces that are hard (hickory, for example), it is equally true that there are hardwoods with soft wood surfaces (butternut, yellow poplar, etc.). Hardwood (as does softwood) refers to the type of tree. A hardwood is a deciduous tree. These are the relatively broadleaved trees that shed their leaves during certain sea-

57

sons of the year. Examples of deciduous trees are the maple, oak, and chestnut. A softwood, on the other hand, is a coniferous tree. These are the needle-bearing or cone-bearing trees of which Douglas fir, white fir, redwood, and ponderosa pines are examples.

## COLOR

A tree contains both *heartwood* and *sapwood*. The heartwood extends from the center of the tree to the edge of the sapwood. This portion of the tree no longer contains living cells. It is usually filled with resins, gums or other materials (e.g. tyloses) that contribute to the coloring. When we mention the color of a wood, we are almost always speaking of the color of the heartwood. The sapwood is found near the outside of the trunk and branches of the tree. This layer contains living cells. Its principal function is the storage of food and the conduction of sap. It should not be confused with the *cambrium* layer. The cambrium layer is located between the sapwood and the bark, and its cells are continually subdividing to produce new layers of both bark and wood. Almost all sapwoods are light in color or virtually white. Any coloring is usually due to a discoloration from fungus or chemical stains (**Fig. 1**).

### Table 1. Wood Terms

| GRAIN | | TEXTURE | |
|---|---|---|---|
| Wide, Conspicuous annual growth rings | Narrow, inconspicuous, annual growth rings | Large pores | Small pores |
| Coarse grained | Fine grained | Open grained or Coarse grained | Fine grained or Close grained |

## GRAIN, TEXTURE, AND FIGURE

Grain, texture, and figure are all terms describing the surface appearance of the wood. Unfortunately, they are used rather loosely and tend to overlap in meaning. This produces a certain amount of confusion.

*Grain* is often used in reference to the fibers of the wood, their arrangement, their prominence, the direction in which they run, or to the annual growth rings and the spacing between them. Painters frequently refer to woods as *open-grained* or *close-*

**Fig. 1. A cross-section of a tree trunk.**

*grained* and mean by this the size of the pore openings. To add to this confusion, *fine-grained* is used synonomously with close-grained and *coarse-grained* with open-grained.

Fine-grained woods are characterized by narrow, inconspicuous annual growth rings. Coarse-grained woods, on the other hand, have wide, conspicuous annual growth rings. Open-grained woods are those having large pores. None of the softwoods and only some of the hardwoods (black walnut, butternut, white ash, etc.) are open grained. Close-grained woods are those having small pores.

The terms open-grained and close-grained would be more appropriately used in reference to texture. Since *texture* is also a term of overlapping and confusing meanings, we will specifically use it here to refer to the size and distribution of the individual cells (pores) on the surface of the wood. This could range anywhere from extremely fine (more frequently a characteristic of the softwoods) to extremely coarse. Table 1 illustrates how the meanings of these terms overlap.

Both grain and texture are aspects of *figure,* a term which gives a more general description of the wood surface. Basically, figure is any distinctive pattern or marking appearing on the surface of the wood. Annual growth rings, knots, irregularities in coloring, rays, and deviations in grain patterns all singularly or in combination produce the distinctive markings known as figure. Some of the confusion in these overlapping terms may be explained in Table 1.

The remainder of this chapter contains a brief description of a number of hardwoods and softwoods used in furniture construction. They have been grouped according to whether they are hardwoods or softwoods. As you will notice, the hardwoods is by far the larger of the two groups.

## HARDWOODS

**RED ALDER** *(Alnus rubra).* This wood is grown all along the Pacific coast from California to Alaska. The color of its wood ranges from an off-white to a pale pinkish brown. It is about avcrage in weight, average in strength, and low in shock resistance. Red alder has a tendency to shrink so it must be properly seasoned before being used. It is used principally in the manufacture of furniture, and can be stained to resemble maple, cherry, and other more expensive woods.

**APPLE** *(Malus pumila)*. A hardwood originally imported from Europe, the apple is now found throughout the United States. The color of apple wood ranges from a cream or off-white to a very light, almost pale brown. This is a very heavy wood, weighing on the average of 48 pounds per cubic foot. Not infrequently a pattern of thin brown lines run at random across the surface of the wood. The grain is very fine, the pores extremely small.

Years ago, apple wood was used quite extensively in furniture along the eastern seaboard. Today it is still used for chair legs. It does not split easily, turns well, but is difficult to carve. Apple wood takes a stain well (a light colored stain is recommended so that the natural color is not obscured). A filler is not necessary.

**BLACK ASH** *(Fraxinus nigra,* brown ash, northern brown ash, and swamp ash). (Fig. 2). This tree is found primarily in the eastern United States, but only in the northern sections. Its range of growth does not extend any further south than Tennessee and Virginia. It has little or no figure, and a straight, uninteresting grain. The color of black ash ranges from medium brown to dark brown. It has an average workability with handtools. Its tendency to split is about average. Its strength, resistance to decay, and its ability to take a clear finish also fall within this grade.

**WHITE ASH** *(Fraxinus americana)*. (Fig. 3). White ash is found throughout the eastern United States except in the coastal plain areas. The color of the wood is a brown to grayish brown with occasional examples of a cream or off-white variety. There is frequently a reddish tint in the coloring. It is similar to black ash in possessing little or no figure. White ash is a fairly heavy wood, weighing about 42 pounds per cubic foot. It has a straight grain, which is not brought out appreciably by staining (stains seem merely to color it), and a texture similar to oak. The pores

Fig. 2. Grain pattern of black ash wood.

are large and visible to the eye. White ash, for the most part, works well with handtools. The only exception is that it tends to split easily. The wood is strong, stiff, and hard. The resistance to shock is good. It is frequently used in furniture construction. White ash bleaches well and may be finished with or without a filler depending upon the effect desired.

**ASPEN** (*Populus tremuloides*, quaking aspen, popple, poplar, cottonwood). Aspen is found throughout most of the northeastern and western United States with the greatest concentration being in the lake states and the New England area. The color of aspen wood ranges from a white to a light brown. It is light in weight, averaging 26 pounds per cubic foot. The pores on the surface are small, and generally not visible, but a filler should be used with most finishes. It reacts well to bleaching. Aspen wood ranks very low in hardness, somewhat higher in shock resistance, and low in

Fig. 3. White ash wood grain (4-piece quartered cut).

strength. These poorer characteristics are offset by a very low tendency to split and a very low rate of shrinkage after proper seasoning. Aspen also works well with either handtools or machine tools. This wood glues easily and reacts well to paint. Aspen is frequently used in the manufacture of high grade excelsior. It can also be found in veneers.

**AVODIRE** *(Turraeanthus africana).* This is a wood grown in West Africa and imported to the United States for use in fine furniture. Avodire wood has a pale yellow to golden coloring with some varieties appearing almost white. Avodire possesses an open grain which takes a stain with average ability. A filler should be used with most finishes. Avodire reacts favorably to bleaching. This wood is about average in weight, possesses an average hand-tool workability, and shows about the same tendency to split. Avodire has a relatively low strength.

**AMERICAN BASSWOOD** *(Tilia americana,* bass, linden). (Fig. 4). This hardwood is grown throughout the eastern United

Courtesy Fine Hardwoods Association

**Fig. 4. American Basswood grain.**

States, particularly in the region around the Great Lakes. The wood has a creamy white to creamy brown coloring with a particularly attractive variety that tends toward a rather light, yellowish-brown. The wood is sometimes highlighted with streaks of a slightly deeper color. American basswood is light weight (26 pounds per cubic foot), with a straight, even grain. Because of the evenness of the grain, stains take very well. This wood is frequently stained to resemble other woods (e.g. cherry, mahogany, or walnut) that are more expensive or difficult to obtain. The pores are quite small, with extremely faint growth rings. American basswood is easy to work with handtools, and does not split easily. It is not a strong wood, and has a low shock resistance. It is used as a core material in high quality furniture veneers (usually over-

*Courtesy Fine Hardwoods Association*

**Fig. 5. American beech wood grain.**

laid with walnut or mahogany). It is also frequently used as a wood for furniture legs and stained to resemble the rest of the piece.

**AMERICAN BEECH** *(Fagus grandifolia).* (Fig. 5). A hardwood found growing primarily in the eastern United States, and as far west as Texas and Missouri. The coloring of the wood ranges from a reddish-white to a reddish-brown. It is heavy (45 pounds per cubic foot), strong, and hard. The grain is even. The pores are so small that they are not visible to the naked eye, but the rays are prominent and cover the surface. A water based stain works well on this grain without causing it to raise. American beech is frequently stained to resemble more expensive woods. This wood strongly resembles sugar maple except that the coloring of the wood is darker, the grain coarser, the weight lighter, and the general strength somewhat less. This wood is difficult to work with handtools. It splits easily and nails are difficult to remove. However, it does machine well, giving a smooth surface. American beech is used in table legs, chair legs, and veneers.

**YELLOW BIRCH** *(Betula allegheniensis,* gray birch). (Fig. 6). This wood is grown in the northern United States and in the Appalachian Mountains as far south as southern 'Georgia. The wood of the yellow birch is a light reddish-brown. It has a fine, close grain, with pores not readily visible. Because the grain is so uniform (it takes a stain very well) yellow birch is used for furniture wood and veneer. Yellow birch is not easily worked with handtools but it machines well. This is a heavy wood, weighing almost 45 pounds per cubic foot. It is hard, strong, and stiff. It has both a high shock resistance as well as a high nail withdrawal resistance. Yellow birch shows a strong tendency to shrink, and should be properly seasoned before using.

**BUTTERNUT** *(Juglans cinerea,* white walnut). Butternut is found growing throughout the northern half of the eastern United States. Its southernmost limits appear to be northern Mississippi, Alabama, and Georgia. The color of the wood is a light brown with traces of red. Its texture is coarse, its pores are open and large. This is a light weight wood, weighing on the average 27 pounds per cubic foot. Butternut is easy to work with handtools

Courtesy Fine Hardwoods Association

Fig. 6. Yellow birch grain.

and machine tools. It takes stains well, and is often stained to re-semble walnut.

**BLACK CHERRY** *(Prunus serotina,* cherry, wild cherry, choke cherry, American mahogany). (Figs. 7 and 8). This is an-other hardwood grown primarily in the eastern United States. The color of the wood is a light to dark reddish-brown. Black cherry weighs, on the average, about 36 pounds per cubic foot, which places it in the average to slightly above average weight category. This wood has a fine, close grain that takes a stain well. A filler is

67

*Courtesy Fine Hardwoods Association*

**Fig. 7. Black cherry grain.**

not required. Cherry has a very poor reaction to bleach. There is a distinctive flake pattern of the rays on quarter-sawed surfaces. Black cherry is often referred to as "American mahogany," although it is stronger and harder than any of the varieties of mahogany. It is also stronger than walnut, but lacks the strength of maple. This wood is stiff, strong, and has a high resistance to shock. Since black cherry has a strong tendency to shrink, it must be carefully seasoned before use. This wood is difficult to work with handtools, but machines easily. Black cherry is considered to be one of the finest furniture woods. Unfortunately, good grades are difficult to find.

Fig. 8. Black cherry wood grain.

**CHESTNUT** (*Castanea dentata,* American chestnut, sweet chestnut). This tree was formerly found in the northern half of the eastern United States. Unfortunately, it has almost been killed off by a blight. The color of the wood ranges from grayish to reddish-brown. The wide-spread prevalence of blight has left only a "wormy chestnut" grade available for commercial uses. This is an open-grained wood with a coarse texture. Because of its large pores, it resembles oak or walnut (chestnut has been used to imitate both these woods in the past). It is very easy to work with handtools, cutting more easily than oak and with less tendency to splinter. Because of its durability and resistance to warp, it is

69

particularly sought after for use in the construction of furniture drawers and veneer cores.

**COTTONWOOD** *(Populus deltoides,* eastern cottonwood, Carolina poplar, yellow cottonwood). This variety of cottonwood grows throughout the eastern United States. The color of the heartwood ranges from grayish white to grayish brown. The pores of the wood are very small, the texture is uniform, and it is generally straight grained. The weight is average to light, weighing about 25 pounds per cubic foot on the average. The wood tends to be softer than most, and shows a lower than average resistance to shock. The handtool workability is about average. It does not split easily and is low in nail withdrawal resistance. Cottonwood

Courtesy Fine Hardwoods Association

**Fig. 9. The American elm wood grain.**

takes paint very well, and is not difficult to glue. It is used as a veneer core and as a furniture wood.

**AMERICAN ELM** *(Ulmus americana,* white elm, gray elm, water elm). (Fig. 9). This hardwood is found throughout the eastern United States except in the Appalachian highlands and southern Florida. The color of the wood ranges from a brown to a dark brown with traces of red. The wood is of average weight (about 35 pounds per cubic foot), hardness, and stiffness. The texture is rather coarse, with large open pores (except in the summerwood where the pores cannot be seen). American elm wood offers a better than average shock resistance. It shows a strong tendency to shrink and must be seasoned properly before use. American elm machines well, but is not easily worked with handtools. It bends very easily and for this reason is widely used in the bent parts of the wood furniture frame. American elm offers no difficulty in gluing.

**ROCK ELM** *(Ulmus thomasii,* hickory elm, cork elm). This wood is also grown in the eastern United States, but does not extend any further south than Tennessee. The color of rock elm wood resembles that of American elm. This is a heavy wood, weighing on the average of 44 pounds per cubic foot. Only hickory and dogwood exceed it in hardness among the American hardwoods. It resembles American elm in shrinkage, handtool workability, and bending qualities. The grain patterns, pore sizes, and texture of the two are also very similar. Rock elm is used in furniture construction and veneers.

**SLIPPERY ELM** *(Ulmus rubra,* red elm). Slippery elm occupies the same areas as the American elm except for the coastal plain areas where it is almost never found. This wood has all the characteristics of American elm. It too is used in the manufacture of furniture and veneers.

**GONCALO ALVES** *(Astronium fraxinifolium,* zebrawood, kingwood). (Fig. 10). This is a wood found in the tropical jungles of eastern Brazil, and imported to this country for use in fine furniture and cabinets. The color of the wood ranges from a yellowish to pinkish to golden background with darker stripes running across it. It has a straight grain with small open pores. A filler is

Fig. 10. Goncalo alves wood grain.

Courtesy Fine Hardwoods Association

generally recommended, but bleaching is not. The texture varies. It is easy to work with handtools.

**HACKBERRY** (*Celtis occidentalis*). This wood grows throughout the eastern United States as far south as Tennessee. The color of the wood ranges from a pale yellow to a greenish or grayish yellow. It is about average in weight and strength (particularly the bending strength). Hackberry is above average in hardness, low in stiffness, and tends to shrink more than average unless seasoned properly. This wood is used primarily in the manufacture of furniture.

**HICKORY or TRUE HICKORY** can be divided into four classes: (1) shagbark hickory (*Carya ovata*); (2) pignut hickory (*Carya glabra*); (3) shellbark hickory (*Carya laciniosa*); and (4) mockernut hickory (*Carya tementosa*). Hickory grows throughout the eastern United States except for southern Florida, northern Main, Northern Vermont, and northern areas in both Michigan and Wisconsin. The color of the wood ranges from brown to dark brown, sometimes with a reddish tint. Hickory is a very heavy wood, averaging 42-52 pounds per cubic foot. It is very hard, strong, and stiff, with a high resistance to shock. Hickory

72

is difficult to work with handtools, and particularly shows a tendency to splinter. The pores are not well-defined. However, cutting along the grain produces pore channels that are distinctive to hickory. Hickory is used in lawn furniture, rockers, and Windsor chairs.

**AMERICAN HOLLY** (*Ilex opaca,* boxwood, white holly, evergreen holly). This tree is found along both the Gulf and Atlantic coasts, and throughout the Mississippi Valley. The color of the wood varies from a white to an off-white, and can be easily stained a variety of different colors. It also reacts well to bleaching. This is a heavy wood, and is well above average in hardness. Its texture is uniform and compact. American holly is frequently used as a furniture inlay.

**IMBUYA** (*Phoebe porosa,* imbuia, Brazilian walnut). This hardwood is found in Brazil and is imported for use in the more expensive furnitures. The color of the wood ranges from a light (almost yellow) brown to a dark brown. Imbuya can be bleached with better than average results. It is a heavy wood, averaging 44 pounds per cubic foot in weight. Imbuya is open-grained with a fine texture, and generally requires a filler. It is about average in hardness, and high in durability. Imbuya is easy to work with handtools, and it machines well.

**KELOBRA** (*Enterolobium cyclocarpum,* parota, guanacaste). This wood is grown in Mexico and northern Central America, and imported to the United States for use in fine furniture. Because of its beautiful grain pattern, it is also used extensively in high grade veneers. It takes a stain well (generally dark brown) and requires a filler. Do not bleach.

**KOA** (*Acacia koa*). Koa is a hardwood grown in Hawaii and used in the manufacture of expensive, fine quality furniture. The color ranges from a gold to a dark brown. Koa will respond well to bleaching. Some varieties have a darker stripe running across a light background. This is a fine, open-grained wood with a texture similar to that of walnut. It requires a filler.

**LACEWOOD** (*Cardwellia sublimis,* silky oak). (Fig. 11). This tree is found in both Australia and Europe. Because of a distinctive figure that sometimes resembles a lace pattern, this

73

Courtesy Fine Hardwoods Association
Fig. 11. Lacewood grain.

hardwood is used as a furniture overlay. The color ranges from a light red (almost pink) to a light reddish-brown. A filler is generally recommended. If necessary, it can be bleached with better than average results.

**CALIFORNIA LAUREL** (*Umbellularia californica,* mountain laurel, pepperwood, myrtle). This variety of laurel is grown along the Pacific coast. The color of the wood ranges from green to brown with mixtures of yellow that produce a variety of shades. It weighs about 38 pounds per cubic foot (kiln-dried weight) which places it in the same weight class as black cherry or mahogany. It produces beautiful distinctive figure patterns that make it highly valued as a decorative wood in fine furniture.

**MAGNOLIA** (Magnolia grandflora, southern magnolia, big laurel, evergreen magnolia). This hardwood is found in the southern United States from North Carolina to Texas. The color of the wood ranges from a light to a dark brown with shadings of yellow or green. It weighs about 34 pounds per cubic foot. The wood is usually close-grained with a close, uniform texture. It is about average in hardness and stiffness, above average in shock resistance, and low in shrinkage. It very closely resembles yellow poplar. Magnolia wood is used in the manufacture of furniture and veneers.

Courtesy Fine Hardwoods Association

Fig. 12. Mahogany wood.

**MAHOGANY** (*Swietenia mahogani,* American mahogany, true mahogany, West Indian mahogany). (Fig. 12). This excellent hardwood is found in the islands of the West Indies and in southern Florida. The color of the wood ranges from various shades of red (including a light pink) to a rich dark brown. Its grain has a fine texture to it and the surface of the wood frequently shows an attractive figure. True mahogany is a heavy wood with about average hardness. It is high in shock resistance, does not shrink appreciably, and has high strength characteristics. This variety of mahogany is easily worked with handtools and machine tools. It is easy to glue, easy to fasten (with nails or screws), and takes both a stain and paint well. In short, this is one of the finest furniture and cabinet woods.

**AFRICAN MAHOGANY** (*Khaya ivorensis,* khaya, Benin mahogany). This wood is imported from West Africa and is used for the manufacture of furniture and veneers. Most of its characteristics resemble those of American mahogany. However, there is a heavier grain pattern and the texture is noticeably coarser.

**HONDURAS MAHOGANY** (*Swietenia mahogani,* Central American mahogany). Honduras mahogany is found in the tropical regions throughout Latin America as far north as southern Mexico. Most of its characteristics resemble those of American mahogany. It is especially noted for its fine grain patterns and even texture. It is a strong, medium hard wood with a weight somewhat above average (about 32 pounds per cubic foot). It is used in the manufacture of furniture and veneers.

**PHILIPPINE MAHOGANY.** This is a commercial trade name given to a variety of hardwoods which belong mostly to the genus *Shorea* (red and white lauans) of the *Diptero-carpaceae* family. The color of the wood ranges from a light khaki or tan to a dark red. It is an open-grained, coarse-textured wood that has an average handtool workability. It machines well. It requires considerable sanding to produce a smooth surface. For this reason, it is used in cheaper grades of furniture than the other mahoganies.

**MAKORI** (*Mimusops heckelli,* African cherry, Makori cherry mahogany). This hardwood is grown on southern Africa and imported to the United States for use in furniture construction.

Makori strongly resembles mahogany, but surpasses the latter in texture, weight, and hardness.

**MAPLE** is a name given to a large genus (*Acer*) of trees many of which have no value as a furniture wood. Two noted exceptions are the **BIG-LEAF MAPLE** (*Acer macro-phylum*) found along or near the Pacific coastal areas of North America, and **HARD MAPLES** which include **SUGAR MAPLE** (*Acer saccharum*) and **BLACK MAPLE** (*Acer nigrum*), both found primarily in the eastern United States.

The hard maples have a light reddish-brown wood. Some varieties of hard maple have a distinctive figure with very small spots of curled grain resembling a bird's eye. For this reason, it

Courtesy Fine Hardwoods Association

**Fig. 13. Narra wood, two piece matched.**

77

is frequently referred to as **BIRDSEYE MAPLE.** All three types of hard maples are used in the manufacture of quality furniture. Birdseye maple is particularly suitable for use in inlays and overlays.

Hard maples are heavy woods, averaging 44 pounds per cubic foot. This wood is generally straight-grained (the birdseye varieties being the exception) with a fine texture. It takes stain and wax well and can produce a high polish. It machines well, but is difficult to work with handtools. This is a strong stiff wood, with a high resistance to shock. The pores are not visible to the naked eye. It has a strong tendency to shrink and must be properly seasoned before use.

**NARRA** *(Pterocarpus indicus,* amboyna, angsana). (Fig. 13). This wood is grown in the East Indies and imported to the United States where it is used in the manufacture of expensive grades of furniture and fine veneers. The color of this hardwood ranges from red to rose to a yellowish brown. This is a heavy wood. It is not as durable as some and is relatively low in strength. Because of its hardness, it is difficult to work with handtools. A filler is recommended for all finishes. Narra can be successfully bleached.

**OAK** is a name given to a large genus *(Quercus)* of trees found in the temperate zones of primarily the northern hemisphere. Three of the most common types used in furniture construction are: (1) the **WHITE OAKS** which include (a) **WHITE OAK** *(Quercus alba)*; (b) **BUR OAK** *(Quercus macrocarpa)*; (c) **CHESTNUT OAK** *(Quercus prinus)*; and (d) **LIVE OAK** *(Quercus virginiana)*; (2) **ENGLISH OAK** *(Quercus robur,* brown oak); and (3) the **RED OAKS** which include among others (a) **SOUTHERN RED OAK** *(Quercus falcata)*; (b) **LAUREL OAK** *(Quercus laurifolia)*; (c) **NORTHERN RED OAK** *(Quercus rubra)*; and (d) **BLACK OAK** *(Quercus velutina)*. (Figs. 14 and 15).

Both white oak and red oak have a grayish brown wood. Red oak wood is distinguished by a reddish tinge. Oak is a heavy wood, ranging in weight from 45 to 47 pounds per cubic foot. The wood is hard, strong, and stiff, with a high resistance to shock. It is

Courtesy Fine Hardwoods Association

**Fig. 14. Oak grain.**

characterized by large, open pores. All white oaks (except chestnut oak) have their pores filled with a hairlike growth called tyloses. Oak is difficult to work with handtools, although it machines well. English oak shares most of the characteristics of the other oaks. However, its color tends to be a deeper brown with a distinctive grain pattern. It is widely used in fine grades of furniture. **QUARTERED OAK** is a method of cutting the wood so that the cuts are formed in a radial direction. This procedure produces very interesting grain patterns of flakes from the wood rays. It is used in the construction of furniture and veneers.

**PEARWOOD** (*Pyrus communis*). A hardwood found in both

79

Fig. 15. Red oak wood grain.

the United States and Europe. The color of the wood ranges from a pink to a white. It reacts well to bleaching. This is close-grained wood with a fine texture, but a filler is generally recommended. It has a grain pattern that is distinguished by a mottled figure. Pearwood is used in high quality furniture and veneers.

**YELLOW POPLAR** (*Liriodendron tulipifera,* tulip). (Fig. 16). The yellow poplar is a hardwood found in the eastern United States. The wood is a brownish-yellow color with tinges of green. The grain and figure is not particularly distinctive. Because the texture is even, it takes a stain very well. Yellow poplar is frequently stained to imitate other more expensive woods. The wood is on

Courtesy Fine Hardwoods Association

Fig. 16. Yellow poplar grain.

the light side (averaging about 30 pounds per cubic foot). It is average in hardness, stiffness, resistance to shock, and bending properties. It also rates average in its machining properties and its ability to take glues. It is easy to work with handtools. Although its nail-withdrawal resistance is low, it does not split easily. Yellow poplar is used extensively in the lower grades of furniture.

**PRIMAVERA** (*Cybistax donnellsmithii*, golden mahogany, white mahogany). (Fig. 17). A hardwood imported from southern Mexico and Central America for use as a furniture and cabinet wood. The color ranges from a light to golden yellow. Primavera reacts well to bleaching. The characteristics of this wood closely resemble those of American mahogany. The grain is straight, the texture coarse. Use a filler.

81

Courtesy Fine Hardwoods Association

Fig. 17. Primavera grain.

**SAPELE** (*Entandrophragma cylindricum,* sapele mahogany, sapeli). A hardwood native to West Africa and imported to the United States for use in the manufacture of furniture, especially as a veneer. It has most of the characteristics of African mahogany, except that it is heavier and harder. Do not attempt to bleach this wood. A filler is recommended with all finishes.

**SATINWOOD** (*Chloroxylon swietenia*). (Fig. 18). A hardwood imported from the East Indies and used for inlays and marquetry in furniture construction. It ranges in color from a golden yellow to a yellowish-brown. This is a strong, hard, heavy wood with a fine grain pattern. There is a West Indian variety

Courtesy Fine Hardwoods Association

Fig. 18. Satinwood grain.

of satinwood (*Zanthoxylum coriaceum*) that strongly resembles the East Indian wood. Its color, however, is more a pale orange. Do not attempt to bleach satinwood.

**SWEETGUM** (*Liquidambar styraciflua,* red gum). Sweetgum is found throughout the eastern United States. The color of the wood is reddish-brown. This is a close-grained wood with a strong figure in some varieties. A filler is not required. Sweetgum stains very well (a maple or walnut stain is recommended), and is frequently used in furniture construction in conjunction with more expensive woods. It is above average in weight (about 35

83

pounds per cubic foot), hard, strong, and moderately high in shock resistance. However, sweetgum machines poorly and has only an average handtool workability. Because sweetgum warps easily, great care must be taken in seasoning it. It does not split easily and it holds nails well.

**AMERICAN SYCAMORE** (*Platanus occidentalis,* button-

Courtesy Fine Hardwoods Association

**Fig. 19. Sycamore wood grain.**

wood). (Fig. 19). A hardwood found in the eastern United States. The color of the wood ranges from reddish-brown to flesh brown. It can be successfully bleached. It is a medium heavy wood, averaging 34 pounds per cubic foot. It has a close, interlocking grain and a coarse texture. The pores are not visible to the naked eye, but the pores are very prominent. It is about average in hardness and strength. It is slightly above average in handtool workability. Sycamore has a tendency to warp and shrink. Great care should be taken to properly season the wood before use. This wood is generally used in cheaper grades of furniture and veneers.

**TAMO** *(Fraxinus mandschurica,* Japanese ash). (Fig. 20). Tamo is a hardwood imported from Japan and used in furniture frames and veneers. The wood has a light yellow color and a pronounced grain pattern resembling that of oak. A filler is gen-

Courtesy Fine Hardwoods Association

**Fig. 20. Tamo wood.**

85

erally required. It can be bleached with better than average results. It has many of the characteristics (strength, stiffness, resistance to shock, etc.) as American ash.

**TEAK** *(Tectona grandis,* teakwood). (Fig. 21). A hardwood

Courtesy Fine Hardwoods Association

Fig. 21. Teak wood.

found in Burma, India, Thailand, and Java and imported to the United States for use in fine grades of furniture. The wood has a yellowish-brown color. A filler is recommended. It is strong, hard, and durable. It strongly resembles walnut in its other characteristics.

**BLACK TUPELO** *(Nyssa sylvatica,* black gum, tupelo gum). This is a hardwood found in the eastern United States, and par-

86

ticularly in the southeastern region. The color of the wood ranges from a pale to a dark brownish gray. This is a fine-grained wood with small pores. There is usually no pattern, although some varieties have black streaks with no discernible arrangement to them. It will take almost any kind of stain, and for this reason is used to imitate other woods. Unstained, the wood closely resembles poplar (the latter is distinguished by the green tinge to the heartwood). Its workability with handtools ranges from average to above average. It carves well. Because of this and its excellent staining properties, it is used extensively in the manufacture of legs for veneered tables.

**BLACK WALNUT** (*Juglans nigra,* American walnut). (Fig.

Courtesy Fine Hardwoods Association

Fig. 22. Black walnut wood grain.

22). A hardwood found in the regions east of the Mississippi, and as far west as portions of Texas and Nebraska. The wood has a chocolate brown color with darker, occasionally purple streaks. This is a heavy wood, averaging 38 pounds per cubic foot. It has a striking grain pattern with large pores that take the form of dark streaks on the longitudinal surfaces. It is strong and stiff with good shock resistance. Black walnut is easily worked with handtools and machines well. The wood takes a high polish, stains well, holds paint with no difficulty, and takes to gluing well. A filler may or may not be used depending upon the desired finish. It is necessary, however, if a smooth finish is desired. All of the excellent attributes of black walnut make it one of the most extensively used woods in furniture construction.

**BLACK WILLOW** (*Salix nigra*). This is a hardwood found primarily in the Mississippi Valley. The wood is a grayish brown or light reddish brown with darker streaks. It has an interlocking grain pattern with a uniform texture. The wood is light, averaging 27 pounds per cubic foot. It is medium soft, rather low in strength, and is moderately high in shock resistance. Black willow wood is used in inexpensive furniture.

## SOFTWOODS

**BALD CYPRESS** (*Taxodium distichum,* southern cypress, white cypress, red cypress, yellow cypress, cypress). (Fig. 23). This softwood grows all along the coastal plains from Delaware to the Mexican border. The wood ranges in color from a light yellowish brown to a reddish-brown. It is a close-grained, even textured wood with little or no figure. Bald cypress is a medium heavy wood, weighing on the average of 32 pounds per cubic foot. It is about average in strength and stiffness. Bald cypress reacts well to most stains. It is easy to work with handtools.

**ALASKA CEDAR** (*Chamaecyparis nootkarensis,* yellow cedar). This tree grows along the Pacific coast from Alaska to as far south as southern Oregon. The wood is a bright, clear yellow. It noes not take a stain well. It weighs about 30 pounds per cubic foot. Alaska cedar rates about average in strength, stiffness, and

Courtesy U.S. Department of Agriculture

Fig. 23. Bald cypress wood.

hardness. It is somewhat higher than average in resistance to shock. This wood is frequently used in furniture construction.

**INCENSE-CEDAR** *(Libocedrus decurrens)*. (Fig. 24). A softwood found in California and southwestern Oregon. The wood has a reddish color. This is a light wood, weighs on the average of 26 pounds per cubic foot. It has a flat, straight grain. In appearance it closely resembles western red cedar. Incense-cedar is a medium soft, rather weak wood, with a low shock resistance. It is easy to work with handtools. It formerly enjoyed widespread use in the construction of cedar chests.

89

Courtesy U.S. Department of Agriculture

Fig. 24. Incense-cedar grain.

**EASTERN RED CEDAR** (*Juniperus virginiana*, red cedar). This tree is found throughout much of the United States east of the Rockies. The wood ranges in color from red to a reddish-brown. It weighs on the average 34 pounds per cubic foot. This is a close-grained, even-textured wood. Because of an oily film on the surface of the wood, it is necessary to seal it (a shellac is often used) before completing the finish.

**WESTERN RED CEDAR** (*Thuja plicata*). This is a softwood that grows in the western United States. The wood has a reddish brown color. It is a light weight wood, averaging 23 pounds per cubic foot. The wood is generally straight grained, and the texture is coarse. It is soft, not very strong, and low in shock resistance. It is subject to only slight shrinkage. It is very easy to work with handtools. Western red cedar does not hold nails well. It is easily glued, holds paints well, and will produce a good finish. It was used as a furniture wood in former times far more extensively than it is today.

**DOUGLAS-FIR** (*Pseudotsuga menziesii,* red fir, yellow fir, Douglas spruce). (Fig. 25). This softwood is found west of the Rocky Mountains in the United States, southern Canada, and northern Mexico. The color of the wood ranges from orange red to

*Courtesy U.S. Department of Agriculture*

Fig. 25. Douglas-fir grain.

91

red with tinges of yellow. It weighs about 33 pounds per cubic foot. It is average in hardness, strength, and resistance to shock. It is a little more difficult than some softwoods to work with handtools. It has above average gluing properties.

**WESTERN HEMLOCK** (*Tsuga heterophylla*). Western hemlock grows on the Pacific coast and in the Rocky Mountains. The color of the wood is white with a purple tinge. It averages about 29 pounds per cubic foot in weight. The texture of the grain is not as coarse as that of eastern hemlock. Consequently, it cuts more easily and produces smoother surfaces. This wood is about average in hardness, strength, and stiffness. Its shock resistance is low. Western hemlock is easy to work with both handtools and machine tools. It is sometimes used in the construction of furniture.

**EASTERN WHITE PINE** (*Pinus strobus,* white pine, northern white pine, soft pine). This wood is found growing in the northern sections of the eastern United States. It extends no further south than northern Georgia. The wood is a light brown color with a frequent reddish tinge. It is a light wood, averaging about 24 pounds per cubic foot in weight. It is about average in hardness, but low in strength and resistance to shock. It has a uniform texture and a straight grain. No filler is required with this wood. Western white pine is extensively used in furniture construction.

**YELLOW PINE** (*Pinus echinata,* shortleaf pine, southern yellow pine). (Fig. 26). This softwood grows throughout the southeastern United States. The color ranges from yellow and orange to a light or reddish brown. A filler is not generally required. It weighs about 36 pounds per cubic foot. It is about average in hardness, strength, stiffness, and shock resistance. Yellow pine is sometimes used in the construction of furniture.

**REDWOOD** (*Sequoia sempervirens*). The redwoods grow along the California coast and into southern Oregon. The color of the wood is a deep reddish brown. It weighs about 28 pounds per cubic foot. Redwood is average in hardness, strength, and stiffness. It is slightly below average in shock resistance. The grain in redwood is generally straight. A filler is not required. It is generally easy to work with handtools. The one exception is

*Courtesy U.S. Department of Agriculture*

**Fig. 26. Yellow pine grain.**

that it shows a tendency to split. Redwood will take a paint well under normal circumstances. Care must be taken to seal the surface of redwood, or the sap will bleed through the paint. This wood is sometimes used in the construction of lawn furniture.

**SITKA SPRUCE** (*Picea sitchensis*). A softwood found along the Pacific coast of North America. The color of the wood ranges from a light pinkish yellow to a pale brown. It is not a heavy wood, averaging only about 28 pounds per cubic foot. The wood has a medium hardness and stiffness, but is high in strength. It is somewhat lower than average in shock resistance. Sitka spruce has a straight grain and a uniform texture. Furniture construction is included among the many uses for sitka spruce.

93

# Chapter 4

# Veneering

Contrary to popular opinion, veneering will produce a stronger and more durable piece of furniture than one constructed from a solid piece of wood. Solid wood is subject to warping, cracking, shrinkage, and other defects resulting from moisture loss, the effects of heat and other conditions. A veneer construction, on the other hand, combines three to five layers of wood glued together to form a single piece. A typical example of veneer construction is illustrated by the piece of furniture in Fig. 1. It should be pointed out that gluing a face veneer to a solid base (such as a furniture table top) is not a true veneer construction, but rather a method of dressing up the appearance of the surface.

It is incorrect to view a veneer as simply the gluing of a thin layer of expensive wood over the surface of a cheaper and less desirable one. Veneering is an extremely old process that requires considerable skill, and the final composition of the veneer is more complex than one would initially suspect.

The term *veneer* can refer to either a face veneer or to each of the several layers (ply) used in the construction of a sheet of plywood or a wood panel. The primary purpose of the face veneer is to provide an attractive surface. These face veneer sheets are either glued directly to a solid base (e.g. a table top) or to the outer surface of a wood panel. The wood panels are usually constructed from three sheets (three-ply) or five sheets (five-ply) veneer. The three-ply panels can have either a veneer core or a lumber core, the latter providing a thicker and stronger panel (Fig. 2).

A *face veneer* is a very thin sheet (generally sold in 1/28 inch thicknesses) of high quality wood selected for its particularly at-

CORE
FACE VENEER
CROSS BANDING
CROSS BANDING
VENEER
VENEER
STRIP OF VENEER TO
COVER END GRAIN
BACK VENEER
STRIP OF VENEER
ON FRONT EDGE
DRAWER SIDE:
THIN BOARD

FACE VENEER
CORE
BACK VENEER
DRAWER BOTTOM:
ONE SHEET OF THICK VENEER
CORNER
SOLID POSTS
SIDE PANEL:
3-PLY VENEER

*Courtesy U.S. Department of Agriculture*

**Fig. 1. Examples of veneer construction.**

tractive figure (the distinctive marking or design created on the wood surface by grain patterns, annual growth rings, coloring, the method of cutting, and other factors). (See Table 1.)

Some woods with attractive figure patterns tend to be very expensive, and furniture constructed entirely from them would, in most cases, be beyond the financial reach of the average person. Other woods with equally attractive figure patterns create a problem by being too weak or too heavy. Veneering is a method of overcoming these problems. The attractive veneer sheet is glued to a core of very strong, lightweight, inexpensive wood.

Unfortunately, veneering is still associated with products of cheap quality. It gained this reputation largely in the nineteenth

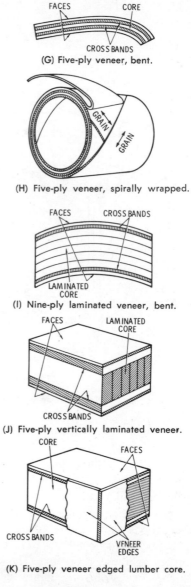

(A) Three-ply veneer.

(B) Three-ply lumber core.

(C) Five-ply veneer.

(D) Five-ply lumber core.

(E) Seven-ply veneer.

(F) Seven-ply lumber core.

(G) Five-ply veneer, bent.

(H) Five-ply veneer, spirally wrapped.

(I) Nine-ply laminated veneer, bent.

(J) Five-ply vertically laminated veneer.

(K) Five-ply veneer edged lumber core.

*Courtesy U.S. Department of Agriculture*

**Fig. 2. Types of plywood and veneered construction.**

century. During the 1860's, veneers were introduced in furniture construction for the first time on a widespread commercial basis. The quality was extremely disappointing. Consequently, veneering

## Table 1. Veneer Thicknesses

Thickness of veneer is expressed in fractions of an inch, or how many pieces of veneer are required, when placed one on top of another, to make an inch. When the wood-worker speaks of 1/24th veneer, he means it is 1/24 of an inch in thickness, or that 24 thicknesses are required to make an inch. The most common veneer thicknesses and their principal uses are listed below:

| | |
|---|---|
| 5/16 inch<br>1/4 inch<br>3/16 inch<br>1/6 inch<br>1/7 inch<br>1/8 inch<br>1/9 inch<br>1/10 inch<br>1/12 inch<br>1/16 inch | SPECIAL COMMERCIAL USES<br>Usually rotary cut, although sometimes sawed or sliced. Mostly "plain" figured wood. Used for boxes; architectural products, such as doors, panels, etc.; cross banding; and the familiar commercial uses for veneer; other than face veneers for furniture. |
| 1/20 inch<br>1/24 inch<br>1/28 inch<br>1/30 inch<br>1/32 inch | FURNITURE, CABINETS, ETC.<br>Usually rotary cut or sliced, although sometimes sawed, such as "quarter-sawed' oak. Used for face veneers on furniture, pianos, theatre seats and similar articles. Fancy figured crotches, burls, etc., are usually sliced. Plainer figures are rotary cut. |
| 1/50 inch<br>1/60 inch<br>1/72 inch<br>1/80 inch<br>1/100 inch | CIGAR BOXES, WALL PAPER, ETC.<br>Usually rotary cut or sliced. Used for special purposes, such as airplane construction, coverings or linings for cigar boxes, etc. Frequently mounted on paper or cardboard backing to give greater strength and to prevent damage in handling. |

quickly became associated in the average person's mind with poor quality furniture. This is no longer true of veneering. New methods of cutting or slicing the veneer sheets, better construction, and a wider selection of face veneers have improved both quality and strength.

Do not confuse veneers with plastic laminates. Veneers are thin sheets of natural wood. Plastic laminates (*Formica* is a common brand name) are composition materials that are sometimes used to imitate wood. This is not to imply that one is inferior to the other. They are simply two entirely different materials. Plastic laminates are described in greater detail in a section at the end of this chapter.

## WOOD FIGURE

Sometimes the term *figure* is used synonymously with that of *grain*. This is incorrect or, at very best, only partially correct.

Fig. 3. Areas of a tree trunk from which different cuts are taken.

Grain is only one aspect of figure. As was pointed out above, the term figure is correctly applied to the distinctive wood surface markings or designs created by such surface factors as grain patterns, annual growth rings, coloring, and texture in combination with the method of cutting or slicing the wood. Thus, a particular figure may have a natural origin (that is, it may be characteristic of a certain wood or woods) or it may depend more on the way in which the wood was cut (for example, the flake figure in black cherry produced by quarter-sawing the wood). Some figure patterns are found in only one or two types of wood (for example,

*Courtesy Fine Hardwoods Association*

**Fig. 4. Mahogany wood, crotch cut.**

99

the lace pattern in lacewood); whereas, others (for example, the stripe or ribbon effect) are found with slight variations in a number of woods.

There are many types of figure patterns and as many names for them. Some of these names describe the pattern (e.g. birdseye, ribbon, mottle), while others refer to the origin of the cut (e.g. crotch). The portion of the tree from which the cut is made will frequently determine the figure (Fig. 3).

The *crotch figure* (Fig. 4) is created by cutting below the point where a fork in the trunk (or large branch) begins. The figure has a splash or swirl pattern to it which results from the

Courtesy Fine Hardwoods Association

Fig. 5. Mahogany wood, swirl cut.

distortion of the fibers during the formation of the fork. A *feather crotch figure* is one characterized by a feather-like spread of the fibers. A *swirl figure* (Fig. 5) originates in the same general area, but on the outside edge of the crotch.

A *plain-stripe figure* (Fig. 6) (or *ribbon figure* or *ribbon-stripe figure*) is obtained from quarter sawed cuts (cuts at a right angle to the annual growth rings). The annual growth rings form the

*Courtesy Fine Hardwoods Association*

**Fig. 6. Sapele, striped figure.**

stripes. The grain is generally interlocking. A *rope figure* (Fig. 7) (often found in avodire) is one characterized by broken stripes, with the breaks in the stripes all running in the same direction.

101

This pattern results from interlocking grains coming together with wavy grains. A *broken stripe figure* (Fig. 8) is, as its name suggests, one characterized by broken stripes. It differs from a rope figure in that the breaks are irregular.

Courtesy Fine Hardwoods Association

**Fig. 7. Avodire, rope figure.**

The *blister figure* shows uneven annual growth rings which are produced through plain-sawing. A *quilted figure* is similar in appearance to the blister figure but usually covers a wider area. As with the butt figure, these are produced through compression of the grain. However, in the case of the quilted figure, this occurs higher on the trunk, generally beneath a large branch.

Fig. 8. Mahogany, broken stripe figure.

Courtesy Fine Hardwoods Association

A *butt* or *stump figure* (Fig. 9) is obtained from the stump or base of the tree. As the tree grows, the wood at the base is compressed. This compression creates the waves and ripples known as butt figure. Walnut is the usual source for this interesting pattern.

A *burl figure* (Fig. 10) results from a strong distortion of the grain pattern caused by the protrusion of a thick twisted growth of wood which extends from the trunk or a branch. The burl usually results from temporary cell division caused by an injury to this area of the tree. A figure which closely resembles a burl is the *snail figure*. This is produced by a compression of the fibers in the trunk. Like the butt figure, it is usually found in walnut.

103

Fig. 9. Butt or stump veneer.

Courtesy Reliance Universal, Inc.

The *birdseye figure* (Fig. 11) receives its name from the many small circular patterns caused by the indention of the fibers.

A *curly figure* results from the grain fibers being twisted during growth. This produces a curly or wavy pattern which usually follows the contours of a knot or some other defect.

A *wavy figure* is characterized by a parallel wave in the grain. The *fiddleback figure* (Figs. 12 and 13) (found in some types of

Courtesy Fine Hardwoods Association

Fig. 10. Carpathian Elm, burl figure.

mahogany) is also characterized by a wavy grain pattern. This wave pattern results from an irregular fiber arrangement. Unlike those in the wavy figure, the fiddleback waves are more broken.

Courtesy Fine Hardwoods Association

Fig. 11. Maple tree, birdseye figure.

Cutting through the medullary waves of the wood with a quarter saw cut will produce a *silver grain figure* (usually found in sycamore and oak) or a *flake figure* (black cherry). Another figure produced by quarter sawing is the *mottle figure* (Fig. 14) found in narra and teak. The grain is either twisted or interwoven with

105

the fibers arranged in short wave-like configurations. The dappled figure shown in Fig. 15 has longer wave-like patterns.

Courtesy Fine Hardwoods Association

Fig. 12. Mahogany, fiddleback figure.

## VENEERING WOODS, TOOLS, AND MATERIALS

Many of the fine woods used in veneering were described in the last chapter (Chapter 3. TYPES OF WOOD). Almost every type of wood color and figure is available to the home crafts-man for veneering. It is a problem of selection, not supply.

106

Courtesy Fine Hardwoods Association

Fig. 13. African mahogany, mottled and fiddleback figure.

The tools and materials used in veneering are largely specific to this type of finishing operation. For veneering, an adequately equipped workshop should include the following:

1. Veneer saw,
2. Veneer roller,
3. Veneer edge trimmer,
4. Veneer groove cutter,
5. Veneer strip and border cutter,
6. Veneer press frame,
7. Veneer repair tool,

8. Veneer tape,
9. Non-flammable contact cement.

Fig. 14. Makori, mottled figure.

A veneer saw (Fig. 16) is a double-edge cutting device used for trimming the edges of a veneer sheet, or for creating tight fitting joints between two or more veneer sheets. The cut should be guided with a straightedge.

The veneer roller (Fig. 17) consists of a free turning, hardwood wheel used for rolling veneer joints and for pressing veneer sheets to core panels. Using a veneer roller greatly reduces or eliminates the possibility of burnishing the veneer.

Courtesy Fine Hardwoods Association

Fig. 15. Walnut, dappled figure.

Sometimes you will find it necessary to make smooth and even cuts on edges of glued veneers. A veneer edge trimmer (Fig. 18) is recommended for this purpose. This tool is designed to cut the veneer with both a forward and backward movement thereby eliminating the usual chips or splits at the ends of the veneer.

A veneer groove cutter (Fig. 19) will enable you to cut straight, curved, and circular grooves in a single operation. The grooves can be of various depths and widths depending upon the adjustment.

The veneer groove cutter is generally used in conjunction with a veneer strip and border cutter (Fig. 20). This tool contains a single retractable knife on one side and a set of two knives with spacers on the other. It is used for cutting and trimming wide borders, or for cutting strips of veneer to a number of different widths.

Fig. 16. A veneer saw.

A veneer press frame (Fig. 21) is recommended for applying the pressure required when gluing veneer sheets to a core with a glue other than contact cement. This tool is constructed from ad-

Fig. 17. A veneer roller.

justable press screws and two or more frames. The frame should be made from a strong, hard wood (e.g. maple, oak, or yellow pine), and all joints should be strongly bolted together.

The veneer repair tool (Fig. 22) is designed for cutting out and replacing (by insertion) small damaged areas or defects on the surface of a veneer. It uses a spring ejector for both removal and insertion. The cuts are made in irregular shapes so that the patch is less obvious.

110

The most suitable glue for veneering is a nonflammable contact cement (Fig. 23). Use of this glue requires that both the core
surface and the bottom of the veneer be coated and allowed to
dry thoroughly before being brought into contact. *Elmer's* white
glue is recommended for joining the edges of matching pieces of

Fig. 18. A veneer edge trimmer.

Fig. 19. A veneer groove cutter.

111

veneer. A veneer tape (or masking tape) is used to temporarily hold veneer sheets together and in the desired position while the glue is drying or the edges are being trimmed.

**Fig. 20. A veneer strip and border cutter.**

*Courtesy Homecraft Veneer*

*Courtesy Adjustable Clamp Co.*

**Fig. 21. A veneer press frame.**

Tools not specifically designed for veneering may also be used for this type of work. For example, an *X-acto* knife (Fig. 24),

*Courtesy Homecraft Veneer*

**Fig. 22. A veneer repair tool.**

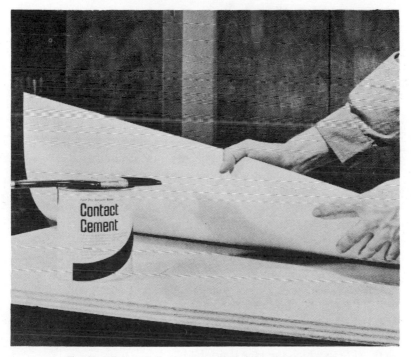

**Fig. 23. Using contact cement to glue a face veneer to a core.**

113

straight-edged razor, or a jack plane can be used for trimming. Feel free to substitute any type of tool that will help you do your work better.

Fig. 24. An X-acto knife.

## CUTTING THE VENEER

The three basic methods for cutting a veneer sheet from the log are:
1. Sawing,
2. Slicing,
3. A number of rotary-cut processes (the straight rotary cut, the half-round rotary cut, and the back rotary cut) (Fig. 25).

In both the sawing and slicing methods, a flitch is used rather than the whole log. (Fig. 26) A *flitch* is a squared longitudinal section of the log with a particularly striking figure or grain pattern. Sawed veneers are produced by placing the flitch on a movable carriage and cutting with a circular saw. Sliced veneers are produced by placing the flitch on a carriage or platform that raises and lowers before the cutting blade. The blade is a stationary one. The flitch is presoaked in steaming water before being sliced.

With sawed veneers both sides of the cut are equally suitable as an exposed surface. In the case of sliced veneers, the side toward the knife (this is called the *open* or *loose* side) suffers imperfections from the knife as a result of the cutting process. This is the side to which the glue is applied.

114

Sawed veneers can be either quarter-sawed or plain-sawed. Quarter-sawed wood (Fig. 27) has a grain which runs parallel to the length of the wood. This type of grain is sometimes referred to as *vertical grain* and results from the cut being made to form a

FLAT CUT: half log is moved up and down against the knife. Slicing is parallel to the center line. Veneer sheets are log length, vary in width. Pattern curvacious at center to ripple striped edges.

ROTARY CUT: whole log revolves against blade, peeling off continuous sheet, wide as log length. Standard size sheets cut from it; pattern quite bold.

RIFE CUT: used for oak, shows striped grain pattern. Quartered log is swung in arc against blade.

QUARTER CUT: quartered log moves against blade at right angles to growth rings. Produces striped veneer pattern; some species pencil lined, others wavy, often flakes.

*Courtesy Fine Hardwoods Association*

**Fig. 25. Various veneer cutting methods.**

radius to the annual growth rings. In plain-sawed wood (Fig. 28) the grain runs along the width of the wood because the cut was made more or less parallel to the annual growth rings.

Actually, only a few veneers are produced by sawing the flitch. These are usually the very hard woods that split easily.

Fig. 26. Preparation of walnut flitch.

The rotary cut method uses the entire log rather than the smaller sized flitch. As with sliced veneers, the log must be softened by steaming in water. The softened log is then placed in a veneer lathe and rotated against a stationary knife. A long continuous sheet is cut from the log by slanting the knife toward the center of the log. Rotary cut veneers also have an *open* (or *loose*) side and a *closed* side. However, it is much more difficult to tell the two apart, particularly in a well cut veneer. Most of the veneers used today are produced by the rotary cut method.

Two important modifications of the standard rotary cut are:

1. The half-round rotary cut,
2. The back rotary cut.

The first method involves cutting the log off center, which produces a broader grain pattern. The cutting is done from the outside (or half-round side) of the log. With the back rotary cut, the cutting is done from the center of the log.

Fig. 27. Quarter-sawed.

117

**Fig. 28. Plain-sawed.**

## VENEER PANELS

A veneer panel is essentially a section of plywood covered on the top and bottom with thin sheets of wood selected for their high quality.

The core (everything exclusive of the face veneers) of a five-ply sheet (or all-veneer sheet) is constructed by gluing together a series of narrow (one to three inch wide) sheets of veneer. The narrowness of width discourages warping. In addition to being narrow, these strips of wood should also be straight grained. This

118

is important because the grain of the next layer will be glued at right angles to the grain of the core wood. Once the glue has dried, the core must be carefully planed so that the entire surface will be even. This should be tested with a T-square. There should not be the slightest depression in the surface of the core piece. This is essential to a proper gluing of the first layer of veneers (or cross bands) across the surfaces of the core. These inner veneer pieces are relatively inexpensive and are glued across the grain of the core for the purpose of giving added strength. They are eventually covered by the higher quality face veneer (the surface exposed to view) and a lower quality back veneer. The inner veneers are glued so that their grains run across the grains of the core wood. On the other hand, the outer veneers are glued with their grains running parallel to those of the core. This change in direction in

Fig. 29. The various layers of a veneer sheet.

which the grains of each layer runs adds to the overall strength of the unit (Fig. 29).

## VENEER MATCHING

Veneer sheets cut from the same flitch are kept together so that they can be matched to form larger sheets. It is almost impossible to match veneers from other than the same sheet because of differences in coloring and figure. Not only can veneer matching produce larger sheets, but special effects can be achieved by the arrangement of the pattern. Some of the more commonly used methods of matching the veneer patterns are:

1. The diamond match,
2. The reverse diamond,
3. The book match,
4. The end match,
5. The four way match,
6. The slip match.

In the diamond match (Fig. 30) pattern, four sheets with a

Fig. 30. Diamond match pattern in veneer.

Courtesy Reliance Universal, Inc.

straight stripe in the veneer pattern are arranged so that the stripes form a diamond. The stripes in the reverse diamond (Fig.

Fig. 31. Reverse diamond pattern.

Courtesy Reliance Universal, Inc.

31) are arranged to run in the direction of the four outside corners. A book match (Fig. 32) has the two sides of veneer sheets joined so that they produce a mirror image. The end match (Fig. 33) uses the same principle but joins the ends of the veneer sheets.

Fig. 32. Book match pattern.

*Courtesy Reliance Universal, Inc.*

The four-way match (Fig. 34) combines the book match with the end match. The veneer sheets are joined in slip matching (Fig. 35) side by side to produce a repetition of the figure.

Fig. 33. Vertical butt match pattern.

*Courtesy Reliance Universal, Inc.*

These matched veneer patterns are used as table tops, the exposed fronts of dresser drawers, the fronts of cabinets, desk tops, and wall panels (Fig. 36).

Face veneers for matching are sold in sheets cut to a $\frac{1}{28}$ inch thickness. These may be purchased from various mail-order houses. Most of these companies offer a wide selection of face veneers including complete kits for the beginner.

121

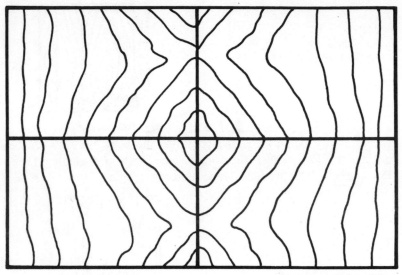

Courtesy Reliance Universal, Inc.

Fig. 34. Four-way center and butt match pattern.

Fig. 35. Slip match pattern.

Courtesy Reliance Universal, Inc.

## VENEERING

Veneering can be as uncomplicated as gluing a face veneer to the surface of a piece of furniture. On the other hand, it can involve the complete construction of a wood veneer panel.

It was pointed out earlier in this chapter that the complete veneering process consists of the gluing of *at least* a face veneer sheet (a back veneer sheet of slightly lower quality is also sometimes added) to a core unit. The core can be a lumber core center with veneer sheets glued to either side; an all-veneer core

122

Courtesy Reliance Universal, Inc.

Fig. 36. Use of veneer in wall panels.

consisting of three-ply (three veneer sheets), five-ply, and even seven-ply constructions (note that the layers are in odd numbers with the middle sheet acting as the core); or the surface of a piece of furniture you wish to cover.

The following is an outline of the veneering process. It can serve as a guide on your own particular projects. Remember to regard it as a guide only. Some of the steps may not apply to what

123

you are doing. On the other hand, you may find it necessary to expand upon it.

The various stages in a typical veneering operation are as follows:

1. Decide first whether you want to use a single face veneer or a matched veneer. Face veneer sheets in both domestic and imported woods are generally sold in 4 inch to 12 inch widths and 3 foot lengths (longer lengths can be obtained on request) with a standard thickness of $\frac{1}{28}$ inch.

2. The single face veneer sheet will have to be cut so that no joint shows. You will also have to do the cutting if you wish to make your own matched veneers. However, matched veneers can also be ordered (the pieces taped and ready for gluing) from a number of mail-order houses in 12 inch by 24 inch sheets, 15 inch by 30 inch sheets, and 30 inch by 30 inch sheets.

3. Lightly sand the surface to which the veneer will be joined until all defects or irregularities are removed and it is uniformly smooth. If several pieces of wood are to be joined together, the joints must be smooth. Any dips in the surface have to be filled and leveled. Any surface bumps must be planed and sanded so that they are even with the rest of the surface.

4. Repeat this procedure for the underside of the veneer sheet.

5. Thoroughly clean the two surfaces you just sanded.

6. Take the veneer sheet and position it on the surface to which it is to be glued. This is the time to decide the direction you want the grain to run as well as the arrangement and positioning of the figure and grain pattern. If you estimated correctly, the total area of the veneer sheet that you purchased (either a single piece or the possible combination of several sheets) overlaps the surface to which it is to be glued at least ½ inch on all sides.

7. Now that you have decided upon the exact positioning of the veneer sheet and this sheet is a single one (that is, it

has not been necessary to cut and join several pieces together to make a veneer sheet large enough to cover the area), take a marking pencil and mark the underside where it meets the edge of the surface to which it is to be glued.

8. You may find it necessary to join two or more veneer sheets together to make one large enough for the surface you wish to cover. Your first problem will be to find two veneer sheets that are very close in figure, grain, and color. You will want to have the grains of the various pieces running in the same direction if you wish to join them so that they appear to be one piece. Above all, the joint between the two pieces must not show.

9. Overlap the two edges that are to be joined (about 1 inch should do). Take a straight edge and draw a line across the veneer sheet at the point you want to make the cut. *X-acto* has a number of blades that will cut through both veneer sheets quite well. After you have made your cut, fold the two sheets over so that the face veneer surfaces are together. Take two 1 × 4 inch boards with straight edges and a length measuring one inch beyond the edge of the two veneer sheets. Take two clamps and attach them to the 1 × 4 inch boards at a point over the outside edges of the two veneer sheets.

10. Allow only about ¼ inch of the veneer sheets to extend beyond the edge (lengthwise) of the 1 × 4 inch boards. Plane off the excess and remove the clamps and 1 × 4 inch boards (Fig. 37). Open up the veneer sheets and place the newly planed ends together. If the match is perfect, glue the edges (Fig. 38). Temporarily tape the good side until you are ready to glue (Fig. 39).

11. The problem now is to determine how close to the core you want to cut the veneer sheet. This, in turn, depends upon whether the top veneer sheet is to overlap the veneer edge strip or the reverse is to be the case. Make your decision about the type of edge you want and then read Step 12 before continuing.

125

12. The excess wood must be cut away from the veneer sheet. Since it is very easy to chip or split the surface, special precautions must be taken. Place straight-edged

C-CLAMP

1"

VENEER
SHEETS

4"

VENEER
SHEETS

HARDWOOD
STRAIGHT
EDGE

PLANE THE EXPOSED
EDGE OF THE VENEER
SHEETS DOWN TO THE
HARDWOOD SURFACE

Fig. 37. Planning the veneer sheets.

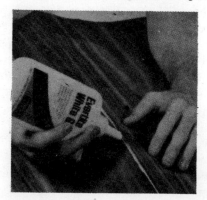

Fig. 38. Gluing the edges of the veneer sheets together.

Fig. 39. Taping the glued veneer sheets
until the edges dry.

wood blocks (made from 1 × 6 inch boards cut to the length of the veneer sheet) on both sides of the veneer sheet so that the outer edge of each block is on the line drawn in Step 9. Use C-clamps to keep the wood blocks in place.

13. Take a veneer saw or knife and cut away the excess wood to about ¼ inch of the line drawn in Step 9. Take a jack plane and trim the rough edge down to the line. Use a sanding block and sandpaper (changing from a medium to a fine grade) to finish the edge.

14. At this point, you must decide what kind of edge you want. Any surface to which a face veneer has been glued must be finished along the edges so that the layers of veneer sheets are hidden from view.

The easiest method of finishing the edge is to take a block of wood and a rough grade of sandpaper (to be followed by medium and fine grades in that order) and sand the edge smooth. After you have finished sanding, wipe away the excess sawdust and dirt and paint the surface of the edge a dark color (flat black, black enamel, red brown, dark brown, ochre, etc.) (Fig. 40).

A more difficult method of finishing the edges is to glue a strip of veneer into place. This strip is usually selected to match the veneer sheet covering the larger surface. The cutting method is the same as the one described in Steps 12 and 13 (Fig. 41).

127

1. SAND THE EDGE OF THE SURFACE

2. PAINT THE EDGE A DARK   OPAQUE COLOR

**Fig. 40. Painting the edge.**

BOTTOM OF VENEER

**Fig. 41. Gluing veneer strip to the edge.**

15. In Step 5 you were asked to thoroughly dust the bottom of the veneer sheet and the surface to which it is to be glued. Dust it again if it needs it.

16. Coat the surfaces to be joined with a contact veneer cement. If you are applying veneer to a table top, desk top, or the top of a cabinet or dresser, coat the edge of the top with cement also.

17. Allow the contact cement sufficient time to dry thoroughly before placing the two recently coated surfaces together. The cement coated surfaces will bond instantly on contact. Therefore, you must exercise great care.

18. Place newspaper so that it completely covers the glue-coated surface of the piece of furniture.

19. Place the veneer sheet on top of the newspaper with the glue coated side down. The dried contact cement will not stick to the paper. It will only bond to the other surface coated with cement.

20. Press down on one end of the veneer while you carefully pull the paper out from the other end. Press against the center of the veneer and outward toward the edges. Use a small veneer roller to press the bonded surfaces into even firmer contact.

21. Press screws are used to construct veneer press frames which are particularly well suited for the type of clamping required in veneering. In the home workshop C-clamps and ¾ inch plywood serve as an acceptable substitute. Clamping pressure is necessary when glues other than contact cement are used.

### REPAIRING VENEERS

Cut away the damaged area in such a way that as many sides of the cut run parallel to the grain as possible. Those sides that cannot do so must be cut so that they form angles that are less than a right angle to the grain. The piece that you remove from the veneer surface will be a trapezoid or some variation of a diamond.

129

Find a wood with a grain matching that of the damaged veneer. The likelihood of finding an exact duplicate is extremely rare (unless you have saved veneer sheets from the same flitch). Because of this, it is best to use a repair piece with a lighter surface color and stain it to match the older veneer.

Measure the opening you have cut in the damaged veneer. Take a piece of stiff paper (poster paper will do) or thin card-

(A) Damaged veneer.

(B) Cutting out damaged section.

(C) Damaged section removed.

(D) Paper pattern.

(E) Replacement insert cut from pattern.

(F) Replacement insert glued into position.

**Fig. 42. Repairing damaged veneer sheet.**

board and, using these measurements, cut out a pattern. Place the pattern on the piece of veneer to be matched. Make certain that it is positioned in such a way that the grains of both surfaces will match. Cut out the veneer patch and insert it in the hole you cut. *Do not force it in.* If it is too tight, remove it and sand the edges. Continue to do this until it will slide smoothly and snugly into the hole. Glue it in place (Fig. 42).

## TRANSVENEER (PLASTIC VENEER TRANSFER)

A *transveneer* (or plastic veneer transfer) is, in many respects, simply a larger version of the decalcomania transfer (transveneers are available in sheets as large as 32 inches by 48 inches, where as decalcomania transfers are sold in sheets of much smaller size).

The transveneer consists of at least three layers:

1. The lacquer background,
2. A paper thin coating of lacquer over which a color print has been superimposed (a photoengraving of wood grain or some other design),
3. A layer of paper (there are sometimes two layers of paper, making a fourth layer for the transveneer sheet).

The paper layer is removed by moistening it with a damp cloth. After the paper is removed, the glue residue is sponged off the sur face of the imprinted layer of lacquer.

The glue suggested by the manufacturer of the transveneer sheet is applied to the sheet and it is then affixed to the surface being covered. Use a roller to remove all wrinkles and air bubbles. Use a damp cloth to remove any excess glue.

Transveneer sheets are successfully applied only over small-pored (close-grained) woods. In woods with larger pores, the grain pattern has a tendency to bleed through the transveneer sheet. If you have any doubts about the surface, it would be wise to sand the surface, fill it, seal it, sand it again, and apply a thin coat of lacquer.

Transveneers are used in place of veneers in the cheaper grades of furniture. The very cheaply priced "complete three-piece bedroom suite" sometimes advertised on television and in the newspaper is most likely to be of transveneer construction.

Humidity will often cause the thin transveneer sheet to peel back at the edges of the furniture. This is particularly noticeable on larger surfaces (such as dressers). A small dab of *Testors* or *Elmer's* white glue can be used to correct this. Press the transveneer down and wipe away the excess glue with a damp cloth.

## PLASTIC LAMINATE

*Plastic laminates* are one of several products resulting from the lamination process. The type of layering (lamina) used in lamination determines the end product. Plastic laminates use a lamina of plastic.

These plastic laminates resemble veneers in that they are built up from several layers of material. In the case of plastic laminates, there are several layers of paper impregnated with resin. The core layers are soaked in phenol-formaldehyde resin; the transparent overlay in melamine resin. The melamine overlay acts as a protective layer for the printed sheet just beneath. All the layers are bonded together under extremely high pressure and temperatures. *Formica, Naugatop,* and *Micarta* are a few of the common trade mark names sold commercially.

These plastic laminates are used primarily for table tops (dining room tables, end tables, coffee tables, etc.) in furniture construction. They provide an extremely durable surface, and resist almost any kind of stain.

# Chapter 5

# Inlaying

*Inlaying* may be defined as the adorning of a wood surface by the insertion of different colored woods. Sometimes the inserted woods form a complex, ornamental design (Fig. 1). Simpler forms of inlay consist of one or more woods arranged to form decorative borders (Fig. 2). Inlaying can be divided into two distinct types:

1. Intarsia,
2. Marquetry.

*Intarsia* is a true inlay process. That is, the wood inserts are glued into a groove or recess that has been cut from the background (base) wood. The wood inserts may be all one color or have several colors. The background wood may be either lighter or darker than the wood inserts, thus providing a contrastive border for the design formed by the wood inserts. The depth of the depression cut into the background wood varies in accordance with the thickness on the inlay. Intarsia is of Italian origin and is historically a forerunner of marquetry.

*Marquetry* is dismissed by some as simply the French word for "inlay" and therefore different in name only. As a matter of fact, the word "marquetry" *is* derived from the French verb *marqueter,* "to inlay", however a distinction can be made between marquetry and intarsia in the method by which the decorative pieces are attached to the background. In intarsia (which is regarded as *true* inlaying), the decorative wood is inserted in grooves and recesses cut from the background wood. Marquetry, on the other hand, consists of cutting a pattern out of a veneer (i.e. not a solid wood background) and inserting a decorative design made

133

from other veneers cut from the same pattern to form a panel. The entire panel can then either be glued to a solid wood background or inlayed in that wood.

Inlaying involves not only the insertion of decorative woods in grooves and recesses cut from solid wood backgrounds, but

Fig. 1. Complex ornamental inlay designs.

also the insertion of such materials as stone, shell, and glass (to mention only a few) into other types of backgrounds. The inlaying of materials other than wood is known as mosaic (mosaicing), and is examined in a later section of this chapter.

134

Fig. 2. Inlay border.

## WOODS, TOOLS, AND MATERIALS

Almost any kind of wood can be used for inlays, but the best inlay woods will have one or more of the following characteristics:

1. Good workability,
2. An even grain with little or no figure,
3. A color light enough to stain,
4. The tendency to take an even, uniform stain.

Using a wood that cuts and trims easily makes inlaying (and marquetry) a lot less difficult. The inlaying procedure frequently involves the cutting and repeated trimming of a wood piece until it is just the right size to fit into the groove or recess. Some woods are subject to splintering or chipping when being cut. The cutting of such woods requires great skill and patience, and sometimes additional time spent in repairing splintered or chipped pieces. Since this can be annoying and time consuming, I would recommend selecting the wood you use with great care.

Very dark inlay woods (e.g. ebony, orientalwood, and walnut) are used for borders or contrastive areas. The light colored inlay woods (e.g. tulipwood, satinwood, holly, and hardwood) are often used because they can be easily stained. This is particularly useful in the restoration of work where matching the color of a missing piece becomes necessary. Stain resistant areas, woods that crack or split easily, and woods that are difficult to cut or trim should be avoided by the beginner.

135

All different types of wood are commercially available to the home craftsman. Mail-order houses that sell woodworking tools and supplies offer a wide range of inlay and veneer woods. They will be happy to send you their catalogs, and in some instances samples of their woods.

One form of inlaying consists of creating borders along square or rectangular shapes with narrow strips of wood. This is sometimes referred to as *line inlay*. The wood strips (inlay bandings) may be one solid piece of wood or built up from a number of different woods. Examples of the multicolored effect possible

Fig. 3. Inlay Bondings.

with the latter is shown in Fig. 3. Inlay bandings are of varying widths, approximately ½₈ inch thick, and sold in 36 inch lengths.

Pre-cut inlay pictures are available commercially from the mail-order houses. As shown in Fig. 4, these are available in a number of different designs. It is also possible to purchase inlay picture kits that are not pre-cut. These are complete kits containing inlay border woods, hardboard mounting panels, all the veneer wood required for the project, master patterns for cutting, and a number of other items necessary for a successful job. Cutting must be done with a suitable saw.

Fig. 4. Pre-cut inlay pictures.

The tools and materials used for inlaying are similar in most respects to those used for veneering. However, there are some that are probably more common to the former. Among the tools and materials you may find useful for inlaying are the following:

1. A jigsaw, hand coping saw, or fret saw,
2. A straight-edged razor,
3. A portable electric router or a router plane,
4. *X-acto* knives,
5. A veneer saw knife,
6. A veneer roller,
7. A try square,
8. Clamps,
9. A miter cutting board,
10. A suitable glue.

Three suitable saws for cutting inlay are the jigsaw, the hand coping saw, and the fret saw. When handcutting, hold the saw so that its blade is always in a vertical position and at a right angle

137

to the wood surface (Fig. 5). Use a blade with a very narrow kerf.

Fig. 5. Sawing at a right angle to the wood surface.

A straight-edged razor is extremely useful for trimming the edge of inlay inserts after they have been cut out with the saw.

Use a router plane (Fig. 6) or a portable electric router to cut the groove or recess in the surface of the background wood. An *X-acto* knife is useful for cutting along the edges of the design before removing the wood from the recessed area. It can also be used to make miter cuts on inlay bandings. For this purpose, a miter cutting board will assist you in making the type of corners required in line inlaying.

138

Fig. 6. Using a router plane.

The veneer saw knife (Fig. 7) is used to make cuts across pieces of veneer. Larger pieces can be reduced to the approximate size required for the job with this tool.

Pressure can be applied to inlay bandings with a veneer roller (Fig. 8). Clamps are also used for applying pressure to the inlay inserts.

Fig. 7. A veneer saw knife.

139

Fig. 8. A veneer roller.

The metal edges of a try square is useful for making both straight edge and miter cuts.

A variety of glues can be used for inlay work. Hot animal glue was once a favorite with many cabinetmakers because it did not discolor the wood. However, it required special preparation and has been replaced in many shops by glues more convenient to use. Casein glue, rubber cement, and a number of others are used today. Whatever your selection, the glue you use should be easy to apply, should form a strong bond, and should not discolor the wood.

## LINE INLAY

There are three basic types of inlaying:
1. Line inlay,
2. Corner inlay,
3. Center inlay.

Line inlay consists of creating borders along square or rectangular shapes with narrow strips of wood. These strips of decorative wood (sometimes referred to as inlay bandings) are inserted into grooves parallel to the edges of the larger wood surface.

The procedure for applying inlay bandings is as follows:
1. Use a ruler and pencil, and outline the position of the groove for the inlay banding.
2. Rout out the groove. The groove must be cut so that it is slightly shallower than the inlay piece. The width of the groove will be exactly the same as the width of the inlay banding.

140

3. Coat the bottom of the recess with glue (some prefer coating the bottom of the inlay banding instead).
4. Place the inlay banding in the groove. If the fit is tight (which is more desirable than being too loose), force it in with a hammer. Do not strike the inlay banding without placing a piece of felt or cardboard between the hammer and the wood. If the fit is loose, it will be necessary to clamp the inlay banding until it has dried.
5. Allow enough time for the glue to thoroughly dry.
6. After the glue has dried, lightly sand the inlay banding until it is level with the surface.
7. Cover the inlay banding with a shellac washcoat before doing any filling or staining of the rest of the surface. Otherwise, you may ruin the inlay colors. It is best to line the edge of the inlay banding strip with masking tape before applying the washcoat.

## CORNER AND CENTER INLAY

Corner inlays consist of decorative designs inserted at corner positions on the wood surface. Center inlays are positioned in the exact center. A decorative design for a center inlay may be relatively small or it may cover most of the surface area. Regardless of size, the design expands outward from a center point on the surface. The size of corner inlays is somewhat limited by the angle of the corner.

The procedure for making corner and center inlays is similar to the one described for line inlay. However, the problem of obtaining a close fit between the inserted piece and the recess cut into the wood surface is usually greater with corner and center inlays than with line inlay work. For a more detailed description, read THE INLAYING PROCEDURE section in this chapter.

### The Inlaying Procedure

The inlaying procedure for line inlay work was described under that chapter sub-heading. This particular section is devoted to a description of the procedure for inserting inlay pictures and

141

other decorative designs into the background wood surface. It is slightly more difficult than line inlay, but most of its procedural steps apply equally well to the latter.

Proper fit is a major problem in inlaying. The inserted pieces must fit snugly into their recesses and grooves. An insert consisting of a few straight edges (e.g. inlay bandings, squares, and rectangles) is relatively easy to use. The problems begin with curved or irregular shaped designs.

The inlaying procedure for center inlay (or corner inlay) is as follows:

1. Take a piece of paper and draw an outline of the decorative design you want to use as an inlay. This will serve as a pattern.

2. Cut out the pattern, position it on the inlay wood, and trace the outline of the design.

3. Using a jigsaw (other suitable cutting tools are suggested in the section WOODS, TOOLS, AND MATERIALS), cut out the inlay design.

4. Lightly sand the edges of the inlay until they are smooth. Do *not* round them. All edges must be vertically straight and square to the surface of the inlay. If this is not accomplished, then the inlay will not fit properly.

5. Place the inlay on the surface of the background wood, position it carefully, and trace its outline.

6. Cut out the area you have outlined with a machine router. Hand cutting can also be done, but it is slower and much more difficult. Before you use the router, cut straight down with a sharp knife along the edge of the outline. This will form the edges of the recess.

7. Be very careful when you cut the recess for the insert. Take your time, because your cuts must be made with absolute accuracy. Otherwise, a space will occur between the edge of the inlay and the edge of the recess. This will fill with glue and give the appearance of a dark, uneven border when the glue dries.

8. The recess should be cut slightly shallower than the thickness of the inlay insert. This will cause the inlay to

142

protrude slightly above the surface, but this will be sanded smooth after the glue has thoroughly dried.

9. The glue may be applied to either the bottom of the insert or the recessed area. For many years hot animal glue was a favorite for inlaying because it left no glue film or discoloration. Specially prepared rubber cements with these same characteristics (though, perhaps, not the same adhesive strength) are now becoming available. Casein glues are also popular.

10. Press the inlay insert into the recess, and immediately wipe off any excess glue that may have squeezed through the edges with a clean dry cloth.

11. A tight fitting inlay (preferably one that requires the use of a hammer to force it into the recess) will generally not require clamping.

12. Allow the glue enough time to dry thoroughly before any sanding is done. The inlay may be subject to both swelling (by absorbing the moisture from the glue) and shrinking (contraction during the drying). Consequently, the true position of the inlay with respect to the surface can only be established after the glue has thoroughly dried.

13. Sand the surface with a fine grade of sandpaper. Dust it with a clean dry cloth, and sand it again with a very fine grade.

14. See FINISHING INLAYS AND OVERLAYS for suggested finishes.

## REPAIRING AND RESTORING INLAYS

Repairing an inlay appears difficult to many people, but it need not be so. It is essentially a problem of replacing an inlay piece with one that matches it in color and shape. Since the procedure for making inlay repairs is identical to the one used for repairing marquetry, all information given in this section will pertain to both.

There are three basic types of repairs associated with inlaying. Beginning with the easiest type of repair and progressing to the most difficult, these are:

1. Re-gluing a loose piece,
2. Replacing a missing piece,
3. Replacing a chipped or broken piece.

Sometimes a piece of inlay will become loose or fall off completely. Since you have the inlay piece in your possession, you do not have the problem of obtaining a replacement. Take the piece of inlay (remove it from its backing if it is still partially glued to it) and clean off all traces of glue on its underside. You will also have to remove any glue found in the groove or recess from which the inlay piece came. The reason you must do this is that a new coat of glue generally will not adhere well if there are traces of old glue on the surface. When you have cleaned all traces of the old glue from both contact surfaces, give it a new coating of glue and reposition it in the groove or recess.

You are faced with a slightly more difficult problem if the piece of inlay is completely missing. You will have to substitute another piece that matches the color and shape of the missing one. Since many mail-order houses that deal in woodworking supplies carry a full line of woods used in veneering and inlaying, it is not too difficult to find a wood that matches or comes very close to matching the wood type and color of the missing piece. You might also be able to find a suitable substitute around your own shop. In any event, once you have obtained a wood to be used as a replacement for the missing piece of inlay, the procedure is as follows:

1. Take a piece of tracing paper, place it over the hole in the inlay and trace its outline. This serves as a pattern for the new piece of inlay.
2. Cut the pattern out slightly larger (about $\frac{1}{8}$ inch larger) than the traced lines indicate.
3. Place the inlay pattern on the piece of wood you obtained and cut out the inlay.
4. Since the inlay pattern was cut out slightly larger than the tracing indicated, it stands to reason that the new inlay

piece will also be slightly larger. This was intentional. The new inlay piece will be trimmed down with a razor until it fits.

5. Place the new, slightly oversized piece of inlay over the groove or recess. Take a single-edged razor or an appropriate *X-acto* knife, and trim the edges of the inlay piece until it fits snugly into the groove or recess. A "good" fit will be one that requires a certain amount of pressure (hammering, etc.) to force it into the depression in the background (base) wood. Do not trim away too much excess wood or the inlay piece will fit too loosely. Trimming should proceed carefully and slowly.

6. After you have trimmed the inlay piece to the desired shape, lightly sand the edges so that they are smooth and straight. Do *not* round the edges as you sand them.

7. Coat the underside of the inlay piece with glue and position it in the recess or groove. Do not use an excessive amount of glue or it will squeeze up between the edges of the inlay piece and smear the surface with a glue film. This, in turn, will interfere with the finishing operation. Wipe away any excess glue with a damp, clean cloth.

8. If the piece of inlay you are using to replace the missing piece does not match the latter in color tone, you can correct this by staining. I would recommend experimenting on a piece of scrap wood first.

Attempting to replace a broken or chipped off piece of inlay is only slightly more difficult than the last described operation. In addition to the eight steps recommended for replacing a missing piece of inlay, you will have to include an additional, preliminary step of cutting off any sharp corners or edges along the break. This can be done with an *X-acto* knife or a straight-edged razor. Make your cut as straight as possible so that the joining edge of the new piece will meet an equally straight edge.

## OVERLAYS

Overlays are wood decorations that are glued directly to the wood surface without routing out a groove or recess (Fig. 9).

145

Fig. 9. Various overlays.

They therefore extend or project slightly above the surface of the wood.

Overlays purchased from mail-order houses or other retail outlets have a protective paper covering the side that faces up. *After* the glue has dried, remove the paper by moistening and then sanding. Remove the dust left by the sanding operation with a dry, lint-free cloth. The surface of the overlay is now ready for a natural finish or a shellac washcoat.

## FINISHING INLAYS AND OVERLAYS

If a natural finish is used, the inlay or overlay wood does not require any additional protection. However, the use of stains or fillers requires that the inlay and overlay woods be protected. A washcoat of shellac will be quite adequate for this purpose. Without this protection, the inlay and overlay woods will show a tendency to absorb color from the stain and filler.

## MOSAIC

*Mosaic* (or *mosaicing*) is the process of inlaying small pieces of tiles, colored glass, stone, or other materials into a background (base) to form a design for a surface decoration.

The most commonly used and readily available material for creating mosaics are the ceramic tiles that can be purchased at most hobby and homecraft centers. These come in several shapes (square, triangular, circular, and rectangular) and a variety of colors. Usually they are used to decorate table tops, but they can also form decorative inlays for chair legs or border strips for furniture frames.

These mosaic tiles may be either inserted into the wood surface or laid across the top. If the former is the case, then it is necessary to cut away a portion of the surface for the insertion of the tiles. The procedure is similar to that described for inlaying pieces of decorative wood (see THE INLAYING PROCEDURE). If the tiles are laid across the surface, then an edging is necessary. This can be either a wood strip or a strip made from anodized aluminum. Whichever is used must be screwed into position or glued to the surface with epoxy glue.

The procedure for creating a mosaic is as follows:

1. Cut a piece of thin cardboard or heavyweight art paper to the exact shape of the area to be covered by the mosaic tiles.

2. Using this cardboard or paper pattern as a temporary guide, arrange the mosaic tiles in the design you wish to create on the furniture surface.

3. The next step is to prepare the surface of the wood. The entire surface must be completely finished before laying the mosaic tile. In the case of an older piece of furniture, this may require removing the old finish, sanding, and applying a new finish. The complete process is described in detail in the appropriate chapters of this book.

4. The tiles must be soaked in warm water first. This will remove the paper backing. In addition, thoroughly soaked tiles will not be able to absorb any more water. The grout (an adhesive used to fill the spaces between the tiles) will then not lose its moisture to the normally highly porous tiles.

5. Using an adhesive, attach the mosaic tiles to their positions on the surface of the furniture. Follow as closely as possible the pattern created in Steps 1 and 2.

6. Mix the grout. The grout dries quickly, so mix only as much as can be used at one time. Water should be added to the dry grout powder until it reaches the consistency of a paste.

7. Fill the gaps around the mosaic tiles with grout. Wipe off the excess grout with a damp cloth. Since the grout dries very quickly, it is best to apply it in several thin applications rather than attempting to do it all at once.

8. A sealer (a varnish or a special sealer for mosaic tiles) should be applied to protect the highly porous tiles from moisture.

# Chapter 6

# Repairing, Restoring, and Stripping

This chapter covers three basic refinishing operations:

1. Repairing,
2. Restoring,
3. Stripping.

Instructions for covering an old finish with enamel or paint have been included for the nonadventurous and weak at heart.

There are a number of different types of repairs that will be considered in this chapter. These range in difficulty from total frame repair (including the disassembly of the frame) to something as minor as removing scratches, dents, or blemishes from the finish. For our purposes, we can divide the different types of repairs into two principal categories:

1. Frame repairs
2. Repairing surface defects.

The first category involves repairs that affect the structure (frame) of the piece of furniture, and includes such things as:

1. Regluing joints,
2. Replacing missing legs, arms, slats and other pieces,
3. Repairing broken sections,
4. Repairing cracks and splits.

Surface defects may involve only the finish, or can be serious enough to have damaged the wood in some way. Crazing, lifting, and cracking are examples of the former; gouges, scratches, and dents of the latter.

149

Restoring is essentially a "touch-up" operation involving minor repairs of either (or both) the finish and the wood portions of the piece of furniture. The old finish is retained, but measures are taken to restore some of its former beauty. Old wax, polish, dirt, grease, and other matter are removed with a suitable cleaning preparation (i.e. one that will not damage the original finish). Sometimes the finish is reamalgamated to eliminate cracks or crazing. Shellac stick and other touch-up materials are used to repair the surface. Minor repair work (such as regluing joints) is also commonly employed. The overall purpose of restoration work, however, is to retain as much of the original finish and structure as possible.

Always attempt to restore a finish before considering the more expensive and time-consuming operation of stripping it. After all, if your restoration attempts fail, you can still remove the finish as well as any evidence of your failure to restore it.

Stripping is the process of removing an old finish down to the bare wood surface. It should be resorted to only if the original finish is in too poor a condition to be effectively restored. Stripping is both messy and time-consuming. Restoring a finish can be reduced to a minimum by careful planning, but I offer no hope for stripping. I strongly recommend that you take your time and work carefully.

Wear old clothes, old shoes, and gloves when you are refinishing. No matter how careful a person tries to be, some of the finishing materials always seem to splatter onto clothing or the skin. These materials are also usually inflammable, so I must caution you once again against working near flames, electric coils, and other heat sources. Sparks are also dangerous because they could set off an explosion. Proper ventilation in the work area is a must, because prolonged inhalation of the fumes from these materials could damage your health. I would recommend using finish removers outdoors.

## TOOLS AND MATERIALS

Many of the tools and materials used in repairing furniture, and in restoring or stripping old finishes have already been described in Chapter 2. Some new items that lend themselves specifically to this type of work are included here.

Those tools and materials that will make *repair* work easier are as follows:

1. Sandpaper,
2. Sanding block,
3. Wood fillers,
4. Glue,
5. Clamps,
6. *X-acto* knives,
7. Small and medium size saws,
8. A hand or power drill.

Both white and epoxy resin glue are very useful in repair work. White glue is commonly used for gluing furniture joints together. Although epoxy resin glue had been more frequently used in the past to join non porous materials (glass, metal, etc.), it is finding increasing use in woodworking. For example, it is useful for regluing a loose joint that you do not want to disassemble. It will even fill in spacing cracks between the joint frames.

A hand or power drill is essential for making new dowel or screw holes (I do not recommend nailing, because it results in the weakest type of construction). Small saws (a jigsaw, coping saw, etc.) are used for cutting wedges or inserts. Larger saws (a handsaw, crosscut saw, etc.) are useful for larger cutting operations such as removing damaged legs or extensive remodeling. *X-acto* knives come in a variety of sizes and shapes, and are excellent tools for trimming.

The clamps illustrated in Figs. 1, 2 and 3 suggest the variety of ways in which pressure can be applied while a joint or surface is being glued.

Sandpaper, sanding blocks, and steel wool are covered in Chapter 2 (TOOLS AND MATERIALS). The various types of wood fillers used for patching wood surfaces (e.g. stick shellac, wax stick, plastic wood, and wood putty) are described in the next section (see USING WOOD FILLERS). Do not confuse these with the type of filler used to fill wood pores during the initial stages of a finishing schedule. They are quite a different thing.

Courtesy Adjustable Clamp Co.

Fig. 1. Wood bar clamp.

The following tools and materials are essential for restoring or stripping finishes:

1. Removers and solvents,
2. Cleaning preparations,
3. Finish lifters,
4. Coarse steel wool,
5. Cheap brushes,
6. Rags,
7. A storage box,
9. Newspapers,
10. Masking tape.

152

Wax, polish, grease, and dirt can be removed from the finish with a suitable cleaning preparation. Mineral oil, or a cleaning preparation containing a mineral oil base, is recommended because it will not harm a shellac finish (preparations containing alcohol will dissolve the shellac). The mineral oil should be warmed slightly and applied to the surface with a soft, clean, lint-free cloth. Lacquer thinner, naphtha, or benzine should be wiped across the wood surface *after* the finish has been removed to eliminate any residue left by the solvent (otherwise, the new finish will have difficulty drying).

*Courtesy Adjustable Clamp Co.*

**Fig. 2. Band Clamps.**

You will need a suitable liquid finish remover such as a paint and varnish remover, denatured alcohol, or lacquer thinner to dissolve the finish. Putty knives, scrapers, or wedge-shaped blocks

153

of wood will be useful for lifting the finish once it has dissolved. A liquid finish remover can be applied with a brush (a cheap one with natural bristles) or a pad of coarse steel wool. Use an old box (e.g. an empty cigar box) to store the pieces of furniture hardware.

Courtesy Adjustable Clamp Co.

**Fig. 3. Steel bar clamps.**

Use large metal cans or containers to catch the dissolved finish. Some finishers refer to it as "sludge" or "slop." I prefer to call it "gunk." In any event, it is still quite a mess and should be carefully stored as the stripping operation progresses. By keeping it in containers, you will drastically reduce the clean-up time at the end of the stripping operation. I do not recommend plastic containers, because they may chemically react with the finish remover and dissolve (and thereby doubling your "gunk").

154

Rags are used for wiping, and should be soft and absorbent. Using the masking tape to mask off areas you do not want stained by the remover. Newspapers will protect the floor and surrounding areas from splatter.

You may not wish to use all the tools and materials suggested in this section, and that is certainly your right. On the other hand, you might want to add a few items to the list. After a little experience, you will be able to determine what works best for you.

## IDENTIFYING FINISHES

Not all cleaning preparations are suitable for every type of finish. Some are simply not chemically compatible, and will cause serious damage to the topcoat. Therefore, it is absolutely necessary that you first correctly identify the type of finish with which you are working before proceeding any further.

Most of the furniture finishes with which you will be dealing can be classified under one of the following types:

1. Shellac,
2. Shellac-lacquer,
3. Lacquer,
4. Varnish,
5. Paint,
6. Enamel.

The easiest method for identifying these finishes is to test them on some inconspicuous spot with a solvent. If you cannot determine the type of finish you have on the piece of furniture, you will have to identify it through the process of elimination by testing it with a number of different solvents. The identification will be made when you find a solvent that will dissolve it.

It is best to start with denatured alcohol, because this solvent will dissolve a shellac finish (and *partially* soften a shellac-lacquer finish), but it will not affect other types of finishes. Soak the end of a clean rag in denatured alcohol and rub it on an area of the finish that is not normally exposed. If the finish begins to dissolve, you are dealing with a shellac finish. However, if your efforts only succeed in partially softening the topcoat, it is more than likely a combination shellac-lacquer finish. Adding an equal amount of lacquer thinner to the denatured alcohol will completely dissolve the topcoat if it is a shellac-lacquer finish. Denatured alcohol will not dissolve any of the other finishes listed above. Consequently, if there is no reaction whatsoever, try the same test with lacquer thinner.

Lacquer thinner will partially soften a shellac-lacquer finish and completely dissolve one consisting only of lacquer. However, it has no effect on varnish, paint, or enamel finishes. These can be dissolved by any of the commercial paint and varnish removers. Table 1 lists the various types of finishes and the solvents used to dissolve them.

**Table 1. Finishing Materials and Their Solvents**

| Finishing Material | Solvent |
|---|---|
| Synthetic Varnish | Turpentine or Mineral Spirits |
| Oil Base Varnish | Turpentine, Mineral Spirits, or Paint Thinner |
| Enamel (Varnish Type) | Turpentine, Mineral Spirits, or Paint Thinner |
| Shellac | Denatured Alcohol |
| Lacquer | Lacquer Thinner |
| Lacquer Sealer | Lacquer Thinner |
| Lacquer Enamel | Lacquer Thinner |
| Paint and Varnish Remover | Denatured Alcohol |
| Water Stain | Soap and Warm Water |
| Spirit (Alcohol) Stain | Denatured Alcohol |
| Oil Stain | Turpentine, Paint Thinner, Naphtha, Kerosene |
| Paste Wood Filler | Mineral Spirits |
| Paint (Latex) | Water |
| Linseed Oil | Turpentine or Mineral Spirits |
| Paint (Milk Base) | Ammonia |

## USING WOOD FILLERS

Wood fillers are used for filling gouges, dents, scratches, and other types of imperfections found on wood surfaces. They should not be confused with the finishing material used for filling wood pores during the preparation of the surface for the topcoats. Each serves a different function, and cannot be substituted one for the other.

The four filler materials most commonly used for repairing and patching damaged wood surfaces are:

1. Plastic wood,
2. Wood putty,
3. Stick shellac,
4. Wax stick.

Plastic wood and stick shellac are more popular with wood finishers for reasons that will be pointed out below. It will be seen that each product has certain advantages and disadvantages.

*Plastic wood* (also referred to as *wood plastic* or *wood dough*) (Fig. 4) is actually a trade name for a wood dough product. Due to popular usage, the trade name is gradually replacing the generic one.

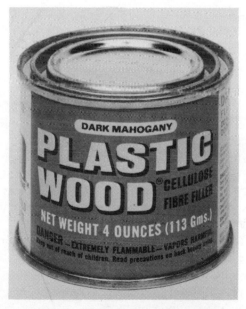

Courtesy Boyle-Midway Div. of American Home Products Corp.

Fig. 4. Small can of plastic wood.

157

Plastic wood is a quick drying filling material so tough that it can be sawed, drilled, sanded, or carved without crumbling or loss of strength. In short, its workability is excellent. Furthermore, it holds nails or screws as well as wood. Unfortunately, it produces an ungrained, opaque surface that is very noticeable unless used under an opaque finish or in areas not normally exposed. Plastic wood is used primarily to (1) repair sections of the frame that require strengthening, (2) fill large dents, gouges, and deep holes (especially knot holes), and (3) build up carvings, moldings, and edges that have been chipped or broken off.

Plastic wood is available in cans and tubes. If it seems too dry (crumbly), it can be restored to a working consistency by adding denatured alcohol, lacquer thinner, or a solvent recommended by the manufacturer. Plastic wood that has dried too hard cannot be restored regardless of the amount of thinner you add. Therefore, it should be stored in an airtight container when not being used.

Coloring plastic wood to match that of the surrounding areas has always been a problem. Some finishers prefer to color it *before* application, others afterward. In the former method, stain somewhat darker than the finish is added to the plastic wood as it is being mixed with the thinner. Apply a portion of the mixture to a piece of wood and let it dry. Drying will lighten the stain slightly. Compare the color of the plastic wood with the color of the wood finish. If you are close to a color match, use it. It is probably as close as you will be able to get.

The method of coloring plastic wood after its application should also be used experimentally on a piece of scrap wood first. Apply the plastic wood and give it sufficient time to dry. After it has dried, stain it and match the dried stain color with that of the finish.

The procedure for using plastic wood to repair and restore damaged areas is as follows:

1. Carefully read the manufacturer's instructions and prepare the plastic wood accordingly. Prepare enough to do the job and have a little left over.
2. Clean the area to which the plastic wood is to be applied.

All wax, polish, grease, and other possible contaminants must be removed. Remove any old finish with a suitable solvent. The area to be repaired must be completely dry before applying the plastic wood.

3. Pack the plastic wood into the depression as deeply as possible, and build it up until it protrudes slightly above the surface. Allow it sufficient time to thoroughly dry. Drying will cause it to shrink to a certain extent. The rest can be sanded level with the surface.

4. The plastic wood may be colored (stained) at this point. Coloring can also be added at Step 1 (thereby eliminating Step 4).

5. Proceed with the various steps in the finishing schedule.

*Wood putty* (also referred to as *water putty*) is also used to fill cracks or other imperfections on wood surfaces that are either not generally exposed to view or will be covered by an opaque finish (e.g. paint or enamel). The reason for this is that it has no grain and there is some difficulty in coloring it to match the rest of the wood. In this respect, wood putty resembles plastic wood very closely.

This is an extremely rapid drying filler and must be applied almost immediately. It is subject to less shrinkage than plastic wood and will result in a smoother finish.

Wood putty is available in a powder form at most hardware and paint stores. Water is added to form a working paste. Wood colors in powdered form can be added to tint the putty the desired color.

The procedure for using wood putty as a wood filler is as follows:

1. Select a container for mixing the wood putty.

2. Pour enough powder into the container to make all the putty you will need to do the entire job.

3. Add the coloring powder, and mix it thoroughly through the wood putty powder. The result should be slightly darker than the finish. It will lighten as it dries.

4. Add water a little at a time to the powder until you have the consistency you want.

159

5. Dampen the area to be filled with a wet cloth.
6. Pack the wood putty into the depression until it extends slightly above the surface at every point. Wipe excess putty from the surrounding areas with a wet cloth.
7. Let dry and sand the wood putty until it is smooth and level with the rest of the surface.
8. Continue with the rest of the finishing schedule.

A semi-hard putty stick under a number of different trade names (e.g. "Patchal Pencil," etc.) can be used for filling scratches and other minor defects. It is rubbed into the depression until the area is built up to surface level, and the excess is wiped away with a cloth or a piece of fine steel wool. No melting or sanding is necessary, which makes it a little more convenient to use than stick shellac. However, it is not as durable as the latter. Putty sticks are already colored.

*Stick shellac* is a wood filler consisting of hard pieces of shellac in a variety of different colors. It is also available in a very light color (neutral in tone) that can be stained to match other colors. Stick shellac is variously referred to by a number of other names including *shellac stick, wood cement,* and *sealing wax.* In any event, they are all one and the same. It is becoming more and more difficult to find stick shellac in the stores, and many manufacturers are apparently no longer making it.

Stick shellac is produced in both transparent and opaque forms. The latter shows no grain. Therefore, when it is used to fill relatively large areas, simulated grain patterns must be put on by hand. This can be done with stain and a pencil brush, but it is a rather difficult technique and requires both a good eye and a steady hand.

When using shellac stick to make surface repairs, select a color that most closely matches the rest of the surface and proceed as follows:

1. Place the shellac stick over a file or the blade of a table knife to shield it from the direct heat of the flame.
2. Hold the file or blade over a hot, carbonless flame. The flame must not emit smoke or it will be incorporated in the melting shellac. Cheap alcohol lamps (available through

mail-order houses dealing in finishing supplies or local paint and hardware stores) are recommended for the heat source.

3. Keep the file or blade over the flame until the shellac stick begins to melt.

4. Pass the file along the surface of the piece of furniture, holding it in such a way that the melted shellac can run into the depressed area. Use enough melted shellac to form a slight ridge above the surface.

5. Moisten your finger and run it along the top of the melted shellac, pressing it lightly as you go. You may then use the flat side of the file or blade to smooth out the shellac filler. If it is still not smooth and level, try rubbing it with a felt pad dipped in FFF grade pumice stone and rubbing oil (only a small amount of rubbing oil is necessary). Use rottenstone and water to complete the rubbing operation. Always rub in the direction of the grain. This holds true regardless of the position of the surface imperfection (e.g. if it lies across the grain).

*Wax stick* is a filler-type material made from colored wax and designed for patching. It is much easier to use than stick shellac. Wax stick is commercially available in a variety of colors or can be made in the home workshop by melting paraffin or beeswax and coloring it with aniline dye powder.

Not only is wax stick easy to apply, it can also be easily removed if the repair work does not look right. It is simply a matter of prying it loose and starting over again. Among its principal disadvantages are its low durability and lack of resistance to wear. Moreover, it has a tendency to bleed into other finishes. The application of a shellac washcoat will eliminate the bleeding tendency and protect the wax stick to a degree.

## REPAIRING SURFACE DEFECTS

Surface defects range in severity from wood damage to various types of problems with the finish. They include dents of various sizes, gouges, scratches, minor splitting and cracking, pit marks, old nail screw, and dowel holes, burns, stains, and a number of other imperfections that ruin the overall appearance of a finish unless dealt with properly. They can be divided into the following three basic categories:

1. Defects that lie on the finish,
2. Defects that have penetrated *into* the finish,
3. Defects that have damaged the wood.

Each type of surface defect will be carefully examined in the sections that follow. The suggested remedies will be based on the degree of damage they have caused (see the three categories listed above).


## SPOTS AND STAINS

The terms "spot" and "stain" are largely synonymous as used in wood finishing. I suppose if you wanted to be technical about it, a spot could be defined as a *deposit of foreign matter on the finish*. A stain, on the other hand, could be regarded as *discoloration caused by a deposit of foreign matter*. There is a little difference in definition, but not much.

The types of spots and stains you will encounter on finishes include the following:

1. Water spots,
2. Alcohol spots,
3. Ink spots,
4. Grease, oil, and dirt spots,
5. Milk spots,
6. Citrus acid spots.

Spots and stains caused by water or moisture on the surface appear as white spots or rings (i.e. blushing) on lacquer and shellac finishes. They can also occur on some cheap varnish finishes. Try wiping the spot lightly with a cloth dampened in naphtha or turpentine. If this fails to remove the spot, wipe the surface with denatured alcohol. Be careful. Too much alcohol will dissolve the finish.

Alcohol will cause shellac finishes, some varnish finishes, and wax finishes to spot white. Wiping the surface with turpentine or denatured alcohol will sometimes remove them.

162

Ink spots can be removed by rubbing lightly with soap and water, or pumice stone (FFF Grade) and water. The latter is recommended only if the stain resists the soap and water treatment. If the ink has penetrated the finish (particularly through cracks), you will have to strip it and bleach the stain out of the wood.

Treat milk spots and citrus acid stains in the same manner as ink stains. Spots other than those caused by water or alcohol can also be eliminated by one of the following methods:

1. Mild soap and water,
2. Mineral oil,
3. Lemon oil,
4. Vinegar and water,
5. Turpentine,
6. Very fine steel wool,
7. Pumice stone and water (or oil),
8. Rottenstone and water (or oil).

## Alligatoring, Scratches, and Cracks

Minor scratches and cracks can usually be eliminated by reamalgamating the finish (i.e. redissolving it with a suitable solvent so that it will flow together and eliminate the defect). It is very important to properly identify the type of finish you are dealing with *before* attempting to reamalgamate it. Consequently, I suggest that you read the section IDENTIFYING FINISHES in this chapter before proceeding any further.

### Table 2. Recommended Solvents for Reamalgamating Various Types of Finishes

| Type of Finish | Reamalgamation Solvent |
| --- | --- |
| Shellac | Denatured Alcohol |
| Shellac-Lacquer | Denatured Alcohol (3 Parts), Lacquer Thinner (1 Part) |
| Varnish | Turpentine (1 Part), Boiled Linseed Oil (1 Part) or Strip the Finish |
| Lacquer-Base Enamel | Lacquer Thinner or Strip the Finish |
| Lacquer | Lacquer Thinner |

*Alligatoring* refers to the development of intersecting cracks or ridges on a finish. In effect, it resembles the skin of an alligator. It usually occurs as a result of overexposure to sunlight. The finish can be restored and the alligatoring effect eliminated by reamalgamation. This consists of partially dissolving the finish with its solvent (Table 2). Apply the solvent with a clean, soft cloth wiped gently across the surface. When the alligatoring cracks and ridges disappear, stop wiping. If the sunlight has affected the stain or wood color, I would recommend stripping the finish and applying a new one. This holds true for crazing or cracking caused by sunlight (see below).

*Crazing* consists of irregular patterns of minute cracks caused by shrinking, excessive moisture, or exposure to excessive amounts of sunlight. You can eliminate crazing by reamalgamating the finish (see Alligatoring).

A *hairline crack* refers to a single, minute crack extending part way or completely across the finish. One or more can occur, but they need not intersect. They are caused by the same conditions that produce crazing or alligatoring. Hairline cracks can also be removed by reamalgamation (see Alligatoring).

A *crack* is a split or break in the finish considerably larger than those caused by alligatoring, crazing, or hairline cracks. However, the conditions causing the crack (i.e. shrinkage, excessive moisture, or too much sunlight) are the same. Reamalgamating the finish should eliminate most cracks.

A *scratch* is caused by a foreign (i.e. externally directed) object being drawn across the surface with enough force or pressure to break the finish. The depth of the scratch will determine the method you use to remove it. Suggested removal methods are:

1. Reamalgamation,
2. Rub with pumice stone (FFF Grade) and oil,
3. Fill with white shellac and stain.

Remove all wax, polish, and other possible contaminants before attempting to repair a finish scratch. Varnish and lacquer can be substituted for white shellac; rottenstone for pumice stone.

## Lifting, Peeling, and Blistering

*Lifting, peeling* and *blistering* are overlapping terms often used interchangeably to describe a condition in which the finish is losing its adhesion to the wood surface. That is to say, it is lifting or peeling off the wood. This condition can usually be traced to one of the following causes:

1. Incorrect application methods,
2. Using two or more chemically incompatible finishing materials,
3. Excessive moisture in the wood.

Because the causes are of internal origin and usually too extensive to effectively repair (in cases where excessive moisture is the cause), a complete stripping of the finish is recommended.

Blistering might prove to be the only exception to the rule. If the blisters are large and cover the entire finish, strip it. On the other hand, if they are isolated in one area or resemble tiny blister-like bubbles, try reamalgamating the finish first.

## Dents, Gouges, and Deep Scratches

Dents, gouges, and deep scratches are all depressions in the surface caused by pressure or impact externally applied. The wood fibers may be torn (as is the case with gouges and scratches) or simply depressed (dents). The force that causes the dent may or may not break the finish.

These types of surface defects can be repaired in several ways depending upon their size. The methods commonly used to make this kind of repair include:

1. Raising the grain,
2. Filling,
3. Fitting wood inserts.

Raising the grain is probably the easiest method but can only be used successfully on relatively shallow dents. The grain raising is accomplished by placing a damp cloth with water over the dent and pressing a heated iron against the cloth. The absorption of water by the wood (in combination with the heat) should cause the fibers to raise and fill the dent. With some woods, only the application of water is necessary. A few hard-

165

woods will resist both the water and the heat, and will have to be filled and sanded.

Large dents, gouges and deep scratches, can be removed by packing them with a filler material and sanding them smooth. Plastic wood, wood putty, shellac stick, and wax stick can be used to repair these surface defects under certain conditions (see USING WOOD FILLER in this chapter). For example, shellac stick and wax stick can be used to repair most scratches unless they have penetrated the wood too deeply. If such is the case, then plastic wood or wood putty are recommended. These two filler materials are also recommended for repairing large dents and gouges. Both plastic wood and wood putty shrink when drying, so be sure to pack enough of either into the depression to extend slightly above the surface. Whatever remains after shrinking can be removed by sanding. Sawdust mixed with glue (or varnish) can also be used to fill depressions. If a sawdust mixture is used, the sawdust should come from the same wood as the rest of the furniture. All splinters should be removed and sharp edges rounded before attempting to repair dents, gouges, or scratches. Except in the case of grain raising, the area should also be thoroughly cleaned of all wax, polish, grease, dirt, old finish, and other substances that might interfere with the proper adhesion of the finishing materials used in making the repair.

If the dents or gouges are particularly large, they can be repaired by cutting a piece of wood to the size and shape of the depression and gluing it in position. Sand the area and apply a stain. Plastic wood or shellac stick can be used to fill any cracks if the fit is not tight enough. This should also be stained or it will leave a noticeable border around the wood insert.

HOLES—Holes in the surface are usually the result of missing screws, nails, dowels, or knots, and will probably extend completely through to the other side of the wood. Tightly fitted wood inserts used in combination with plastic wood or shellac stick are the recommended method of repair (see above).

BURNS—A burn can be caused by a cigarette, cigar, or a burning match dropped on the finish. It can also be caused by setting a hot pan or plate down on the surface. Usually this will make the finish blister or dissolve. If a cigarette or cigar is allowed to remain long enough, it could burn into the wood and result in a dent-like depression.

Superficial burning of the finish on a small area can be repaired by first sanding the spot smooth with a very fine sandpaper, and matching the rest of the surface with an appropriate shade of shellac stick or wax stick (see USING WOOD FILLER in this chapter). After the shellac stick has cooled, rub it down with linseed oil and a lightweight emery cloth. The whole surface may then have to be rubbed in order to make the overall gloss (or lack of gloss) uniform.

If the burn is deep enough to have caused a dent-like depression, it may have to be filled in with plastic wood, stained, and sanded. This is particularly true along edges (where most such burns occur), because you will have to do a certain amount of rebuilding of the edge.

## MISSING PIECES OF VENEER AND INLAY

The problem of replacing missing pieces of veneer and inlay is described in Chapter 4 (VENEERING) and Chapter 5 (INLAYING).

### Worn Edges

Worn edges can be caused by heavy use over a period of time or careless handling when moving the piece of furniture. If the former of the two is the case, then the wear will be evenly distributed over those portions of the frame where one would normally expect to find it. If you are dealing with a genuine (or suspected) antique, I would not recommend doing anything about it. These naturally acquired signs of wear will add a certain charm to the furniture, and does not reduce its monetary value (refinishing it most certainly will). If you possess a piece of furniture with no appreciable value other than sentiment, I would recommend antiquing it (see Chapter 16).

Wear caused by improper or careless handling is usually unevenly distributed on the frame. This can be repaired by either

167

replacing a section of the frame (e.g. the top of a table, a table leaf, a chair leg, etc.) or by building up the defect with plastic wood or wood putty. The latter (filling) is recommended if the wear is not extensive and occurs along an edge of the frame.

## Making Frame Repairs

The preceding sections of this chapter described various types of surface defects that can cause damage to the finish or the wood surface. A second major category of furniture repairs are those that involve damage to the structure or frame. Although it may not be possible to list every type of repair problem found in this category, such a list should include the following:

1. Split or missing frame sections,
2. Broken or missing hardware,
3. Warping,
4. Loose frame,
5. Wood dry rot.

## Split or Missing Frame Sections

If any portion of the wood frame has been split, it is best to remove that particular section and replace it with a new piece of wood. It is important that this new piece be seasoned (kiln dried), because unseasoned wood will shrink. This could result in unsightly gaps after the glue has dried. The best solution to this problem would be to take an identical section from damaged furniture of the same age and style.

All of the old glue must be removed from the surfaces to which the split section was attached (a new coat of glue applied over an older one will result in a weak joint). A glue used in furniture construction must penetrate the wood in order to set properly.

It is not difficult to replace pieces of the seat foundation or the back, because they are, for the most part, hidden from view. However, arms and legs present a totally different problem. This is largely because they are in full view and must therefore be identical in appearance to the remaining original sections after the repairs have been made.

Some legs and arms are quite ornate and consequently difficult to replace. If they are badly damaged, you may be able to obtain a matching leg or arm from an identical piece of furniture in a similar condition. In other words, it may be possible to make one good chair from two damaged ones.

Whether or not you are reassembling the entire frame, or simply reattaching a certain piece (arm, leg, etc.), the following steps are recommended:

1. Remove all glue from both surfaces. Never place a new layer of glue over an older one.
2. Before regluing, test the pieces for fit.
3. Do not use nails in the reassembly. If these were used in the original construction, remove them, and fill in the holes with wood filler. Should you feel that a reinforcement is needed in addition to gluing, use such recommended forms as wood corner blocks, wood screws, wood dowels, or metal fasteners.
4. If the frame consists of mortise and tenon joints, use thin pieces of wood (shims) or cloth glued to the tenon to tighten the fit.
5. Reglue the frame. Remember: clamping pressure is necessary.

## BROKEN OR MISSING HARDWARE

Sometimes you will find that one or more pieces of furniture hardware (knobs, handles, hinges, etc.) are broken or missing. If you have an antique, you should make every effort to repair the broken piece of hardware or replace it with an identical piece of reproduction. Remember though, there is an inverse ratio between the amount of replacement and the value of the antique. The more you replace, the more it drops in value. This is not the same problem with furniture not classified as antique. In this case, I would recommend one of two possible solutions. Order a completely new set of hardware from a mail-order house that sells wood finishing materials or take the hardware from an identical piece of furniture in too poor a condition to restore.

169

## WARPING

Warping results from a piece of wood being able to absorb moisture from one side but not from the other. In wood finishing, the finish will serve as the waterproofing coat. Since the bottom of a table leaf, table top, or other sections is often left unfinished (it is cheaper that way), it is this side of the wood that absorbs the moisture and causes the warp. The result is a shape having both a concave (unfinished) and convex (finished) side (Fig. 5).

Fig. 5. The convex and concave sides of a warp.

In some cases, the warp can be removed by applying both moisture and pressure (with weights or by means of clamps). Lay the board on wet grass with the concave side down and place some heavy weights on the convex side for pressure. If the warp disappears, clamp the board in a flat position so that the warp will not return as the board dries. After the wood has thoroughly dried, apply a finish to *both* sides. Wet burlap folded flat can be substituted for the wet grass as a source of moisture.

Other methods of removing warp include cutting grooves into the underside of the board, or sawing the board into strips and regluing it. These are really too complicated for anyone but the professional to attempt. If you are not successful with the pressure and water method, I would recommend replacing the warped section or taking it to a cabinet shop.

## LOOSE FRAME

Examine the frame for loose joints. If you do not intend to refinish the piece of furniture, the frame can be reinforced with wood blocks. Sometimes a damaged section (table top, frame side, the back of a dresser or cabinet, etc.) will cause the looseness in the frame. If the part is salvageable, it should be refastened with wood screws and glue. Should you have to replace it, try to find a section the same age as the one being replaced. This can be taken from another piece of furniture that is in too poor a condition to be repaired.

If a joint is loose without being damaged, try to pull it apart and remove all the old glue. This is important because new glue applied over old glue seldom forms a strong bond with the wood. A frequently effective method of removing glue is to pour hot white vinegar over the surface. Allow the vinegar time to work on the glue and wipe it off with a rag (some of the modern glues have to be chipped off). Sand the surfaces of the joint, and wipe them with turpentine to remove any traces of the old glue. The joint can be made especially tight by coating the glued surfaces with ground steel wool, inserting a thin shim, or wrapping the tenon (of a mortise and tenon joint) with a small piece of cloth.

Loose joints that cannot be separated can be reglued by drilling a hole into the joint, and inserting the glue with a glue injector. This is not as satisfactory as complete disassembly of the joint, because there is no way of removing the old glue.

If the entire frame is loose, it would be best to completely disassemble it, remove all glue from the exposed surfaces, and reglue it.

## WOOD DRY ROT

Moisture not only causes the wood to warp, it also indirectly contributes to dry rot. Dry rot is a crumbling or powdery condi-

171

tion of the wood resulting from a fungus which attaches itself to the moist areas. This condition generally develops over a long period of time, but it can be corrected quite easily. Simply scrape out the dry rot area, and coat the new surface with a dry rot retardant which can be purchased in most paint and hardware stores. If the area is not too extensive, fill it with plastic wood or wood putty and stain it to match the rest of the surface (see USING WOOD FILLER). Smaller areas can be patched with shellac stick.

## STRIPPING FINISHES

*Stripping* is the process of removing an old finish down to the bare wood surface. This can be accomplished mechanically or with a chemical solvent. Machine sanding or hand sanding is used in the mechanical method of removal, but this generally results in removing not only the finish but also some of the wood surface. As a result, certain very attractive aspects of the wood coloring gained through aging (i.e. the patina) will have been destroyed. Therefore, mechanical removal is only recommended if the wood is not particularly attractive and if you intend to cover it with a semi-opaque or opaque finish. Using a chemical solvent, on the other hand, will remove the finish without damaging the wood. This is the most commonly used method for stripping finishes. It is particularly recommended for woods with attractive grain patterns and coloring.

The removal method you select will be the *second* decision you make when stripping a finish. Of far more importance is whether or not you decide to remove the finish or leave it intact. Sometimes all that an old finish needs is a good cleaning. Once the old dirt, grease, and wax is removed you might be surprised and pleased with the attractiveness of the finish. Try rubbing the finish with a clean preparation that will not dissolve it (water and a mild soap can be used on all finishes except lacquer or shellac where it has a tendency to cause blushing (the formation of white spots, rings, or film).

Not all finishes should be removed even if they show signs of age. This is particularly true of an antique. The original finish is an intrinsic part of its monetary value, and by removing the finish you will have considerably reduced this value. Consequently, I would *never* recommend removing a finish from an antique without first seeking and obtaining professional advice. Furthermore, I would strongly recommend retaining any old finish if it is attractive and its condition is not too bad. Signs of aging will frequently add to the overall appearance of a piece of furniture rather than detract from it.

The third decision you must make when removing an old finish is the type of remover or solvent to use, because not all of them work equally well on all finishes. Therefore, you must be able to identify correctly the type of finish you are about to remove. This can usually be done quite adequately by testing it with one or more thinners or solvents. For example, denatured alcohol will remove shellac (but not varnish, lacquer, and other types of finishes). A lacquer thinner is best for a lacquer finish. Varnish and paint remover will remove most other types of finishes.

## STRIPPING PROCEDURE

The stripping procedure described in this section is a generalized one, and therefore cannot be expected to fit every situation. As you gain experience, you will substitute your own variations.

The procedure for removing (stripping) an old finish is as follows:

1. *First,* identify the finish. Your identification will determine the type of cleaning preparation and remover you select (see IDENTIFYING THE FINISH in this chapter).
2. Clean the surface with a cleaning preparation that will not dissolve the finish. The cleaning preparation you select will be determined by the type of finish you are removing.
3. Examine the cleaned finish and decide whether you want to remove it, restore it, or leave it in its present condition. If the finish shows signs of brittleness, cracking, or poor adhesion (lifting, peeling, etc.), it is best to remove it completely.
4. If you have decided to strip the finish, remove all the hard-

ware (handles, knobs, hinges, etc.), and store them in a safe place. (Fig. 6).

*Courtesy Glidden Coatings and Resins*

**Fig. 6. Removing furniture hardware.**

5. At this point, some finishers prefer to disassemble the piece of furniture *before* they strip the finish. Others do not. However, using a finish remover does frequently loosen joints, and regluing a disassembled frame will result in stronger joints.

6. Apply the paint and varnish remover to the surface in liberal amounts (Fig. 7). It can be applied by flowing it on

**Fig. 7. Brushing on a finish remover to the wood surface.**

174

with an old clean brush or a new inexpensive one. Allow the remover several minutes to work down into the old finish. When you feel that you have allowed enough time for the remover to penetrate the finish layers (there will be visual signs such as wrinkling of the surface), gently remove the old finish with a lifter. (Fig. 8) Do *not* bear

Fig. 8. Removing the softened finish with a lifter or scraper.

down with any great force, because you will run the risk of gouging or scratching the surface of the wood. If some of the old finish proves stubborn, apply another coat of remover and repeat the process. A tooth brush is excellent for removing finish from moldings, carvings, and other tight contours.

7. Now that you have pushed away the bulk of the dissolved finish with the lifter, wipe it free with clean rags and then rub the surface with a fine grade of steel wool and some denatured alcohol (or turpentine). This will not only enable you to remove the last traces of the old finish from

the larger areas, but also from corners, carved moldings, and other difficult to reach spots.

8. Take a clean cloth, soak it in turpentine, and wipe the entire surface. This will eliminate any traces of the remover left on the wood. This is particularly important if the remover contained any wax (some paint and varnish removers do), because the traces of wax will prevent the new finish from drying properly. After you have finished, take a clean dry cloth and wipe the surface dry.

## COVERING AN OLD FINISH

If the old finish is still in good condition, then you can save yourself a great deal of time and trouble simply by covering it with paint or enamel. By "good" condition, I mean that the finish is not cracking, is not brittle, and still adheres strongly at every point on the surface. Run your hand over the surface of the old finish. If it feels smooth to the touch, then it will probably accept a covering coat well. If even minor repairs (small areas of cracking, etc.) are required, I would recommend that you refinish it. The time spent preparing the area so that it will match the rest of the finish would be better spent completely removing it. Remember: a paint or enamel finish is opaque, and should only be applied over wood surfaces that are not particularly attractive.

A much more detailed description of painting or enameling furniture is given in Chapter 12 (PAINT AND ENAMEL FINISHES). A much briefer outline for the procedure for covering an old finish with paint or enamel is as follows:

1. Thoroughly clean the surface of the old finish. This means removing all the dirt, furniture wax and polish, and other contaminants that have accumulated over the years. It is quite possible that a good cleaning will restore the surface to a condition that will not require covering. Use warm water and a mild detergent for cleaning (or another suitable cleaning preparation if you are working with a shellac or lacquer finish). Work quickly — do not allow water to soak in or stand on the surface. If you have done your

job well, the water will run off the surface without beading (the formation of moisture beads on the surface is an indication that some wax still remains). Decorative carvings can be cleaned with a soft toothbrush. Wipe the surface clean with a clean, lint-free cloth, and allow it time to dry.

2. If the old finish has a gloss, it will have to be removed. The new finish will not adhere to a surface with a gloss. Use a very fine grade of sandpaper to lightly scuff the surface. This will satisfactorily remove the gloss and provide a base for the topcoat.

3. It may be necessary to reglue joints loosened by the cleaning. When you have accomplished this, check the wood surface for glue film. This must be removed or it will prevent the topcoat from properly adhering to the surface.

4. Brush on the first coat of paint or enamel. Allow it about twenty-four hours drying time and apply the second coat. Read Chapter 12 for further and more detailed instructions.

# Chapter 7

# Wood Preparation

The first step to be considered in any finishing or refinishing procedure is the preparation of the surface for the finishing materials. If this is not done properly at this stage, the results will be very disappointing. This cannot be emphasized to strongly. Remember: the quality of the finish is directly related to the care you take in preparing the wood surface. Take your time. Many beginners are in such a hurry to see how the final finishing coat will look that they take short cuts and try to use labor saving techniques. The results are usually disappointing.

You are faced wih one of two possible situations:

1. An old finish that needs to be removed or covered,
2. A new wood surface that requires finishing.

The procedures involved in removing or covering over old finishes were described in considerable detail in the last chapter (also see Chapter 12 PAINT AND ENAMEL FINISHES). This chapter concentrates on describing the procedure to be followed when preparing a bare wood surface and includes those surfaces from which previous finishes have been completely removed.

Wood is a highly complex material and extremely varied in its characteristics. Two pieces of the same type of wood can vary in color, moisture content, and porosity. Different types of woods will show an even greater variance. Nonuniformity is the rule rather than the exception. As a result, the worker must employ a variety of techniques to create a suitable surface for whatever finish has been selected.

A number of operations have become standard procedure in wood preparation. They include:

1. Sanding,
2. Sizing (grain raising)
3. Bleaching,
4. Wood coloring,
5. Applying a washcoat,
6. Using a filler,
7. Sealing.

Some of these operations are optional. For example, if the color of the wood is uniform and the shade you desire, there is no need to bleach it (remove the color) or stain it (add color). Sanding, on the other hand, is an operation used at various stages in the finishing schedule right up to the application of the final fin-

SANDING BARE WOOD

APPLYING FIRST FINISHING COAT

SANDING FIRST FINISHING COAT

APPLYING SECOND FINISHING COAT

**Fig. 1. Sanding should be done on the bare wood surface and on the various coats of finishing material.**

ishing coat (Fig. 1). The finishing operations that you choose to use will depend upon the overall effect you are trying to achieve.

179

## SANDING AND SMOOTHING THE SURFACE

Sanding is the first step in wood preparation. The wood must be sanded so that it provides a smooth and uniform surface for the finishing materials. All surface imperfections (scratches, dents, pits, etc.) must be removed or they will ruin the overal appearance of the finish. Wood fibers raised above the level of the surface have to be cut down so that the finish appears completely uniform. You must be careful when sanding not to scratch the surface. If you are using a portable electric sander, it is all too easy to leave machine marks on the surface. Hand sanding across the grain or using a grade of sandpaper too coarse for the wood will also leave unsightly scratches. Remember: any type of imperfection left on the surface will be readily apparent once the finish is applied. At that point it will be too late to correct without going to the trouble of stripping the finish and starting all over again.

As a general rule, sanding a surface in preparation for the finish begins with the coarser grades of sandpaper and progresses to the finer ones. Normally, a satisfactory surface can be produced by starting with a 3/0 sandpaper, switching to a 4/0 sandpaper, and finishing with a 6/0. Once again, the coarsest grade you use will depend upon the softness of the wood. If the sandpaper is too coarse, it will scratch the wood and damage the fibers. It is probably better to use a paper with too fine a grade, although here you will encounter the possibility of clogging the wood pores and reducing stain penetration.

Use a sanding block with some sort of backing inserted between the paper and the surface of the block. Cork or hard rubber sanding blocks are better than the metal or hardwood variety because they greatly reduce the possibility of scratching the surface with the hard edge of the block.

Sand with the grain, in long even strokes almost as if you were ironing a piece of clothing (Fig. 2). Do not bear down heavily or you will lose some of the handling and directional control necessary to good sanding. You also run the risk of cutting too deeply and unevenly. Use a moderate to light pressure and take your time. The old adage "haste makes waste" is certainly appropriate here.

Change your sandpaper frequently. If you continue to use it after it has become worn smooth, it will smear the surface of the wood. This will prevent stains from penetrating into the wood, because the pores will have become blocked. This can also occur if you using too fine a grade of sandpaper.

Fig. 2. Correct and incorrect sanding techniques; (A) Correct. Sand straight and parallel with the grain; (B) Incorrect. Sanding strokes are not straight which cut into the grain; (C) Incorrect. Never sand across the grain.

Use a clean, dry lint-free cloth or a brush to clean the dust from the surface of the wood left by the sanding operation. As a final touch, pass a damp clean cloth over the surface of the wood.

181

This will cause the grain fibers to swell and raise slightly (for a more detailed description of this aspect of wood preparation, see GRAIN RAISING in this chapter). Sand these raised fibers down level with the surface, and brush away the sawdust.

Regardless of whether or not you have an old furniture frame from which a finish has been removed, or a new one that has never had a finish, the wood surface probably has some dents and scratches. These must be removed before the preliminary stage of sanding is completed.

Raise the dents by applying a wet cloth to the area of the dent, or by applying an iron to a wet cloth held over the dent (Fig. 3).

Fig. 3. Removing shallow dents by using a moist cloth and a hot iron.

This causes the wood fibers to swell and raise above the surface. Shallow dents can be filled in by this grain raising action. The raised fibers are removed by sanding. By the way, make certain that the cloth you use is a clean one. Otherwise you may leave dirt and grease blemishes on the surface.

Scratches, pit marks, old nail and screw holes, gouges, and deep dents can be removed by filling them with wood putty, plastic wood, or a stick shellac. The latter is recommended for use beneath natural finishes. Stick shellacs are particularly useful, because they are available in a number of different colors. This enables you to very closely match the color of the wood. Additional information on removing surface defects can be found in Chapter 6 (see section REPAIRING SURFACE DEFECTS).

182

## GRAIN RAISING

Most woods are subject to a certain amount of grain raising when the surface comes into contact with moisture. When some of the wood fibers become wet they rise above the general surface, dry, and stiffen. The result is a rough, uneven surface that destroys the overall appearance of the wood. The task of the wood finisher, then, is to reduce the effects of grain raising. This is accomplished by deliberately raising the wood fibers and sanding them down to the level of the surface. This operation *must* be done before the first of the finishing coats is applied. It is recommended that it be completed before any staining is done.

*Sizing* is an operation used by the furniture industry to remove wood fibers and fuzz, and is used as a matter of practice just before the last sanding stage in wood preparation.

*Size* is made by dissolving a stiffening material (such as certain types of glue) in water until it reaches a very thin consistency. The sizing solution is then applied to the wood surface causing the wood fibers to raise and stiffen. These raised and stiffened fibers are then removed by sanding. This reduces the amount of grain raising at later stages in the finishing schedule such as when a water stain is used. Sizing also acts as a sealer coat for soft areas on the surface. As such, it allows the stain to be applied more uniformly, and reduces the chance of a splotchy appearance. In this respect, it has the same function as a pre-stain washcoat.

Rags, pads, or sponges are used to apply size. Be certain that the size is completely dry before attempting to sand it. Remember: sizing is a pretreatment stage in wood preparation. It is not intended as a filler or sealer.

Another method of raising and stiffening wood fibers is by applying a sanding sealer. The sanding sealer functions in the same way as sizing.

Many finishers accomplish grain raising simply by sponging the surface of the wood with cold water. (Fig. 4) Sponge the water onto the surface until it is thoroughly soaked, wipe off the excess and let it dry. As soon as the fibers have dried and stiffened, lightly sand them down to surface level. Remove the dust

Fig. 4. Sponging water on the surface in order to raise the wood grain.

and the residue left by the sanding operation with a tack rag or a clean lint-free cloth.

## BLEACHING

Examine the surface of the wood. Sometimes an old finish has penetrated deeply into the wood pores. This stains the wood, making it somewhat darker than its original natural color. You will also find cases in which the coloring is uneven or too dark. This condition can occur with unfinished wood or wood from which a surface has been removed. Bleaching is used to remedy this situation.

Bleaches are used to lighten coloring or to remove it from a a wood surface. Whatever the sought after results, they must be *completely uniform*. You have not bleached properly if there are spots still on the surface showing different shades of coloring. The bleach may be applied to local areas or over the entire surface. In any event, the main purpose in applying the bleach is to obtain not only a lighter coloring, but also the even distribution of the same shade. A good bleaching, then, will succeed in removing all dark spots from the surface (spots that will ruin the appearance of clear and semi-opaque finishes). It will not affect the grain pattern of the wood.

Synthetic (*not* natural) fiber brushes are recommended for applying bleach. Brushes made from natural fibers show a ten-

184

dency to break down when coming in contact with the strong chemicals found in bleaches. Commercial one-solution bleaches can also be applied to the surface with a sponge (Fig. 5).

Fig. 5. Apply liquid bleach
with a sponge.

Bleaches should be mixed in glass or enamel-lined containers. Other types of containers may also be used as long as they prove resistant to the bleaching solution chemicals.

Although both one-and two-solution bleaches are available commercially, the latter is by far the more effective form with woods that resist lightening. In the two-solution bleaches, the first solution produces the chemical change in the pigments and the second solution removes the residue.

Bleaching should be used only as a last resort, because (unless extreme care is taken) the strong chemicals used in the bleaching process can harm the skin or ruin the wood surface by destroying the fibers.

The procedure for mixing and using your own bleach to lighten a wood surface is as follows:

1. Use a brush with a synthetic fiber. Natural fiber brushes disintegrate under the action of the bleach solution. Wear rubber gloves to protect the hands, and make certain that you have proper and sufficient ventilation.

2. Apply an oxalic acid-water solution to the surface of the wood. A mild bleach can be produced from three ounces of oxalic acid (usually obtained in crystal form) dissolved in a quart of hot water and allowed to cool.

185

3. Mix sodium hypochlorite (household bleach) with hot water in the same proportions as the oxalic acid solution. Allow it to cool before application.

4. After the two solutions have been prepared and cooled, apply the oxalic acid solution. After it has dried, then apply the second solution.

5. As soon as the sodium hypochlorite has dried, wipe the surface with a solution of borax and water. Again, allow the solution enough time to cool before applying it to the surface). The borax will neutralize the acid in the bleaching operation.

Step 3 will further lighten the wood, though it is not absolutely necessary to apply sodium hypochlorite after the application of the oxalic acid solution. Household bleaches work best at lightening natural wood colors, although they can also be used with success on water stains and ink. Oxalic acid-water solutions also work on water stains, chemical stains, and as a color lightener. If you would prefer not mixing your own bleach solution, there are a number of commercially prepared bleaches available.

Commercially prepared two-solution bleaches enjoy widespread use. A popular brandname is *Dexall*, a commercial wood bleach manufactured by the *Sherwin-Williams Company*. Other reliable two-solution bleaches are *Albino* and *Blanchit*.

*Clorox* is a commonly known one-solution bleach. It is a chlorinated liquid form that will continue to lighten the wood with successive applications.

A special word of caution should be given about bleaches. Do not allow them to come into contact with your skin. The ingredients in the bleaches will frequently cause extreme skin reactions. This can be avoided by wearing rubber gloves and using some caution. Bleaches using oxalic acid solutions are particularly dangerous to the eyes and lungs. The threat is greatest when sanding a wood surface that has been treated with an oxalic acid solution. The dried oxalic acid adheres to the sawdust particles and is easily inhaled and brought into contact with the eyes. Excessive inhalation can cause the throat muscles to contract. It is recommended that you wear some sort of protective face mask (with goggles) when working with this type of bleach. I would also recommend that you work outdoors.

## WASHCOATING

Washcoating involves the application of a thin fast drying material over a stain, toner, or the bare wood surface prior to filling or using a pigment uniform stain.

The purpose of applying a washcoat over a stain or toner is to seal these two materials and prevent them from bleeding through into the filler and subsequent finishing coats. It also provides a better surface for the application of the filler. Finally, it serves to raise loose wood fibers so that they may be sanded down close to the surface. When a washcoat is applied directly over a bare wood surface, it seals off the wood (particularly important if a bleach has been used) and provides a base for the stain. Stains will be much more uniform if applied over a washcoat. This is particularly true of open-grained woods.

Sometimes the terms "washcoat" and "sealer" overlap in meaning thereby causing a certain amount of confusion. The difference between the two lie in their functions, and to a lesser extent in their composition. A sealer should be a thinned coating of whatever finish is to be placed on the wood. If the surface is to be varnished, then the sealer should be a much thinner varnish. A washcoat, on the other hand, may be a thinned shellac (50% shellac, 50% denatured alcohol), a thinned lacquer (or vinyl type material), or a sealer. Sealers are always used after staining and after filling. Either a sealer washcoat or one of the other types of washcoats is used after a stain or on the bare wood surface. With these possibilities in mind, you could follow either of the two finishing schedules illustrated in Table 1. Finishing Schedule B should only be used with close-grained woods. Otherwise, the stain will penetrate too deeply and unevenly into the wood.

A good washcoat properly applied will coat the inside of the wood pore, not close it off. The pore must remain open so that the filler can be packed into it. Thinning, then, is a very important consideration when making a washcoat.

## Table 1. Finishing Schedules for Washcoats and Sealers

| Finishing Schedule A | Finishing Schedule B |
|---|---|
| 1. Sanding | 1. Sanding |
| 2. Washcoat or Sealer | 2. Staining |
| 3. Staining | 3. Washcoat or Sealer |
| 4. Sealer | 4. Filler |
| 5. Filler | 5. Sealer |
| 6. Sealer | 6. Various Coats of Finish |
| 7. Various Coats of Finish | |

As was mentioned before, the three basic types of washcoats are:

1. Thinned shellac,
2. Thinned lacquer (or vinyl type material),
3. A washcoat sealer.

Shellac washcoats are made by thinning orange or white shellac with denatured alcohol. The mixture is commonly 50% shellac thinned with 50% denatured alcohol, although thinner solutions can be used effectively. Shellac washcoats are preferred by many finishers because they are inexpensive, easy to make, and easy to apply. However, they should be used immediately and not stored, because shellac has a tendency to break down over a period of time and lose its effectiveness. Non-grain raising and water stains will frequently bleed in a shellac washcoat and give the appearance of greater depth (particularly with cordovan and dark mahogany finishes), brilliance, and clarity.

Sealer washcoats (made from a lacquer sealer) are reduced with a lacquer thinner on a one-to-one basis. However, not all lacquer sealers can be properly reduced and you might encounter some difficulty in making this type of washcoat. It all depends on the quality of the sealer.

Lacquer washcoats are fast drying (faster than shellac) and easy to use. They are also very easy to sand. I would recommend purchasing a lacquer washcoat rather than attempting to make one. It is not as simple as reducing a lacquer with a lacquer thinner.

All bleached surfaces must be sealed with a washcoat, because the alkali contained in bleach has a tendency to cause other finishing materials to decompose. The best washcoat for this purpose is the vinyl type since it is not as susceptible to the decomposing action of bleach as are the other washcoats. Vinyl washcoats are very similar to the lacquer type, except that they are based on vinyl or modified vinyl resins. As such, it functions as an excellent sealer for some resinous woods.

Washcoats can be lightly colored or pigmented with dye in order to create certain color effects. In this manner, they are very similar to toners in both function and composition.

*Always* lightly sand the washcoat after it has thoroughly dried. This will cut down any wood fibers that may have been raised, and produce a smooth, even base for the stain or filler.

## STAINING

Stains are frequently used to add color to a wood by darkening areas so that they match other equally dark areas of color. Using stains to add color to the wood *before* a final finish is applied gives to staining a function exactly the opposite of bleaching (that is, the addition rather than the removal of color). It is that function of staining in the wood preparation stage of finishing that will be discussed here. Because staining is a very complex subject and only one aspect of it pertains to the preliminary stage of wood preparation, a detailed examination of both stains and staining techniques will be discussed in the next chapter.

A typical staining procedure is illustrated in Fig. 6. A more detailed description of finishing schedules for specific types of stains is found in Chapter 8.

## SEALERS

A sealer or sealing coat functions primarily as a barrier between two mutually incompatible substances. For example, a sealer is frequently used over fillers or stains to prevent bleeding through into the finish. An abbreviated schedule including the sealer step would appear as follows:

1. Staining,
2. Sealer,
3. Final finish (varnish, shellac, lacquer, etc.).

# WOOD PREPARATION

(A) Removing all hardware and repairing scratches and other surface imperfections.

(B) Removing old finish.

(C) Sanding the bare wood.

(D) Applying a filler to open grained wood such as oak, mahogany or walnut.

(E) Applying the stain.

(F) Removing the stain for various tone effects.

*Courtesy Sherwin-Williams Co.*

**Fig. 6. Preparing the wood surface for staining.**

The addition of a filler would expand this schedule with the following steps:

1. Staining,
2. Sealer,
3. Filler,
4. Sanding,
5. Sealer,
6. Final finish.

Note that a sealer coat is used after the application of both the stain and filler to prevent any possibility of combining with the next layer. Fillers are not required for close-grained woods (those having small pores). With these types of wood, the sealer functions as a substitute for the filler.

Sealers are available commercially or may be made in the home workshop. The latter is simply a washcoat of white shellac (1 part shellac mixed with 1 part denatured alcohol).

The shellac washcoat is applied to the surface with a brush. Allow the wood to absorb the sealer. If the wood is particularly porous, it may be necessary to apply several coatings before the pores are completely filled. You will know that a sufficient amount of sealer has been added to the wood surface when the soaking action of the pores has ceased. Wipe off the excess sealer and allow the surface to dry for one to two hours. These shellac sealers are frequently used as base coats for a varnish finish.

Commercial sealers containing penetrating oils and resins are also available. These commercial sealers are variously referred to as *sealers*, *penetrating sealers*, *sealer stains*, or *penetrating resin finishes*, and may be purchased in a clear form or with stains added. These sealers are applied to the surface until it is sufficiently saturated. It is then allowed to sit for ten or twenty minutes, and the excess is wiped away with a soft cloth. It provides a protective coat as tough as varnish, but (unlike varnish) it penetrates deeply into the pores of the wood where it hardens to form its special lamination-like effect. Moreover, these commercial sealers enhance and emphasize the grain of the wood. At least twenty-four hours of drying time should be allowed between each layer of sealer.

Shellac or varnish may be applied over the commercial sealers, or it may be waxed and serve as the finish itself. Should the latter be the case, it is recommended that the dried sealer be rubbed with steel wool (000 grade), and then wiped clean *before* waxing.

Sanding sealers are usually vinyl-based finishing materials designed to make the sanding operation easier. They are sold in liquid form and are brushed or sprayed onto the surface. If the sanding sealer is sprayed, it should be thinned to the proper spraying consistency. A sanding sealer properly used will make sanding smoother and will reduce the amount of dust that adheres to the sandpaper.

A sanding sealer may be applied to the surface of the wood to stiffen fibers raised by wetting. In this respect, it has a function similar to that of a shellac washcoat or sizing.

When varnishing, a sanding sealer is sometimes used before the first coat of varnish is applied. It provides protection to the wood, stain, and filler. It also functions as a smooth bonding surface for the varnish topcoat.

Wherever you use the sanding sealer, it should be lightly sanded afterward. Make certain that it is thoroughly dry before sanding. Use a tack rag or a clean lint-free cloth to remove the dust and other residue left by the sanding operation.

## FILLERS

Open-grained woods (those having large pores) must have their pores filled before the finish coats are applied. Otherwise, the finish will seep down into these large pores, resulting in a very uneven coat. Another reason for filling is to provide a color contrast between the pore and the flake of the wood.

Fillers are produced in either a paste or liquid form. Both are manufactured from a base which includes quartz silica mixed with some sort of drier, a thinner (usually turpentine or oil), and a vehicle.

Fillers may be sprayed or brushed onto the surface, with the latter method being the most common in the home workshop.

The procedure for brushing a filler onto a wood surface is as follows:

1. Apply a washcoat to the untreated wood surface.
2. Thin the filler to the thickness you find suitable for working. Follow the manufacturer's recommendation for the selection of a thinner.
3. Brush in the filler in the direction of the grain. Allow the filler sufficient time to dry to a dull sheen. Do not let it become completely dry or it will be difficult to rub off.
4. Rub the filler *across* the grain with a piece of burlap.
5. Take a clean burlap cloth and rub across the grain a second time.
6. Take a clean soft cloth and wipe the surface in the direction of the grain.
7. Allow the filler enough time to dry completely and then sand lightly to restore the smooth surface.

Most filling problems can be traced to one or more of the following causes:

1. Improper application,
2. Poor drying,
3. Use of the wrong filler.

The most common problems related to the improper use of a filler are:

1. Puffing,
2. Shrinkage,
3. Ashing,
4. Pinholing.

*Puffing* refers to the swelling of the filler after the sealer and topcoat have been applied. It results in the filler pushing itself out of the wood pore, and is caused by not allowing sufficient time for the filler to dry. *Shrinkage,* on the other hand, has the opposite effect. Although a filler will be subject to some shrinkage as it dries, an excessive amount is caused by coating the filler before it is completely dry.

*Ashing* refers to the grayish color a filler will acquire after a topcoat has been applied. This, too, is due to improper drying. *Pinholes* are also caused by applying a sealer or topcoat to a filler before it has had time to dry. However, pinholing can also be traced to other causes unrelated to the filling procedure, such as

193

vapor trapped in the pores or excess moisture in the wood. The pinholes resemble tiny eruptions on the surface of the finish.

One aspect of improper application is wiping the filler too vigorously and before it has dried sufficiently. This results in removing some of the filler from the pores and giving the surface an appearance similar to one caused by excessive shrinkage.

Poor filling can also be caused by any of the following factors:

1. A washcoat that is too thick or thin,
2. A filler that is too thick or thin,
3. A surface that is poorly sanded.

A washcoat that is too thick will bridge (close) the pores, and prevent packing by the filler. A washcoat that is too thin will cause the filler to wipe hard. This produces a nonuniform appearance. A filler that is too thick will not pack the pores properly. On the other hand, one that is too thin will not fill them adequately. Poor sanding produces rough spots and results in a nonuniform application of the filler.

All of these filling problems can be prevented by properly preparing the wood surface, and carefully following the manufacturer's instructions for using the filler.

# Chapter 8

# Staining

A *stain* is a solution of coloring matter (usually an aniline dye or a pigment) in a solvent. The coloring matter is dissolved or suspended in the solution depending upon the type of stain. Dye-type stains are transparent unless modified with opaque pigments. Pigment-type stains, on the other hand, are characterized by a certain degree of opacity. It all depends on the amount of pigment color suspended in the solution.

*Staining* is the process of applying a stain to a wood surface. Stains may be applied over a smoothed, bare wood surface (almost always close-grained woods), over a washcoat or sealer (open-grained woods), or over finishes (shading, antiquing, etc. See Chapter 15). They may also be applied to portions of the surface or to the entire surface.

The primary purpose of staining is to alter or change the color of a wood, and *not* to provide a protective coating. Generally, a stain is unsuitable as a protective coating because it lacks toughness and its color is subject to fading. A "stained finish" is usually one that has some sort of clear, transparent finish or wax applied over the stain to lock-in the colors and to provide a protective coating. This protective finish is applied after the stain has dried. Examples of how a stain can be finished are:

1. A shellac washcoat and a wax,
2. A sealer and a clear varnish,
3. A lacquer sealer and a lacquer.

The washcoat or sealer prevents the stain from bleeding into the wax or clear top coat, but at the same time does not obscure or alter the color of the stain.

As was previously mentioned, the primary purpose of staining is to alter or change the color of a wood. Reasons for this vary. For example, the colors of many woods are too light or pale. Consequently, the figure and grain appear indistinct. Staining these woods will enhance their beauty. Staining is also used to create a uniform color over the surface. Frequently a wood surface will

Fig. 1. Spraying a stain coating on a wood chair.

have a number of spots that are lighter or darker than the rest of the wood. Staining will correct this unevenness. Another way in which a finisher can use a stain is to change the color of a wood to represent that of one more expensive or more difficult to obtain.

Finally, staining can be used to create special coloring effects. There are red, green, and other non-wood color stains on the market that can change a cheap, uninteresting wood surface into an attractive addition to any room.

Wood stains can be purchased in hardware stores, paint stores, art supply stores, and many other retail outlets. Stains may also be purchased from mail-order firms that specialize in wood finishing materials.

The finisher should carefully follow the instructions and recommendations of the manufacturer when using a stain. One word of caution: always purchase enough stain of a particular name brand to complete the job. The color produced by one manufacturer does not always match the same color available from another manufacturer, and many complications can be avoided by not mixing the two brands.

**Fig. 2. Brushing on a stain.**

Before applying a stain to a wood surface, the finisher is advised to test it on a piece of wood of similar composition. If this is not available, select a section of the piece of furniture (e.g. a back rail, underside, etc.) that is usually out of view and apply

197

the stain. If, when testing the stain, you find that it is darker than you want, thin it with turpentine. Stains that appear to be too light can be darkened by adding a second coat. After the stain sample has dried, coat it with the various finishing materials (e.g. filler, sealer, and topcoats) you plan to use. This will give you a very close idea of how the completed job will look. Remember: even a clear finish will alter a stain color slightly.

Stains can be applied with a brush, pad, lint-free cloth, or by spraying them onto the surface (Figs. 1, 2 and 3). The last method finds its greatest use in shading, toning, or applying stain to areas that offer difficult access. Brushes with synthetic bristles and rubber ferrules are recommended for brushing on a stain.

**Fig. 3. Wiping on a stain.**

In addition to the surface preparation procedures described in Chapter 7, it is recommended that the following additional precautions be taken when applying stains:

1.  Whenever possible, place the surface being stained in a horizontal position (i.e. the working surface face up). This will minimize the problem of the stain running.

198

2. Only overlap wet surfaces. If a wet brush stroke overlaps a dry one, it may result in unsightly lap marks on the surface. This is always a problem with water stains (it decreases in varying degrees with other types of stains).

3. Work from a light to a dark tone when staining. It is always easier to darken a color by adding more stain.

4. Apply the stain in the direction of the grain whenever possible.

5. Remove badly stained areas with a commercial bleach.

6. For large surface areas, mix two or three containers of the same stain color before starting the work. Mix only stains from the same manufacturer. Different manufacturers may have different chemical formulas for the same stain color. Mixing them may cause problems.

7. If the stain is too dark, lighten it before application by adding a lighter stain of the same type and from the same manufacturer.

8. If you have already applied the stain and feel that it is too dark, you can lighten it considerably by wiping part of it off the surface before it has had time to penetrate very far into the wood.

9. Always stain the largest exposed areas of a piece of furniture last.

Many of the stains used in wood finishing can be grouped into three principal categories depending upon the base used in their composition. These three categories of stains are:

1. Oil stains,
2. Water stains,
3. Spirit (alcohol) stains.

## OIL STAINS

Oil is used as the base in the production of oil stains. These types of stains are commercially available in a wide variety of colors, are relatively easy to apply, and will usually not raise the grain of the wood. On the other hand, oil stains do show a tendency to fade over a period of time. Although an oil stain will impart a deep rich tone to the wood, it also has a tendency to reduce the clarity of the grain pattern. Finally, untreated end grains will become considerably darker than the rest of the wood when covered with an oil stain. This can be avoided by applying a coating of linseed oil, thinned shellac, or mineral spirits as a sealer before staining.

Oil based stains are the easiest for the beginner to apply. If the surface is carefully prepared, and the manufacturer's instructions faithfully followed, even the most inexperienced should have no difficulty.

A generalized procedure for applying an oil stain to a wood surface is as follows:

1. Prepare the surface according to the instructions described in Chapter 7.

2. Cover all end-grains with a washcoat of thinned shellac or a similarly suitable sealer( linseed oil, mineral spirits, etc.). This will prevent excessive penetration of the porous end-grains by the stain.

3. Apply the oil stain with a brush or cloth until the entire surface is covered. Brush or wipe with long, straight strokes.

4. Continue to apply the stain until the wood pores will absorb no more.

5. After about 15 to 20 minutes, wipe off the excess stain. Wipe the dark areas more than the light ones, and you will be able to obtain greater uniformity in tone and color.

6. Allow the stained surface to dry for approximately 24 hours.

7. Smooth the surface with a very fine grade of steel wool, *only* if you feel it absolutely necessary. The danger of using an abrasive on a stain is that you may cut through it and show light spots. It is far better to remove all rough spots from the surface *prior* to staining.

8. Remove all residue left by the smoothing operation. A soft clean dry brush may be used.

9. Apply a sealer coat of thinned shellac to the stained surface. This will seal in the stain and provide a degree of added protection to the surface.

Remember that this finishing schedule for staining is very generalized. The staining instructions from the manufacturer may suggest modifications of this schedule.

Oil-base stains may be divided into several types depending upon their composition. The two types most frequently used in furniture finishing are:

1. Pigment oil stains,
2. Penetrating oil stains.

## PIGMENT OIL STAINS

Pigment oil stains (not to be confused with pigmented wiping stains) are composed of ground color pigments suspended in a solvent (e.g. turpentine, linseed oil, or naphtha). These are non-penetrating oil stains that at one time enjoyed widespread use in furniture finishing. They have now been largely replaced by non-grain raising stains, water stains, spirit (alcohol) stains, and other more convenient to use.

Pigment oil stains are particularly useful for blending and re-touching colors. This is primarily due to the fact that the stain is mixed by the finisher himself to match the color of the surface and there are literally hundreds of different color tones possible.

The disadvantages of using pigment oil stains are as follows:
1. The color pigments have a tendency to settle to the bottom of the container and must be thoroughly stirred before and during use.
2. Oil pigment stains have a tendency to fade as well as cloud the finish.
3. These stains require a comparatively longer drying time.

## PENETRATING OIL STAINS

Penetrating oil stains consist of aniline dyes dissolved in a solvent (turpentine, naphtha, tolvol, or some other hydrocarbon

201

solvent). These stains are available in a ready-mixed liquid form or powders.

Penetrating oil stains are very easy to apply, and the lightness or darkness of the overall color can be controlled by wiping. Unfortunately, they tend to penetrate unevenly on certain woods. These stains generally penetrate the wood more deeply than other types, and are therefore much more difficult (and sometimes impossible) to remove once they have dried. Penetrating oil stains are produced in clear, transparent colors and are used most effectively on open-grained woods (those having large pores). Their primary advantage is that they will not clog the pores of these woods.

The color of penetrating oil stain has a tendency to fade. Moreover, this type of stain exhibits bad bleeding characteristics. This is particularly true under lacquer or varnish topcoats where it usually bleeds through and creates a spotted or mottled appearance.

## WATER STAINS

Water stains are produced by dissolving powdered aniline dye in hot water. These stains are particularly effective in bringing out the natural color of the wood. The most serious drawback encountered when using water stains is their tendency to raise the grain of the wood. As a result, certain wood fibers swell and harden, extending permanently above the surface of the wood. They must be removed by sanding before the finishing schedule can proceed any further. The problem of raised grains can be handled in several ways, including:

1. Raise the grain *before* applying the stain by sponging the surface with warm water, allowing it to dry (1 to 3 hours), and sanding down the raised grain.

2. Sand down the raised grain after having stained the surface (this is the least desirable method, because you run the risk of sanding through the stain).

3. Use a non-grain raising (N.G.R.) stain.

The procedure recommended for applying a water stain to a wood surface is as follows:

1. Prepare the surface according to the instructions given in Chapter 7.
2. Raise the wood grain by sponging it lightly with warm water. Allow the surface sufficient time to dry and the wood fibers time to harden.
3. Sand the raised grain down with a fine grade of sandpaper. Do *not* sand against the grain.
4. Remove all dust caused by the sanding operation. Use a soft, clean cloth for this purpose.
5. Apply the water stain with even, straight brush strokes. Do not wipe off the excess. This will be absorbed by the wood or will evaporate during the drying period.
6. Allow the stained surface to dry for approximately 24 hours.
7. Sand the surface lightly with a fine grade of sandpaper if further grain raising has occurred. It may be necessary to apply a second coat of stain, especially if the sanding has caused light spots to appear. Always sand in the direction of the grain (never across the grain).
8. Remove all dust caused by the sanding operation (see Step 4).

A water stain may be sprayed, brushed, or wiped onto the surface. Brushing is often followed by wiping, because a water stain can be uniformed by the wiping action. Drying time is rather long (usually 24 hours), but this allows the stain to penetrate more deeply into the wood. A water stain is flooded onto the surface. This ensures uniformity in application, but the excess stain should not be allowed to sit too long. The longer the stain is allowed to sit after it has been applied, the darker the color will be. A very light color can be obtained by wiping off the stain almost immediately after application.

Water stains are noted for their rich, deep colors. The intensity of the color is determined by the amount of water added to the aniline dye powder. As the amount of water in proportion to the powder increase, so does the intensity of the color decrease.

Water stains are non-bleeding, and can therefore be used safely under a lacquer or varnish topcoat. These stains should be applied on a horizontal surface in order to reduce the chance of running.

A washcoat is mandatory after applying a water stain, because it creates a smoother surface for the next layers of finishing material. It is particularly important that end-grains be sealed when working with this type of stain. A shellac washcoat will do nicely.

Water stains should not be applied over surfaces that have been stripped, because oil films from the old finish will interfere with a uniform penetration of the stain.

## SPIRIT (ALCOHOL) STAINS

Spirit (alcohol) stains are formed by dissolving aniline dye powders in alcohol. These stains are commercially available in a wide variety of ready-mixed colors, or you can mix your own by purchasing packets of the aniline dye powder.

Like oil stains, the color of a spirit stain tends to fade over a period of time. In addition to that, these stains exhibit extremely bad bleeding characteristics and will bleed into most finishing topcoats unless properly sealed. Never use a shellac washcoat under a spirit stain. Alcohol will dissolve shellac.

A spirit stain will dry in about a half hour. Because of its rapid drying rate, spraying is recommended as the method of application. Brushing requires quick, long, even strokes parallel to the longer edges. Overlapping should be avoided. Do not sand a spirit stain except as a last resort. Any grain raising and sanding should take place before the stain is applied. Avoid applying a spirit stain if the humidity is particularly high. Otherwise, the wood will absorb a certain amount of moisture from the air and grain raising will usually ocur after the spirit stain is applied.

## NON-GRAIN RAISING (N.G.R.) STAINS

A non-grain raising stain consists of:
1. A primary solvent (e.g. methanol),
2. A secondary solvent to hold the colors in solution,

3. A coal tar dilutant to reduce grain raising.

4. An aniline powder (the same acid dye used in water stains).

Non-grain raising stains are the most commonly used stains in furniture finishing. Among their principal advantages are:

1. Color permanency (they show very little tendency to fade),
2. Color uniformity,
3. The absence of bleeding.

The major disadvantage of using non-grain raising stains is their relative costliness as compared to water stains. On the other hand, they are still cheaper than the spirit stains.

Non-grain raising stains dry more quickly than water stains, usually requiring only 15 minutes to 1 hour. This makes brushing them somewhat difficult. Furthermore, brushing a non-grain raising stain tends to cause a certain amount of grain raising. For this reason spraying is recommended because very little or no grain raising takes place with this method of application.

Because non-grain raising stains dry so rapidly, a relatively wide brush (2½ to 3 inches) is recommended for applying. The rapid drying speed of non-grain raising stains also results in lap marks when brushed onto the surface. These can be reduced to a minimum by applying several thinned coats of this stain rather than one overall coat.

The most notable feature of non-grain raising stains is that they will not raise the wood grain appreciably if properly formulated.

## VARNISH STAINS

A varnish stain consists of an aniline dye dissolved in a varnish solvent. It should never be used on a fine wood surface, because it tends to obscure the grain pattern and color. Moreover, it has no penetrating power, and sits on the surface in a manner similar to paint or enamel.

Varnish stains are generally sold under the names of woods that approximate their color (e.g. "walnut" for a walnutlike color), and are easily applied to the wood surface with a brush. In the furniture industry, they are used to apply a quick, inexpensive stain coating to wood surfaces not generally exposed to view (chair bottoms, insides of cabinets and drawers, the backs of chests, dressers, and dish cabinets, etc.) Pigmented wiping stains are recommended for use in place of varnish stains.

## SPRAY STAINS

Wood stains are available in aerosol spray cans (16 oz. capacity) for coating areas that are difficult to reach with a brush or cloth, and for shading and toning. These are quick drying stains requiring only about 20 to 30 minutes to become completely dry. They are produced in a number of different colors and are sold under such names as "Spanish Walnut," "Modern Walnut," or "Cherry."

These are lacquer-base stains that both seal and stain the wood in one application. Because lacquer is used in their composition, the same safety and health precautions recommended for a lacquer topcoat should also be used when spraying with these stains.

The nozzles of some spray cans are adjustable for either a vertical or horizontal spray pattern. When spraying, hold the can approximately 12 inches from the surface, and move it according to the instructions given in Chapter 2.

Spray stains can be applied over old finishes as well as bare wood surfaces. If you are spraying an old finish, make certain that no lifting or crazing has occurred (otherwise, it will have to be stripped). Clean off all dirt, grease, polish, wax, and other substances that might contaminate the new stain with a suitable solvent (e.g. mineral spirits). Do not use a solvent strong enough to dissolve the old finish. Sand the surface with a very fine grade of sandpaper and remove the dust left by the sanding operation with a clean, lint-free cloth. Spray the stain onto the surface with quick, uniform movements. Allow the stain to dry thoroughly (about 30 to 45 minutes) and apply additional coats until you have obtained the desired uniformity and depth of color. When the last coat has completely dried, spray several coats of a clear finish compatible with the stain onto the surface.

## STAINING OVER SURFACE DEFECTS

Stains are designed to reveal and enhance the wood grain. Unfortunately, they also reveal surface defects equally well. Consequently, stains should not be used as finishes (e.g. stain and wax finish) over surfaces on which extensive repair or build up has been done.

In Chapter 6 the use of wood putty, plastic wood, and shellac stick for filling dents and other surface imperfections was described. All of these materials can be closely matched with the natural color of the wood or the finish; however none of them contain wood graining. Therefore, their extensive use will be quite conspicuous under any of the clear finishes. Opaque finishes (paint, enamel, etc.) are recommended for surfaces that require more than minimal repair.

## SAP STAINS, OVERALL STAINS, AND ACCENT STAINS

*Sap stains, overall stains,* and *accent stains* are terms referring to specific staining functions. For example, sometimes wood surfaces will have color streaks or nonuniform sections of coloring. *Sap stains* (water stains, non-grain raising stains, or modifications of these two) are used to equalize the overall color of the surface by eliminating these color irregularities. Sap stains are also used to equalize the color differences between the various parts of a piece of furniture (legs, arms, rungs, etc.) and the veneer.

*Overall stains* (usually water or non-grain raising stains) refer to stains applied to the entire surface of a piece of furniture. *Accent stains,* on the other hand, are stains applied to accent wood grain before an overall stain is applied. These are usually spirit or water stains. Accent stains can also be applied over the filler, sealer, or first coat of lacquer for a highlighting effect.

## TONERS

A toner is used to partially or completely change the natural color of a wood to a simulated one. The toner covers the surface of the wood and does not penetrate into the pores. It generally consists of an opaque or semiopaque pigment suspended in a lacquer. A synthetic or natural resin base may also be used as a vehicle for the toner. Sometimes a toner will contain a dye instead of pigment which results in a more transparent coating than the pigment-type will give.

The disadvantages of pigment-type toners is that they obscure the grain figure and often succeed in giving the wood a painted effect. However, if the toner is too transparent, the uniforming effect decreases. A good toner will have the following characteristics:

1. Maximum uniformity,
2. Little build up,
3. No obscuring of the grain,
4. A smooth base for the other finishing materials.

## EQUALIZERS

Equalizers are similar in composition to toners, but differ in their function. As was already mentioned, toners are used to partially or completely change the color of a wood. Equalizers, on the other hand, are designed to uniform a wood of variegated colors.

## PADDING STAINS

A padding stain is essentially a glaze and takes its name from the method by which it is applied. A pad moistened with shellac or lacquer (in this case a special padding lacquer) is dipped into a colored powder and then rubbed onto an older surface for a special color effect. Note that it is not rubbed onto a bare wood surface.

## TOBACCO AND OTHER ORGANIC-BASE STAINS

Cornell University has developed a tobacco stain for use on pine that leaves a very interesting warm brown color.

The stain is made by mixing a cut up plug of tobacco with a pint of clear household ammonia in a quart jar. The mixture is sealed and allowed to soak for 7 to 10 days, and then applied to the wood surface. A soft, lint-free cloth is recommended for application. Because this is in a sense a wiping stain, the excess not absorbed by the wood should be wiped off as soon as possible. Allow the stain to dry for approximately 24 hours, remove any dust particles or other matter with a tack rag, and apply a sealer coat.

Other organic-base stains have been made from berries, roots, bark, and other types of vegetation. The coloring matter is ground and dissolved in a solvent in much the same manner as aniline dye powders used in water stains. The method of application is also similar. The colors of these stains fade more rapidly than do the water stains, and it is for this reason that they were largely replaced by the latter.

## SEALER STAINS

Sealer stains (or stain sealers) are designed to add color and seal the wood in the same operation. These stains are basically sealers produced by thinning such finishes as varnish, shellac, or lacquer and mixing in color dyes.

Sealer stains usually dry a uniform tone without the occasional dark spots found with other types of stains. They are also characterized by the absence of lap marks during their application. Sealer stains generally exhibit less surface penetration than do other types of stains. Pigmented wiping stains and *Minwax* are examples of sealer stains.

## PIGMENTED WIPING STAINS

*Pigmented wiping stains* (known also as *wiping stains, oil stains, uniforming stains,* or *unifying stains*) consist of finely ground color pigments suspended in a solvent (naphtha, mineral spirits, turpentine, or linseed oil) which is usually combined with oil or a synthetic resin binder.

209

These stains are more closely related to an enamel or paint (they are actually a thin paint by composition), and are frequently used to cover or mask an undesirable grain pattern or wood color. When they do emphasize a grain, it is accomplished by filling in the open pores with color pigments. Essentially, then, the grain is outlined by the wiping stain. These stains are frequently used to fake the color of a more expensive wood.

Pigmented wiping stains are second only to non-grain raising stains in popularity. This is due not only to their low cost but also to their ease and flexibility of application. They may be brushed, wiped, or sprayed onto a surface, and various color effects can be obtained by the manner in which they are wiped off. These are rather long drying stains and wiping generally takes place 5 to 10 minutes after application.

Either size or a washcoat should be applied to a bare wood surface before using a pigmented wiping stain. This reduces penetration, increases color uniformity and develops better wiping properties for the stain.

Two stain systems are possible by applying a pigmented wiping stain over a water or non-grain raising stain. This will result in combining the best properties of the dye-base stains (depth and brilliance of color) with those of the pigmented wiping stain. An abbreviated finishing schedule for such a two-stain system is as follows:

1. Wood preparation steps prior to staining (see Chapter 7).
2. Apply a water or non-grain raising stain to the wood surface and allow it sufficient time to thoroughly dry.
3. Lightly sand the surface with a very fine grade of sandpaper. Be careful not to scratch through the stain spots.
4. Wipe away the dust left by the sanding operation with a clean lint-free cloth.
5. Apply the pigmented wiping stain.
6. Concluding steps of a finishing schedule following the application of a stain (see Chapter 7).

A pigmented wiping stain can also be applied over a toner when the latter substitutes for the primary stain (i.e. in Step 2 of the above finishing schedule).

210

All pigmented wiping stains should be carefully mixed before using. The ground color pigments have a tendency to settle to the bottom of most containers when not being used. Pigmented wiping stains are available in cans, bottles (with dauber tops), aerosol spray cans, and tubes (cream or paste form).

Most pigmented wiping stains (with the exception of those in aerosol spray cans) should be thinned before use. Follow the manufacturer's recommendations for thinning.

## MINWAX

*Minwax* is a trade name for a finishing material that functions as both a stain sealer and a finish. It penetrates, stains, and seals the wood in a single action, and dries to a relatively tough scratch resistant finish.

The recommended finishing schedule for applying *Minwax* is as follows:

1. Prepare the surface (sanding only) according to the recommendations suggested in Chapter 7.

2. Thoroughly mix the *Minwax* before applying it to the surface.

3. Apply the first coat of *Minwax* with a brush or a clean lint-free cloth and wait 10 to 15 minutes for it to penetrate the wood.

4. Wipe away the excess with a clean cloth and allow it to dry for about 24 hours.

5. Apply a second coat of *Minwax* (follow Steps 2, 3, and 4).

6. Apply a paste finishing wax and polish with a clean soft cloth.

A tougher finish with a deeper richer color can be obtained by modifying the finishing schedule as follows:

6. Apply a shellac washcoat and allow it sufficient time to dry thoroughly.

7. Apply one or two coats of clear varnish.

## BLONDING

*Blonding* is a staining procedure used to lighten the color of a wood without resorting to bleaching. This is accomplished by applying a very light tinted or white pigmented wiping stain to the wood and wiping it off. This procedure does not work on dark colored woods, and produces only a slight lightening effect on the light colored ones.

## SHADING WOOD STAINS

Wood stains can be given a shaded effect by wiping or brushing harder at the center of a wood surface than at the edges or in the corners. The stain will then be darker at these points and will appear to frame or outline the panels and other sections with a gradual change of color from very dark to very light.

The procedure for shading wood stains is as follows:

1. Follow the instructions for preparing the wood surface given in Chapter 7.

2. Apply a thinned oil stain to the surface and wipe it off almost immediately afterwards. This will prevent the stain from penetrating the wood pores to any great extent and provides the lighter shades.

3. Apply a second unthinned coat of oil stain to the edges and corners. Wipe off the stain with a cloth using circular hand movements. Wipe harder on those areas that will be a lighter shade or color.

Refer to Chapter 15 for a more detailed description of shading procedures. See the same chapter for information on SHADING STAINS and GLAZING STAINS.

## GELLED WOOD STAINS

Wood stains are also available in gelled form in ½ pint, pint, and quart cans. The advantage of gelled wood stains is that the color pigments are distributed evenly throughout the container. Consequently, there is no settling out of the color pigments (as is the case with liquid oil stains) and the same color is maintained from top to bottom.

These stains can be applied over latex or flat oil type bases with a brush or a cloth wiping pad. As such, it is an excellent stain for antiquing (see Chapter 15). Gelled wood stains are available in a variety of different colors, including red mahogany, brown mahogany, butternut, fruitwood, and walnut.

## Chapter 9

# Shellac Finishes

The word "shellac" is formed by combining the words "shell" and "lac". The latter word is of ancient origin being found in Persian (as *lak*), in Hindu (as *lahk*), and in Sanscrit (as *laksha*). In any event, all three refer to the tiny lac insect and its resinous excretion used in the production of shellac. The word translates in each of the three original languages as "hundred thousand" and is descriptive of the manner in which the insect rapidly multiplies until it completely covers the host plant. The lac insect, then, is literally the "hundred-thousand bug."

The lac insect seeks out certain types of host plants to which the larvae attach themselves and feed upon the sap. However, prior to feeding, the lac insect covers itself with a protective cover or shell by excreting a sticky resinous substance. It is this substance (also referred to as *lac*) that forms the basis for the manufacture of shellac.

### USING SHELLAC ON FURNITURE

Much of the furniture of the eighteenth century was finished by applying many thin layers of shellac. This technique, known as *French polishing,* was developed in France and eventually found its way to England and America. This is a tough, transparent finish that greatly enhances the beauty and grain pattern of such woods as mahogany, walnut, and birdseye maple. Although it takes many hours of painstaking care in application, this technique is still used by many finishers today in order to obtain that velvet sheen characteristic of French polishing.

The introduction of production line, mass-produced furniture in the second quarter of the nineteenth century resulted in the eventual disappearance of multilayered shellac finishes from all but the most expensive pieces. The determining factor, of course, was an economic one. Because these shellac finishes required a number of different coats, it was quicker and cheaper to use a finish that needed only one or two applications.

Shellac has a variety of other uses in furniture finishing besides that of a top coat. For example, it enjoys widespread use as a washcoat and undercoating for other types of finishes such as lacquer or varnish. It functions very efficiently as a sealer to prevent other substances (e.g. stains, fillers, etc.) from bleeding through into the top coat. In Europe and other areas, it was popular for a long time as a combination filler and sealer. In this case, the shellac was thickly applied, allowed to dry, and sanded smooth. This technique was not uncommon even as late as the 1940's.

## TYPES OF SHELLAC

Shellacs are available in several types and are distinguished by colors ranging from very dark (almost a black) to very light (orange). Shellac can also be bleached (the so-called white shellac) and completely purified of all wax content. The latter is a clear shellac having no color at all.

White and orange shellacs (frequently referred to as *shellac varnishes*) are available in a ready-mixed liquid form or in dry flakes that must be combined with a vehicle. The liquid form is the most common. *Note*: because the liquid form of shellac is ready-mixed, many beginners make the mistake of using the shellac directly from the can without thinning. Do *not* try to do this. The shellac is too thick and must be thinned before use (50-50 is a good rule-of-thumb formula for thinning). Otherwise, the shellac will tend to thicken and pile up on the surface causing all sorts of finishing problems.

White shellac is a purified and bleached form of shellac from which virtually all traces of color have been removed. It is used primarily to apply a clear finish to light colored woods. Orange

215

shellac, on the other hand, is recommended for surfaces having darker colors (e.g. redwood or gumwood). Orange shellac can be stored longer than white shellac. It will also prove to be a more durable finish in the long run. The major objection to using orange shellac is that it is too dark for the lighter woods. Using an orange shellac on a light colored wood will all too frequently leave a yellowish cast.

Shellac substitutes should be avoided because they usually require refinishing long before surfaces on which a genuine shellac has been used. These shellac substitutes( as well as cheap shellacs) will gum during sanding and clog the abrasive. As you can see, there is really no advantage to using shellac substitutes.

## PIGMENTED SHELLAC

Anilines used to produce alcohol stains can also be dissolved in shellac. The result is a pigmented, opaque shellac that produces a finish similar to paint. The color and shade of the shellac will naturally depend upon the type of aniline dye selected and the amount used. Pigmented shellac can be used to touch up worn areas on a piece of furniture or to completely refinish it. Because pigmented shellac is an opaque finish, it can be applied directly over an older finish.

## ADVANTAGES AND DISADVANTAGES OF USING SHELLAC

Among the principal advantages of using shellac in wood finishing is that it is easy to apply and it permits the natural grain of the wood to show through. It is a quick drying finish, and mistakes made during application can be corrected quite easily. A shellac finish polishes well and imparts a mellow tone to the color of the wood.

Unfortunately, shellac finishes are not the most durable. They are easily scratched, they form white spots when they come in contact with water, and both water and alcohol will cause them to dissolve.

216

## BRUSHES AND BRUSH CARE

Soft bristle brushes, two to four inches wide, are recommended for applying shellac to wood surfaces. These are the same kind of brushes used for applying varnish or enamel. The wider brushes should be used where it is necessary to cover large areas (e.g. table tops, desk tops, etc.). The brush should be kept wet with shellac at all times. If the brush is allowed to become dry, the shellac coat will more than likely be uneven. Skipping spots, streaking and lapping are all characteristic results of using a dry brush improperly.

If the shellac is allowed to dry on the brush, the brush can be cleaned and softened again by soaking it in denatured alcohol. Always clean shellac brushes in denatured alcohol. After the brush is completely cleaned, dry it, wrap it in paper, and store it in a flat position.

*Never* dip a brush wet from water into the shellac. Water is the natural enemy of shellac finishes. Not only will a wet glass bottom cause a white ring to form on a shellac finish, it is possible to remove the entire finish simply by rubbing it with soap and water.

*Never* allow a shellac brush to be used for any other purpose. You do not want to run the risk of contaminating the shellac when you use it for that purpose again.

## SPRAYING SHELLAC

The equipment used for spraying shellac should be absolutely clean. Any dirt or residue from other finishes found in the equipment will probably be combined with the shellac and sprayed onto the surface.

Thin the shellac to approximately a 1½ to 2-pound cut (see Table 1) for use in the spraying equipment. Maintain a distance of 7-8 inches between the surface and the nozzle of the spray gun. Move the gun in a straight line parallel to the surface. Resist the temptation to swing the gun nozzle in an arc.

The major problems encountered when spraying are runs and uneven deposits of shellac. The latter results in surface sags and is generally caused by failure to maintain an even distance between the spray gun and the surface. Runs are caused by spraying too much shellac onto the surface.

Always spray where there is proper ventilation. If you are indoors, the work area should be equipped with an acceptable exhaust fan. Do *not* use portable electric house fans for this purpose. The smallest spark could set off a dangerous, perhaps fatal, explosion.

The shellac will have to be thinned before it can be used in a spray gun. This will generally be thinner than the consistency for brushing.

### Table 1. Formulas for Thinning Shellac

| Desired Cut For Finish | Consistency of Purchased Cut | Alcohol | Shellac | Consistency |
|---|---|---|---|---|
| 1-Pound Cut | 3-Pound Cut | 4 Parts | 3 Parts | Thin |
| 1-Pound Cut | 4-Pound Cut | 2 Parts | 1 Part | |
| 1-Pound Cut | 5-Pound Cut | 2 Parts | 1 Part | |
| 2-Pound Cut | 3-Pound Cut | 2 Parts | 5 Parts | Average |
| 2-Pound Cut | 4-Pound Cut | 3 Parts | 4 Parts | |
| 2-Pound Cut | 5-Pound Cut | 1 Part | 1 Part | |
| 3-Pound Cut | 3-Pound Cut | ———* | ———* | Thick |
| 3-Pound Cut | 4-Pound Cut | 2 Parts | 1 Part | |
| 3-Pound Cut | 5-Pound Cut | 1 Part | 2 Parts | |

*No Dilution. The Shellac is used at full strength.

## THINNING SHELLAC

The consistency of the shellac is determined by the size of the cut purchased and the amount of denatured alcohol used to thin it. For example, a 4-pound cut indicates that four pounds of shellac have been dissolved in one gallon of denatured alcohol. A 5-pound cut, on the other hand, means that an additional pound of shellac has been dissolved in the same amount of alcohol (one gallon), whereas a 3-pound cut contains one pound less. With each of the three different cuts (3-pound, 4-pound, and 5-pound), the same amount of denatured alcohol has been used. Regardless of the size of the cut, the consistency of the shellac can be further thinned by adding more denatured alcohol. Table 1 indicates the recommended amounts for the various consistencies.

Once again, no shellac should be used straight from the can without thinning. Not only is thinning a relatively simple procedure, it makes the shellac much more easy to work with.

Denatured alcohol is used as thinner for shellac, and is available in most paint stores, hardware stores, and other outlets where paint supplies are sold. Do *not* use methyl alcohol or wood alcohol for thinning.

Old drinking glasses or jars are excellent containers for mixing shellac with the thinner. Make certain that the container you use is perfectly clean and dry. Any dirt left will combine with the shellac and eventually find its way into the finish. Rubber gloves and old clothes are recommended for wear when working with shellac.

## A STANDARD SHELLAC FINISH

The standard shellac finish is relatively easy to apply. It does not require the addition of special oils or other ingredients (as is the case with the French polish technique), nor as long drying periods between coats necessary. The steps in the finishing schedule are fairly simple and should (if followed faithfully) provide the finisher with satisfactory results.

The procedure for applying a standard shellac finish is as follows (Fig. 1.):

1. Sand the wood surface until it is completely smooth. Wipe a damp cloth across the surface to remove the dust and to raise the grain. Sand the surface a second time to remove the raised grain. Clean off all dust resulting from the sanding operation. More detailed instructions for preparing the surface are given in Chapter 7.

2. Prepare the shellac. The shellac should be thinned prior to use. This can be best done in a large drinking glass or glass jar. Add enough denatured alcohol to obtain the desired consistency. The initial coats of shellac will be very thin; subsequent coats are generally thicker.

219

3. If the wood is an open grain one (e.g. pine, mahogany, chestnut, etc.), the pores should be sealed with a thin shellac washcoat. This will insure uniformity in the subsequent coats and prevent the stain (should one be used) from sinking too deeply into the pores of the wood. Lightly abrade the shellac sealer coat with a very fine grade of sandpaper or steel wool.

4. If staining is necessary, the stain should be applied immediately after the initial washcoat.

**STEP 1**   PREPARE THE WOOD SURFACE.

**STEP 2**   PREPARE THE SHELLAC ACCORDING
TO DESIRED CONSISTENCY (BOTH
WASHCOATS AND TOPCOAT).

**STEP 3**   APPLY A THIN SHELLAC WASHCOAT.

**STEP 4**   APPLY A STAIN (OPTIONAL).

**STEP 5**   APPLY A THIN SHELLAC WASHCOAT
(IF A FILLER IS TO BE USED IT SHOULD
BE APPLIED AFTER THIS STEP AND
BEFORE STEP 6).

**STEPS 6-10**  APPLY THE SHELLAC COATS.

Fig. 1. Procedure for applying shellac.

5. Using a stain will require a second sealer coat of very thin shellac. This is applied directly over the stain so that it will not bleed into any of the finishing materials that follow.

6. Apply the thinned coat of shellac and allow it sufficient time to dry (about 2 to 3 hours).

7. After the coat of shellac has dried, *lightly* sand it with a fine grade of sandpaper or steel wool. It is very important not to cut through the shellac coat. Otherwise, it will be necessary to start all over again, because it is very difficult to repair this kind of mistake. Remove the dust

left by the sanding operation with a dry, lint-free cloth or by other suitable means.

8. Repeat Steps 6 and 7 until at least four or five layers of shellac have been applied to the wood. These coats should be somewhat thicker in consistency than the washcoats used for sealing. *Note*: after the last coating of shellac has been applied, substitute a fine grade of steel wool for the sandpaper that was used in the previous steps.

9. Apply one or more coats of wax and polish with a soft, clean lint-free cloth. If you use a self-polishing wax, the polishing operation is eliminated. However, you may buff the surface lightly with a soft cloth after the wax has thoroughly dried. See Chapter 14 WAXING AND POLISHING FINISHES for further information.

10. A tougher, more durable surface can be obtained by covering the final coat of shellac with a thinned coat of clear varnish. If this is desired, then eliminate Step 9 in the finishing schedule.

## SEMIDULL FINISH

A semidull finish can be obtained by lightly dry rubbing the final coat of shellac with a No. 000 or No. 0000 grade of steel wool. Do not rub too hard or you may cut through the finish. Remember, you are only trying to reduce the sheen. Be sure to remove all dust particles left by the sanding operation before applying the wax.

## DULL FINISH

Some finishers recommend a rubbing paste made from pumice stone, vaseline, and paraffin oil as a means of obtaining an interesting dull finish. The vaseline and pumice stone (FF grade) are mixed on a one-to-one basis. The paraffin oil is added until the mixture reaches the consistency of thick paint. The rubbing paste is then applied to the shellac surface with a pad of No. 0000

221

steel wool. Rub the shellac in the direction of the grain. Once again, you are cautioned to rub lightly to avoid scratching through the surface. The paraffin oil will leave oily residue. This can be easily removed by sprinkling a layer of clean sawdust across the surface and then brushing it off. The sawdust will absorb the paraffin oil.

## SATIN FINISH

Allow at least 24 to 48 hours for the last coat of shellac to dry. When you are certain that it is thoroughly dry, remove the sheen by rubbing it lightly with No. 000 or No. 0000 steel wool. Remove the dust left by the steel wool rubbing operation with a dry line-free cloth. Brush (lightly) a FFF grade of pumice stone across the surface. Make certain that every portion of the surface is brushed with the pumice stone. Wipe off the pumice stone powder and lightly sand it again with a No. 000 or No. 0000 steel wool. Wipe off the dust with a dry lint-free cloth.

## FRENCH POLISH

*French polish* is a shellac top coat finishing technique originally developed in France some three centuries ago. It is a durable finish produced by building up layer after layer of thinned shellac after an initial application of linseed oil to the surface. The French polishing technique results in imparting a velvet sheen to the surface, and in enhancing both the grain pattern of the wood and its natural color. This finishing technique gives better results when applied to close grained woods. Open grained woods will require a certain amount of staining and filling before the layers of shellac are applied.

The procedure for French polishing is essentially as follows:

1. Sand the wood surface until it is completely smooth. Raise the grain of the wood by wiping a damp cloth across the surface, and sand it again. See Chapter 7 for more complete instructions describing the preparation of the surface.

2. Remove any dust or other particles left on the wood surface by the sanding operation with a lint-free cloth, soft brush, or by vacuuming.

3. Stain the surface for the desired coloring. Allow the stain sufficient time to be absorbed by the wood pores. Do not proceed to the next step until you are certain that the stain has completely dried. As a result of the staining operation, the surface should now have an even, uniform color.

Fig. 2. Making and using a French-polishing pad.

4. Apply the linseed oil to the surface, and allow it sufficient time to soak in and dry. Wipe away any excess.

5. Sand the surface with a very fine grade of sandpaper. Remove the dust and allow about 24-hours to make sure that the wood has completely dried.

6. Apply a thin solution of shellac to a rubbing pad made from a section of soft linen wrapped around tightly wound strips of muslin (Fig. 2). The shellac must be evenly distributed over the entire rubbing surface of the pad.

7. Using a circular movement, rub the surface of the wood with the pad (Fig. 2). Add an occasional drop of raw linseed oil while rubbing. Continue rubbing the surface for 45 to 50 minutes, and then allow it to dry for approximately 24 hours.

8. Repeat Step 7 and allow 48 to 72 hours drying time.

9. Repeat step 7 and allow one week to ten days drying time.

10. A soft cloth (preferably one that has been used to apply shellac) slightly dampened with denatured alcohol is quickly and lightly passed over the surface to remove any oil residue left from the raw linseed oil.

Some finishers prefer to add the raw linseed oil directly to the shellac before it is applied to the surface. This is usually at the ratio of $\frac{1}{4}$ ounce of raw linseed oil for *each* pint of denatured alcohol. If this is desired, then eliminate Step 4 in the French polish schedule.

The shellac itself will generally serve as an adequate filler for close grained woods. On large (open) grained woods, an additional agent is required. One method used by many finishers is to sprinkle a fine grade of pumice across the surface when applying the second coating of shellac. The pumice is rubbed into the pores of the wood with a circular movement of the rubbing pad, and the excess is removed after the operation is completed. The filling operation should take place after Step 7 of the finishing schedule described for the French polishing technique.

## PIANO FINISH

A *piano finish* is obtained by rubbing a clear or pigmented shellac until the surface has a near perfect gloss or "egg shell" finish.

The procedure for applying a piano finish is as follows:

1. Sand the wood surface until it is completely smooth. Raise the grain of the wood by wiping a damp cloth across the surface, and sand it again. See Chapter 7 for more complete instructions describing the preparation of the surface.
2. Remove any dust or other particles left on the wood surface by the sanding operation with a lint-free cloth, soft brush, or by vacuuming. Wiping the surface with a cloth dampened in denatured alcohol will remove any last traces of dirt.
3. Apply a water stain to the surface for the desired coloring. Allow the stain 24 hours to completely penetrate and dry.
4. Apply a thinned washcoat of shellac (generally about 4 parts denatured alcohol to 1 part shellac in a 3-pound cut).
5. Brush on a filler and allow approximately 24 hours to dry.
6. Sand the surface with a fine grade of sandpaper *in the direction of the grain.* Sanding across the grain may leave scratches on the surface.
7. Remove any dust or other particles left on the wood surface by the sanding operation with a lint-free cloth, soft brush, or by vacuuming.
8. Apply the first coat of shellac that will form the top coat. This will be thinned to a medium consistency (about 2 parts denatured alcohol to 5 parts shellac in a 3-pound cut).
9. Allow the shellac 2 to 3 hours to dry.
10. Lightly sand the surface with a fine grade of sandpaper. Patch the surface dents and scratches with shellac stick matching the color of the stained wood as closely as pos-

sible. Sand again with the fine grade sandpaper until the surface is smooth and even to the touch.

11. Remove all dust or other particles left by the sanding operation with a lint-free cloth, soft brush, or by vacuuming

12. Apply the second coat of shellac and follow Steps 8 through 11.

13. Continue to apply as many coats of shellac as necessary to obtain the desired gloss (3 or 4 should do it), but rub each coat with pumice and raw linseed oil.

14. Before applying the final coat of shellac, allow the surface to dry for 3 or 4 days.

15. Apply the final coat of shellac, allow it sufficient time to dry and rub it with rottenstone, a felt pad and raw linseed oil.

16. Clean the surface by wiping it gently with a soft, lint-free cloth.

17. Wax the surface to protect it from water damage. Polish the waxed surface with a dry, soft cloth.

## SHELLAC AS A SEALER AND BASE COAT

Shellac can be used as a sealer coat over wax finishes, dents and other minor defects. A shellac sealer coat will be adequate for filling in these minor surface imperfections and for providing a flat, smooth surface for subsequent finishing coats. The sealing of a wax finish will prevent the wax from bleeding through into the new top coat. This is particularly important for such finishes as varnish or lacquer.

Shellac should be applied as a sealer over all types of stains and especially as a base coat for a varnish finish. A base coat of shellac and a single coat of varnish is far quicker and simpler to apply than the often recommended multiple layers of varnish.

A shellac sealer coat is an absolute necessity over any wax stick patching to prevent the wax from bleeding through into the top coat. The sealer should be applied over the entire surface rather than just the patched portion.

Shellac also serves well as a sealer over an old coating of paint, because the paint will not bleed through it.

Shellac is often used as a sealer over unfinished wood, particularly a wood with large open grain. The shellac sealer results in an even, uniform surface over which fillers, stains, and finishes can be applied. Regardless of the type of finish to be used, the shellac sealer coat should be lightly abraded with a fine grade of sandpaper or steel wool. This will enable the other finishing coats to adhere better.

### REAMALGAMATION OF SHELLAC FINISHES

Shellac finishes showing minor defects (e.g. scuffing, wear, etc.) can be restored through the process of reamalgamation. Essentially this consists of dissolving the shellac with denatured alcohol and allowing it to reform and thereby erase the defect. Older shellac finishes often contained special substances that increased their durability or decreased the drying time. Unfortunately, these special substances also tend to resist the dissolving effect of denatured alcohol. The addition of a little lacquer thinner to the alcohol should overcome this resistance.

### STICK SHELLAC PATCHING

Stick shellac is sold in a great variety of colors that approximate or match the numerous different finishes and woods. It is difficult to use, and requires a period of practice before the beginner can expect to obtain satisfactory results. A detailed description of stick shellac patching is found in Chapter 7 of this book.

### POINTS TO REMEMBER

Anyone using shellac in wood finishing should be aware of a number of precautions that must be taken to insure an acceptable standard of work. The four principal precautions are as follows:

1. Never store shellac for more than 90 days.

2. Never store shellac near a source of heat.
3. Never apply shellac to a wet surface.
4. Never use a damp brush to apply shellac.
5. Never apply shellac in a room with any appreciable degree of humidity.
6. Never use shellac near a heat source.

You will note that the avoidance of water and dampness is emphasized. Water should never be used to polish shellac. Because finishes are highly flammable, they should be kept well away from any heat source. Shellac also tends to evaporate rapidly. Because of this it is recommended that glass containers with screw-top covers be used for storage. The container *must* be tightly sealed when the shellac is not being used.

Air bubbles in the shellac will detract from the appearance of the finish. This can be greatly minimized by *not* shaking the shellac container excessively before application.

Shellac should be applied as rapidly as possible. When using a brush, *flow* it onto the surface always in the same direction. Never go over the shellac a second time or you will cause it to pile up. For this reason, the first application must be correct. The thinner the shellac, the less likelihood there will be for mistakes of this nature to occur. You can always add two or more coats until you have obtained the desired thickness.

# Chapter 10

# Varnish Finishes

Varnish is one of the toughest finishes used on wood surfaces. It is a clear finish that enhances and emphasizes the grain while at the same time imparting a special warmth to the wood coloring. Varnish finishes demonstrate an especially strong resistance to the effects of water and alcohol. Furthermore, they will resist impact, abrasion, and heat to a much greater degree than other finishes.

Although there are many different types of varnish available for use on wood surfaces, this chapter will be limited to a description of the two types most commonly used as furniture finishes. These are:

1. The oleoresinous (or oil-base) varnishes,
2. The synthetic resin varnishes.

The oleoresinous or oil-base varnishes have been used for centuries in various forms. It is made by combining a drying oil (commonly linseed oil), natural resins, and other additives such as a solvent or thinner. Turpentine was used for years as the solvent for oleoresinous varnishes, but due to its expense and increasing scarcity was later replaced by mineral spirits (petroleum spirits). A recent improvement of oleoresinous varnishes was brought about by the substitution of China wood oil for the linseed oil.

The solid film of the oleoresinous varnish is produced by the evaporation of the solvent and the drying of the oil by oxidation. The drying rate of these varnishes is rather slow when compared with the newer synthetic resin-types, and it is for this and other reasons that they have been largely replaced by the latter. Other factors contributing to the decline of their popularity include their lack of color retention, durability, and (in some cases) resistance to wear.

The synthetic-resin varnishes are an improvement over the oleoresinous (natural resin) type. They exhibit better durability, better color retention, and greater hardness. They also show the same resistance to water, alcohol, fruit juices, mild acids, and other substances that the oleoresinous substances do. They are faster drying, but still not fast enough to compete with the lacquer finishes that have replaced them in the furniture industry. However, unlike lacquers, they exhibit good resistance to fingernail-polish type solvents.

The synthetic resins used in the production of varnishes are basically of four types:

1. Urethane,
2. Alkyd,
3. Phenolic,
4. Vinyl.

Others are continually being developed in the laboratories and added to the list.

Not all synthetic resin varnishes will produce a completely satisfactory finish (at least not if durability is one of your requirements). Some, such as the urethane-type, will lift off the surface when the finish is cut or struck by a sharp object. The chances are that the finish will then peel off in thin plastic-like sheets. It may be that after experimenting with different varnishes you will find that you prefer the older oleoresinous varnishes to the newer synthetic resin-type. It becomes a matter of personal choice.

Color is also a problem when selecting a varnish. Some varnishes are extremely clear (e.g. the vinyl types), whereas others have traces of color in them (e.g. the alkyd and phenolic resin varnishes). However, their color after application will depend on so many variables it is almost impossible to predict the results. Never hesitate to ask your local paint or hardware store sales personnel for their advice. They have had a great deal of experience with this sort of thing, and will usually try to give you a product that will suit your specific needs.

One of the major disadvantages of using varnish is that it is a relatively slow drying finish. As such, it is very susceptible to dust and other particles being trapped in the finish before it is completely dry. This problem can be greatly minimized by observing the following procedures:

1. Apply varnishes in rooms that are as dust-free as possible.
2. Work in a room in which the temperature is maintained at 65 to 70°F.
3. Remove dust from the wood surface with a tack rag before applying the varnish.
4. Lightly sand each coat of varnish with a very fine grade of sandpaper.
5. Give the final coat a careful rubbing.

Dust particles and other objects (e.g. hair, lint, sand, etc.) can be removed by lifting them with a sharply pointed brush (an artist's brush will do) that is slightly wet with varnish. A specially constructed picking stick will also serve the same purpose (Fig. 1). These are sticks with small, tightly rolled balls of cotton attached at one end. The cotton ball is rolled in varnish, and then squeezed until all excess varnish has been removed. Shape the cotton so that you have a pointed end for picking up the various foreign objects from the surface. The cotton should be tacky, not wet.

## THINNING VARNISH

Both mineral spirits (paint thinner) and turpentine can be used to thin varnish. Usually this is on a 5-1 formula (5 parts varnish to 1 part thinner), but it can range as high as 8-1 depending upon the consistency desired. Your safest bet is to use the thinner recommended by the manufacturer of the varnish. Some varnishes are formulated to be applied by brush without thinner. I would recommend testing these on a piece of scrap wood and being your own judge of the manufacturer's claim. For spraying, use one pint of VM&P Naphtha for each gallon of varnish.

231

1. COTTON WAD GLUED TO THE END OF A STICK

3. SHAPE TIP AND ALLOW IT TO DRY UNTIL IT BECOMES TACKY

2. DIP IN VARNISH

4. USE THE TACKY TIP TO PICK UP HAIR, DUST PARTICLES, AND OTHER FOREIGN OBJECTS ON THE SURFACE

Fig. 1. Constructing and using a picking stick.

## APPLYING VARNISH WITH A BRUSH

Before applying any varnish to the surface, make certain that the brush you intend to use is suitable for varnishing. Furthermore, the brush must be perfectly clean and in fairly good condition. Examine it carefully for any loose bristles that may detach themselves during the varnishing operation. Many finishing problems can be avoided by using a new brush of good quality (a cheap price does not always indicate a bargain, and particularly not when you are trying to brush varnish onto a surface).

Thinning the varnish will usually reduce brushing problems, but you should not be too concerned about minor brush marks on the surface. Varnish, like enamel, tends to flow together or level itself as it dries.

Try to work so that the surface you are varnishing is in a horizontal position. Turn the piece of furniture so that you are always working on a flat, horizontal surface.

Lighting is also very important. Place the piece of furniture in such a way that the light will reflect on the surface and indicate any spots that you may have missed. This holds true when spraying a varnish, too.

Always keep your brush wet, but be careful about overlapping it with too much varnish. Otherwise, the excess varnish may drop onto the surface. If this should happen, try to pick up the drops of varnish with the tip of your brush. Never allow drops or pools of varnish to stand on the surface. Always remove them immediately. The problem of excess varnish on the surface is especially bad along edges. If it is not noticed and allowed to dry, it forms a hard ridge of varnish along the edge.

Try not to overlap your strokes. Begin each new stroke on a dry spot where the last one ended. One method of applying varnish is to cross and tip off the brush strokes so that a series of intersecting and interlocking bands is formed. This pattern is followed until the entire surface is covered. It is started by laying a series of parallel (but separated) strokes in the direction of the grain. Cross these with a series of strokes in the same manner *across* the grain. Tip off the brush by filling in the uncoated areas. If you intend to apply more than one coat of varnish, make certain that the previous one has thoroughly dried before applying the next.

## VARNISH FINISHING SCHEDULE (BRUSHING)

The finishing schedule for applying varnishing to a wood surface bears many similarities to other types of finishing schedules, particularly during the initial steps. However, varnishing does have certain features that are characteristic to it alone and especially when it is applied with a brush.

Prepare the wood surface according to the instructions given in Chapter 7. It is essential that the surface be smooth and clean.

233

Roughness, grease or oil stains, and other surface imperfections will be emphasized by the varnish topcoat. These will ruin the overall appearance of the finish.

The procedure for applying varnish to a wood surface with a brush is as follows (Fig. 2):

1. THE FIRST BRUSH STROKES ARE MADE PARALLEL IN THE DIRECTION OF THE GRAIN

2. THE SECOND SERIES OF BRUSH STROKES CROSS THE GRAIN

3. UNCOATED AREAS ARE FILLED BY TIPPING OFF IN THE DIRECTION OF THE GRAIN

Fig. 2. Brushing technique used when varnishing.

1. Raise the grain of the wood by dampening the surface with water or some other suitable means. Flooding the surface with water and wiping off the excess will usually be adequate.
2. Allow the surface sufficient time to dry, and for the raised fibers to stiffen and harden.
3. Remove the raised wood fibers by sanding lightly with a fine grade of sandpaper. Sand with the grain. Sanding across the grain will produce surface scratches.
4. Remove any dust or other particles left by the sanding operation with a tack rag or clean lint-free cloth.

5. Apply a thin washcoat of shellac to the wood surface. This is particularly necessary for open-grained woods in order to prevent uneven penetration. Washcoating will give the stain a uniform appearance.

6. Allow the washcoat sufficient time to thoroughly dry and remove any raised fibers by sanding lightly with a fine grade of sandpaper.

7. Remove the dust left by the sanding operation with a tack rag or a clean lint-free cloth.

8. Stain the surface. A water or non-grain raising stain is suggested for use with varnish because of their high non-bleeding characteristics. Allow the stain sufficient time to dry. Sanding a stained surface is *not* recommended, because you may scratch through it in spots and produce light spots in the surface coloring. That is why it is advisable to complete all grain raising in Steps 1 through 7.

9. Seal the stain by applying a shellac washcoat. Allow it sufficient time to dry and then sand it lightly with very fine sandpaper.

10. Remove the dust left by the sanding operation.

11. A liquid or paste filler can now be applied if you want a particularly smooth surface. Reread the section on wood fillers in Chapter 7, and the manufacturer's suggestions for application.

12. After you have applied a filler (and properly sanded and cleaned the surface), you will have to seal it so that it does not bleed into the varnish topcoat. Apply a suitable sealer (a shellac washcoat will be adequate), and allow it sufficient time to dry.

13. Rub the entire surface (in the direction of the grain) with very fine steel wool.

14. Remove the dust left by the rubbing operation. Be particularly careful to get the surface clean, because steel wool will leave behind minute metal particles.

15. Thin the varnish with a suitable thinner and apply it to the surface. Follow the manufacturer's recommendations for thinning.

16. Brush the varnish on with light, even strokes. Do not press down with the brush. Work on one section of the furniture at a time.

17. When the surface has been completely covered, tip it off (first across the grain and then with the grain). Do not worry about a few brush marks. These will generally flow together as the varnish dries.

18. Remove dust particles, hairs, and other forms of matter trapped in the finish with a sharp pointed artist's brush. This should be done *immediately* after applying the varnish.

19. If additional coats of varnish are to be applied, the first one must be lightly abraded (scuffed) with a very fine grade of sandpaper. This will give the surface stronger holding power for each topcoat that follows. Remove all dust left by the sanding operation with a tack rag or a clean lint-free cloth, *before* the next topcoat is applied. See Fig. 3.

| | |
|---|---|
| **STEPS 1–4** | PREPARE THE WOOD SURFACE. |
| **STEPS 5–7** | APPLY A WASHCOAT. |
| **STEP 8** | STAIN THE WOOD. |
| **STEPS 9–10** | APPLY A SEALER. |
| **STEP 11** | APPLY A FILLER. |
| **STEPS 12–14** | APPLY A SEALER. |
| **STEPS 15–20** | APPLY THE VARNISH. |

Fig. 3. Varnish finishing schedule.

20. Do not sand the final topcoat. This one will be rubbed to the desired sheen. See Chapter 14 for a number of techniques that can be used.

A sanding sealer compatible with varnish can be substituted for Step 16 (i.e. the *first* varnish topcoat). This will dry more quickly than the varnish and provide a smoother finish for the next coat of varnish after it has been sanded. Make certain that the sanding sealer has thoroughly dried before you sand it. Lightly sand it with a fine grade of sandpaper in the direction of the grain. Remember to remove all dust left by the sanding operation before applying the varnish.

Shellac can be substituted for the intermediate coats of varnish (see Steps 16 and 19). These will not be as thin as a shellac washcoat, and their consistency should approach or equal that of a shellac topcoat.

## VARNISH REAMALGAMATION

Reamalgamation refers to the partial dissolving of a finish to eliminate cracking, crazing, alligatoring, and other minor imperfections on the surface of the finish. As the finish dries, it flows together (i.e. reamalgamates) and eliminates these imperfections.

The reamalgamation process is quite successful with lacquer and shellac finishes, but is generally unsatisfactory when applied to varnish. Solvents for reamalgamating varnish finishes are sold under a variety of different trade names in local paint and hardware stores.

Another method of reviving a varnish finish is to lightly rub the entire surface (always in the direction of the grain) with a very fine steel wool. Remove the dust from the surface, and apply a coat of boiled linseed oil, or linseed oil mixed with varnish (on a 1:1 basis) and thinned with pure turpentine. Several coats may be necessary.

If these suggestions for restoring the finish do not work, your only recourse is to strip it. This is usually the advice given when anyone mentions reamalgamating a varnish finish.

## REVARNISHING

An old varnished surface may be revarnished if it is still in good condition and adheres well to the surface of the wood. If you are planning to revarnish, you should prepare the surface in the following manner:

1. Wash it with warm water and a mild soap to remove all traces of old polish, wax, dirt, and other contaminants.
2. Sand the surface smooth with a fine grade of sandpaper.
3. Remove all dust left by the sanding operation with a tack rag or a clean lint-free cloth.

Step 1 is important because any contaminants left on the surface will prevent the varnish from properly adhering. Remember this when you are stripping a varnish finish, because some varnish and paint removers contain wax. The wax traces can be eliminated by wiping the surface with turpentine.

The sanding operation (Step 2) roughens the surface thereby providing a better holding action. Any gloss must be removed by sanding or the new finish will not adhere properly.

## VARNISH STAINS

A varnish stain is essentially a pigmented varnish. Coloring has been added to the varnish in sufficient amounts to obtain a particular shade, but not enough to obscure the wood grain entirely. It has no penetration power and remains on the surface in the same manner as a varnish. Varnish stains are not generally used on furniture surfaces exposed to view (see Chapter 8. STAINING).

## VARNISH AND LINSEED OIL FINISH

A very fine varnish and linseed oil finish has been used over the years on mahogany, walnut, and other open-grained woods. It is made by mixing 1 part varnish (a spar varnish is often used), 1 part boiled linseed oil, and 5 parts turpentine.

Prepare the wood surface as you would for a varnish finish (see VARNISH FINISHING SCHEDULE in this chapter), and proceed as follows:

1. Apply a sealer coat of thinned varnish (thinned 1:1 with turpentine).

2. After the sealer has thoroughly dried, sand it lightly in the direction of the grain with a very fine sandpaper.
3. Remove all dust left by the sanding operation with a clean lint-free cloth or a tack rag.
4. Wipe on a coat of the varnish and linseed oil. Allow it sufficient time to completely dry.
5. After waiting four days, rub the surface with pumice stone (FFF Grade) and rubbing oil.
6. After waiting another four days, rub the surface with rottenstone and rubbing oil.

If more than one coat of varnish and linseed oil is desired, sand each coat (except the last one) with a very fine sandpaper. Be sure to remove all the dust left by the sanding operation before applying the next coat.

## CLEANING THE BRUSH

Pure turpentine is used to clean varnish from the brush. A paint and varnish remover can also be used, but with caution. Some removers will destroy the bristles of the brush.

Read the appropriate section in Chapter 2 (TOOLS AND MATERIALS) for a more detailed discussion of brush care.

## VARNISHING HINTS

Varnish is certainly not the easiest finish to apply, but a careful reading of the recommendations given in this chapter should lessen much of the difficulty. Here are some additional suggestions to help you.

1. Varnish (for brushing) cannot be properly mixed by vigorously shaking the can up and down. This will cause bubbles to form in the varnish which will result in an unsatisfactory finish. Mix the varnish by gently tipping the can back and forth.
2. Work in a room with a temperature ranging from 65°F to 70°F. Avoid working in room temperatures below 60°F since it will interfere with drying. Varnishes should be

allowed to dry in a warm room for about three or four days. If the weather is especially damp (rain or high humidity), give it twice as long. It is best to avoid varnishing in wet weather altogether.

3. *Always* wait for the varnish to become completely dry before sanding or using some other kind of abrasive. If you do not wait long enough, you will destroy the finish.

4. Observe all the precautions for safety and health described in previous chapters.

# Chapter 11

# Lacquer Finishes

Lacquer as a furniture finish originated in the Far East and was first introduced to the countries of Western Europe in the late sixteenth and early seventeenth centuries. Not long after, the cabinetmakers in France, Holland, and England were producing imitations of the Oriental pieces. In England, lacquer finishing (referred to at this time as "japanning") became quite popular. Although at first inferior to the Oriental product, English lacquer work was soon characterized by a high degree of quality. Many of these early examples of English lacquer furniture indicated that the cabinetmakers preferred to cover the base wood with a veneer over which a lacquer finish was applied. Colored backgrounds of black, red, blue, green, and pale yellow were used with these lacquer finishes. After enjoying a period of relatively widespread popularity (from the late sixteenth century to the middle of the eighteenth century), the interest in lacquered furniture began to decline. Its revival occurred in the form of cellulose nitrate lacquers after World War I. The spraying technique of application contributed greatly to its revival. Lacquer now represents the most widely used finish in mass-produced furniture.

Lacquer is a tougher, more durable finish than shellac, and it will dry much more quickly than varnish. Unfortunately, its extremely rapid drying rate (9 to 12 seconds) makes it very difficult to apply with a brush—particularly for a beginner. As a result, most lacquer finishes are applied with spraying equipment.

When properly rubbed, lacquer will produce a gloss or satin finish. Others, the flat lacquers, dry to a dull or flat finish. Mixing a clear gloss lacquer with a flat lacquer will result in variations of a semi-gloss finish.

241

Lacquers are available in spray cans and are particularly effective in this form for covering small areas. (Fig. 1) These spray cans may be purchased in both refillable and disposable containers. Lacquer can also be used in the various types of spraying equipment. Small spray guns and compressors are available for the home workshop and are adequate for most finishing work.

*Courtesy Deft, Inc.*

**Fig. 1. Lacquer spray stains that both stain and seal the wood in one application.**

However using such equipment does require proper ventilation (see Chapter 2 TOOLS AND MATERIALS).

The lacquer solvent is so strong that only finishing products (e.g. sealers, stains, fillers, etc.) that are compatible with lacquer should be used. Otherwise, surface defects will develop ranging in seriousness from small pinholes to a soft surface that will not properly dry. Lacquer solvent is not alcohol, but rather a special thinner that contains acetone (the ingredient that causes the rapid rate of drying).

## TYPES OF LACQUER

Modern lacquers can be divided into two basic categories:
1. Nitrocellulose base lacquers,
2. Cellulose acetate butyrate base lacquers.

Lacquers represented by the first category (i.e. nitrocellulose base lacquers) are the most widely used as a top coat in furniture finishing.

Nitrocellulose base lacquers are composed of nitrocellulose, various resins, plasticizers and a solvent. These are low cost, fast drying lacquers that produce a durable, attractive top coat. They are available in any sheen from dead flat to high gloss. It should be pointed out that a sheen can be altered by rubbing. For example, a high gloss sheen can be rubbed to a dull flat, or a dead flat sheen can be rubbed to a high sheen. It all depends upon the rubbing method used. Usually a lacquer will be chosen on the basis of the type of sheen desired on legs or other sections that cannot be easily rubbed, but where one would like to give the effect of a rubbed surface. Lacquer top coats are frequently given numerical designators that indicate the type of sheen they will impart.

Most lacquers are supplied in a condition ready for spraying. A reducer or retarder may be added to increase the flow characteristics of the lacquer or to reduce blushing under conditions of high temperature and humidity. The manufacturer of the lacquer will generally recommend the amount to be added.

Lacquer dries by the evaporation of its solvent. This usually occurs 25 to 30 minutes after it has been applied, although this should not be regarded as a complete drying. At this point the surface is still not ready for rubbing. Complete drying takes 2 to 24 hours after the application, depending upon (1) the solid content of the lacquer, and (2) the number of coats applied. Premature rubbing will cause shrinkage.

Nitrocellulose lacquers will range in color from a very pale (the so-called "water white lacquers") to an amber. All nitrocellulose base lacquers will yellow to some extent over a period of time. Excessive exposure to sunlight will increase the rate of yellowing.

Nitrocellulose base lacquers are noted for their excellent resistance to water (hot or cold), mild soap, citric acid (in fruit juices), and other substances commonly spilled on surfaces. Fingernail polish will damage a lacquer top coat, because it contains the same type of solvents found in lacquer.

Lacquers in the second category are based on cellulose acetate butyrate (rather than nitrocellulose) in combination with suitable resins, plasticizers and a solvent. Neither sunlight nor aging will cause these lacquers to yellow. For that reason they are commonly used as top coats over white finishes. All other properties (drying time, durability, etc.) are the same as those described for the nitrocellulose base lacquers.

### LACQUER THINNER

Lacquer thinner is sold in pint, quart, and gallon containers, and is used to thin both brushing and spraying lacquer. It is also recommended for cleaning spray guns and brushes. When it is used for the former purpose, the lacquer should be sprayed through the gun immediately before and after use.

Lacquer thinner contains acetone (the ingredient that causes the rapid rate of drying), and is so strong that it should be used only with finishing materials compatible with lacquer.

### SPRAYING A LACQUER

Although lacquer is available in aerosol spray cans, this method of application offers certain difficulties that can prove quite frustrating for the beginner. For example, the spray can nozzles are not always reliable, and the containers cannot always be depended on to give a steady uninterrupted pressure. Better and more efficient results can be obtained when using aerosol spray cans to apply lacquer if the following recommendations are observed:

1. Shake the container well before using.
2. Test the nozzle by directing the spray against a piece of scrap wood.
3. Spray lacquer at a greater distance than other finishes.
4. Spray lacquer horizontally (not downward) at a surface. (Fig. 2).
5. Hold your finger back from the opening of the nozzle when spraying.

**Fig. 2. Spraying lacquer horizontally.**

Do not try to apply the entire lacquer at one time. This has a tendency to cause runs and build up. Splattering will be the major problem you encounter when spraying, and is generally caused by, (1) overlapping the nozzle with the finger (thereby touching and deflecting the spray. (Fig. 3), and (2) spraying vertically (downward) against the surface.

**245**

Fig. 3. Overlapping the nozzle with the finger tip.

## USING A BRUSH TO APPLY LACQUER

The inexperienced finisher should avoid using a brush to apply lacquer. It dries much too quickly for anyone but the most experienced. If a brush is used, one made from camel's hair is recommended. Nylon brushes will disintegrate when exposed to a lacquer thinner. The lacquer must be flowed on as rapidly as possible. A wide brush is recommended because it reduces the number of strokes that are required to complete the job. Each stroke of the brush should slightly overlap the preceding one (Fig. 4). A lacquer thinner is necessary to insure that the lacquer will flow freely and evenly. Be certain that you have approximately the same amount of lacquer thinner on hand as you do lacquer. If several layers are applied, lightly sand each layer before flowing on the next coat. This will remove air bubbles and irregularities caused by dust or other particles trapped by the lacquer.

## BASIC LACQUER FINISHING SCHEDULE

Before following any schedule for applying a lacquer finish, the surface should first carefully be prepared. This procedure has already been thoroughly described in Chapter 7, and it is recom-

Fig. 4. Brushing lacquer with slight overlap of brush strokes.

mended that these instructions be reviewed before proceeding any further.

As soon as the surface has been prepared and you are satisfied with the results, you should give some consideration to the type of stain you will be using. Water and non-grain-raising (NGR) stains work well under lacquer, but oil stains should be avoided as they have a tendency to bleed through into the lacquer coat. However, experienced finishers have successfully used oil stains under lacquers by making certain that an adequate sealer has been layed over the stain. Shellac (1 pound or 1½ pound cut) is recommended for the sealer. Allow the sealer to dry 24 hours before applying the lacquer.

247

## Lacquer Finishes

The schedule for applying a lacquer finish is essentially as follows (Fig. 5):

**STEP 1**    PREPARE THE WOOD SURFACE.
INCLUDE STEP 2-5

**STEP 6**    STAIN THE SURFACE.

**STEPS 7-8**    APPLY A SEALER.

**STEPS 9-10**    APPLY A FILLER.

**STEP 11**    APPLY A LACQUER SEALER.

**STEPS 12-14**    APPLY THE LACQUER.

Fig. 5. Basic lacquer finishing schedule.

1. Prepare the surface according to the instructions given in Chapter 7.
2. Raise the grain of the wood by dampening the surface with water. A soft cloth or a sponge soaked in clean water may be used for this purpose.
3. Allow the surface to dry.
4. Remove the raised wood fibers with sandpaper (use a 5/0 or 6/0 grade for this purpose).
5. Remove the dust left by the sanding operation. Some finishers prefer to remove the dust by vacuuming; others find a soft, clean cloth or a round horsehair brush effective.
6. Stain the surface. A water or non-grain raising stain is suggested for this purpose. Allow at least 16 hours for the stain to dry.
7. Apply a sealer (a shellac washcoat works well).
8. Allow the washcoat about 2 hours to dry and then sand it very lightly with a 5/0 or 6/0 grade sandpaper. Remove the dust by the methods suggested in Step 5 above.

9. Apply a wood filler. The type of wood filler used (paste or liquid) depends upon the size of the wood pores. Paste fillers are recommended for open-grained (large pore) woods; liquid fillers for closed-grain woods. A piece of burlap is suggested for applying a paste filler. Use a circular movement to ensure penetration.

10. Take a piece of burlap and wipe *across* the grain to remove the excess filler. Allow the filler sufficient drying time (follow the manufacturer's recommendations found on the container or with accompanying literature).

11. Apply a lacquer sealer (spraying is the most effective method of applying the sealer). Lacquer sealers are designed and produced specifically for the purpose of sealing the wood and providing a base for the finishing coats of lacquer. They are *always* used *after* a stain and filler have been applied.

12. Spray a coat of lacquer on to the surface. The lacquer may also be applied by brushing, but this is recommended only for the most experienced finisher (see the brushing instructions for lacquer found elsewhere in this chapter). The manufacturer's recommendations for spraying should be carefully followed.

13. Allow the first coat of lacquer sufficient time to dry and then rub it lightly with steel wool (a 000 grade of steel wool is recommended). Remove all dust left by the rubbing operation (see Step 5 above).

14. Apply one or two more coats as described in Steps 12 and 13. Allow at least 24 to 30 hours drying time between coats. A wax may be applied after the final coat of lacquer for added protection.

15. Varnish can also be applied over lacquer, but a lacquer sealer is recommended as a base coat.

If you are applying the lacquer with a brush, I strongly recommend that you try to make do with just one coat. Lacquer has the unfortunate tendency to dissolve previous coats of lacquer. Because of its rapid rate of drying, you cannot avoid leaving brush marks in the dissolved lacquer.

249

The longer you allow a coat of lacquer to dry, the smoother the surface will be. If a lacquer top coat is applied to a lacquered undercoat before the latter has had sufficient time to dry, it will damage it.

## MODERN PROVINCIAL FURNITURE

Modern provincial furniture can be finished in a soft warm brown on walnut, and then coated with lacquer. To obtain this coloring, the following finishing schedule is recommended:

1. Prepare the wood surface according to the instructions given in Chapter 7. The essential point to remember is that the surface must be smooth and clean.
2. Trace the cathedrals* with a very dark non-grain raising (NGR) stain. This stain can also be used to add cathedrals to an area where they do not naturally exist (e.g. in radially cut veneer).
3. Allow sufficient time for the stain to dry.
4. Apply an overall non-grain raising stain of light warm brown, and allow sufficient time to dry.
5. Apply a sealer over the stain. As soon as the sealer has dried, lightly sand the surface. Do *not* sand through the sealer into the stain.
6. Remove any dust or other particles left by the sanding with a lint-free cloth or tack rag.
7. Apply a dark wood filler (one with little staining power) to accent the grain pattern of the wood. Remove excess filler by rubbing across the grain with a piece of burlap. Allow the filler sufficient time to dry.
8. Apply an overtone that is lighter than the filler and darker than the overall stain used in Step 3. This will add depth to the finish.
9. Shade the light areas to obtain a uniform color over the the entire surface.

*Note*: The arch design usually found at the top (front) of furniture or wall-bookcases is called the cathedral. It can be a molding design on front or sides of furniture or panels actually cut to produce the cathedral effect.

10. Opaque spatter and distress color may be applied at this point, although it is optional.
11. Apply a lacquer sealer.
12. Apply the lacquer top coat.

Sometimes cheaper more readily available woods are used for posts or legs. Generally woods for this purpose are also lighter in color. To minimize the amount of shading necessary, it is recommended that they be given an initial dark purplish stain prior to Step 2 above.

## LACQUER REAMALGAMATION

As is the case with shellac, lacquer is also subject to the white spotting caused by water or moisture resting on the surface. The white spot (blush) can be removed through careful application of lacquer thinner. The lacquer thinner causes the lacquer finish to redisolve and flow together. This process is referred to by finishers as *reamalgamation*. Lacquer finishes are subject to cracking, too, which also can be remedied by reamalgamation.

The important thing to remember about the reamalgamation process is that too much lacquer thinner will result in the removal of more of the lacquer finish than is desired. Consequently, it is advisable to begin with as little thinner as possible and carefully watch the results before proceeding with more. It is recommended that the finisher begin with a clean, soft cloth dampened with thinner and wipe it lightly across the area containing the white spot or crack until the defect has disappeared. If the defect is not removed, add more thinner to the surface. After the successful reamalgamation of the surface, the entire finish should be lightly rubbed with steel wool (000 grade) and waxed.

## SHADING LACQUERS

After the completion of the lacquer finishing schedule described in this chapter, a shading lacquer may be sprayed onto the surface to highlight the wood and to add a special shaded effect. These shading lacquers are transparent colored lacquers formed by

251

adding dry aniline dyes to a gloss lacquer. Although designed primarily for shading, these shading lacquers can also be used to apply a stain and a lacquer in one operation.

A shading lacquer can also be used to slightly change the color tone of the stain. This will alter the lacquer finishing schedule after Step 6 (see BASIC LACQUER FINISHING SCHEDULE). According to the schedule, the stain was applied in Step 6 and the sealer in Step 7. Change the finishing schedule as follows:

1-5. (previously described).
6. Stain the surface. Allow sufficient time to dry.
7. Spray on a shading lacquer. Allow sufficient time to dry. *Do not sand.*
8. Apply a lacquer sealer over the shading lacquer. The remainder of the finishing schedule follows Steps 8-14 described in the BASIC LACQUER FINISHING SCHEDULE.

## LACQUER TONERS

Lacquer toners differ from shading lacquers by being *semi-transparent* colored lacquers (shading lacquers are transparent colored lacquers). In other words there is a certain degree of opacity to lacquer toners. This may be attributed to their composition. Lacquer toners are made by mixing color pigments with a clear gloss lacquer. The recommended mixture is approximately ½ pint of tinting color with each gallon of lacquer. If the amount of tinting in the lacquer is increased, a pigmented lacquer results.

Lacquer toners are used to color the wood but still reveal the grain. They produce a more uniform coloring than do shading lacquers. In addition to shading and applying a stain and a lacquer in one operation, lacquer toners are also used for uniforming and toning.

## LACQUER SANDING SEALER

A clear lacquer sanding sealer is designed not only to seal the wood, but also to function as a base for the finishing coats of lacquer. As such it is chemically compatible with lacquer. If a stain or filler is used in the finishing schedule, the lacquer sealer is applied after these steps.

## POINTS TO REMEMBER

Using lacquer is really not recommended for the beginner. It is difficult and tricky to apply, and requires a certain amount of practice and skill before good results can be obtained. For those among you who still wish to apply a lacquer finish I would like to draw your attention to the following important points:

1.  Lacquer fumes are highly toxic and can damage your health if inhaled.
2.  Lacquer fumes are explosive. Do *not* use lacquer around flames, heat sources, or where sparks may occur. Even a metal spark could cause an explosion.
3.  In view of Points 1 and 2, *always* apply lacquer outside. Never apply lacquer inside a building unless you have present all the safety conditions required by the professional (suitable exhaust system, spraying booth, etc.). A common electric house fan is not considered a suitable ventilation or exhaust system for lacquer spraying. Faulty wiring in the fan could cause a fatal explosion.
4.  Lacquer can only be applied over a lacquer sealer, another top coat of lacquer, or a suitable washcoat. Lacquer will dissolve most other finishes in much the same manner as a paint remover. This is particularly true of varnish.

# Chapter 12

# Paint and Enamel Finishes

Paint essentially consists of pigments suspended in a vehicle. Many other substances such as drying oils (castor oil, linseed oil, etc.), thinners or solvents, and natural or synthetic gums are added in various combinations to provide the special characteristics of a particular paint. The pigments (white or colored solids) give paint both its opacity (non-transparency) and its color. The vehicle or liquid must be of a type in which the pigments are soluble.

Although there are many different types of vehicles used in the manufacture of paints, this chapter will be limited to a description of the following four:

1. Oil-base paints,
2. Alkyd resin-base paints,
3. Latex paints,
4. Milk-base paints.

Enamels are sometimes classified or grouped with paints, while at other times they are given separate consideration. It is true that enamels and paints do have many common characteristics, and it is perhaps for this reason that there is some looseness about how these terms are used. For example, it appears to be an advertising prerogative to call certain types of interior wall paints "enamels," even though they are only paints. Essentially, enamel is an approved form of varnish (the vehicle used for many enamels). However, because it has many characteristics in common with paint, its specific characteristics are such that it will be covered in this chapter. Other paintlike, opaque finishes such as pigmented shellacs and pigmented lacquers will be covered in the chapters dealing with their vehicles (see Chapter 9 SHELLAC FINISHES and Chapter 11 LACQUER FINISHES).

Paints are available in many different types of retail outlets, but more commonly and in greater variety, in paint and hardware stores, arts and crafts stores, and hobby shops. Almost every imaginable color is available or can be mixed to obtain the desired shade.

Paint is an opaque finish, and it will completely obscure the underlying wood surface. This is especially advantageous when a finisher must cover a cheaper wood of particularly poor appearance. Another important function of paint is the decorative one. Brightly colored painted furniture can be as attractive in the proper setting as furniture done with various clear finishes. Finally, as is the case with all finishes, paint is designed to preserve the wood.

Paint finishes are easy to maintain, because they can be washed with soap and water without suffering any ill effect to the finish itself.

## EQUIPMENT AND SUPPLIES

The selection of a suitable brush is very important. A flat brush with a width of 1 to 4 inches is recommended for most work. This is the same type of brush commonly used to apply enamel or flat varnish. The wider brushes should be used to apply paint to large surface areas (e.g. table tops, cabinet doors, panels, etc.), the narrower ones for trim, scrollwork, and other small detail. An oval brush is frequently useful for painting round surfaces.

Brushes should always be cleaned immediately after you are through painting. The cleaning solvent is generally the solvent used for the particular paint (see the section on thinners in this chapter). Soak the brush for several minutes in the cleaning solvent and work the paint from the heel of the brush to its tip. Shake out the excess solvent and wash the brush in soap and water (lukewarm). This will remove the last traces of paint and cleaning solvent. Comb the bristles out straight, wrap the bristles in paper, and store the brush in a flat or hanging position.

Old drinking glasses, large glass jars, or certain types of cans are useful for mixing, cleaning, and storing paints. Using these containers for storage requires that each one has an air tight cover. Regardless of the type of use to which the container is put, it must be thoroughly cleaned. Dirt and other contaminants will combine with the paint and eventually find their way into the finish.

Other equipment and supplies recommended for painting include:

1. The necessary equipment and supplies for preparing the surface.
2. Several clean lint-free cloths or tack rags.
3. A suitable thinner (follow the manufacturer's recommendations).

## BRUSHING TECHNIQUES

Select one surface at a time for painting. Moving from one section to another before completing the previous one will cause lapping and other problems that detract from the overall appearance.

If at all possible, follow the direction of the wood grain. This will reduce the tendency of the paint to ripple. Paint with the flat side of the brush, not the edge (unless a narrow section is being painted). It is best to cover as large an area as possible with each brush stroke. Paint the edges, scrollwork, and trim first. The larger surface areas will be painted last.

## PAINTING PROCEDURE

Paint can be both brushed and sprayed onto a surface. Brushing and spraying instructions are basically the same as those given for other types of finishes. When spraying, the spray gun should move in a straight line at an equal distance from the surface of the piece of furniture. The finisher should not swing the spray gun so that it forms an arc or heavy build ups—weak spots will develop. Brush marks will be left on the surface if brushing is maintained too long after the application of the paint. This is particularlly true of wood surfaces that are absorbent, and which therefore cause the paint to dry more quickly. In this case, a sealer coat is recommended to prevent uneven penetration of the wood by the paint.

The procedure for applying paint to a wood surface is as follows (Fig. 1):

| | |
|---|---|
| **STEP 1** | PREPARE THE WOOD SURFACE SO THAT IT IS EVEN AND SMOOTH. |
| **STEPS 2-5** | APPLY A SEALER. SAND SMOOTH ANY WOOD FIBERS RAISED BY THE SEALER OPERATION AND REMOVE THE DUST. STAINING IS NOT DONE UNDER AN OPAQUE TOPCOAT. |
| **STEP 6** | THIN THE PAINT TO THE PROPER WORKING CONSISTENCY. |
| **STEPS 7-8** | APPLY THE PAINT. |
| **STEP 9** | APPLY A CLEAR TOPCOAT (OPTIONAL). |

**Fig. 1. Painting procedure.**

1. Prepare the surface according to the suggestions offered in Chapter 7. Basically the surface must be smooth (no raised grains, dents, or scratches), clean, and dry.
2. Seal the surface with a washcoat of thinned shellac. No stain is used under a paint top coat, because the latter is an opaque (nontransparent) finish.
3. Allow the sealer sufficient time to thoroughly dry.
4. The wood grain of previously unfinished surfaces will rise and harden as a result of having applied the shellac sealer coat. Remove the raised wood grains by sanding with a fine grade of sandpaper.
5. Remove all dust left by the sanding operation with a soft lint-free cloth or tack rag.
6. Thin the paint with a suitable thinner until it flows fairly easily.
7. Do not attempt to paint the entire piece of furniture all at one time. Proceed section by section allowing sufficient drying time to prevent the paint from running or streaking. Cover the entire section with the paint and then tip it off.

257

8. If several coats of paint are applied, sand each lightly with a fine grade of sandpaper. Be certain that the paint is completely dry before sanding. Remove the dust left by the sanding operation with a lint-free cloth or a tack rag.
9. A clear finish (lacquer, varnish, etc.) can be applied over the paint for greater durability. Make certain that both are compatible or you will ruin the entire finish.

## OIL-BASE PAINTS

In oil-base paints, the color pigments are suspended in an oil vehicle. One of the most frequently used vehicles is linseed oil, an inexpensive, dependable drying oil derived from the crushings of flax seeds. Other oil vehicles include castor oil (a plasticizer for lacquers), China wood oil or tung oil (used in varnishes or alkyd wood finishes), Oiticica oil (pigmented enamels), and soya bean oil (a plasticizer for lacquers).

## ALKYD RESIN-BASE PAINTS

The synthetic alkyd resin is used as both a plasticizer and as the liquid base (vehicle) for paints and other finishing products. Its use is quite widespread, dating back to the 1920's. Among other synthetic resins used in the production of paints and finishing products are acrylic resin, urea resin, vinyl resin, silicone resin, and styrenated alkyd resin.

## LATEX PAINTS

The water-soluble latex paints developed and used primarily for painting interior and exterior walls can also be used on furniture, particularly unfinished furniture. There is resistance to their use by some finishers because of their grain raising effect on the wood (water is the vehicle used in these paints) and the difficulty found in removing them. However, these objections are not serious ones. The raised grains can be removed by sanding and a second coat of paint can then be applied to the surface. Latex paints can be easily covered with another latex paint or some other opaque finish (if a suitable sealer has first been placed over the original finish). It is doubtful that anyone would profit by stripping off a latex paint. Wood surfaces over which a paint has been applied are generally unattractive.

Latex paints are commercially available in a great variety of colors and shades. Special colors and shades can be mixed to meet individual needs.

A latex paint can be made more durable by covering it with a thin coat of clear lacquer or some other type of clear finish.

## MILK-BASE PAINTS

An early method used for making paints consisted of mixing berry juices, colored clays, or blood with milk. Later, dry colorants were substituted as coloring agents. Packages of these dry colorants are available at most paint and wallpaper stores, and find extensive use as tints for exterior house paints. However, by mixing them with dry powdered milk and water, a suitable milk-base paint can

**Table 1. Paints and Their Thinners**

| Type of Paint | Thinner |
|---|---|
| Oil-Base Paints | Turpentine |
| Alkyd Resin-Base Paints | Naphtha or Mineral Spirits |
| Latex Paints | Water |
| Milk-Base Paints | Water |

be produced. The dry colorants are extremely bright, and should be dulled by mixing in black or brown.

## PAINT THINNERS

The manufacturer will generally recommend a suitable thinner for use with his paint. If such is not the case, it will be necessary to experiment on a section of furniture that is not exposed to view. Table 1 gives a listing of suggested thinners for various finishes. Note that latex paints use water as a thinner. Other types of paint use such thinners as turpentine, benzol, naphtha, and benzine.

## PAINTING FIR PLYWOOD

Fir plywood is frequently used by home craftsmen in the construction of furniture. Because good grain patterns are generally found in only the highest quality plywood, an opaque finish (paint, enamel, etc.) is often selected as a finishing top coat.

The grain in fir plywood is subject to unequal absorption. Consequently, using a finish on fir plywood without the prior application of a sealer will result in dark spots appearing on the surface. The use of a sealer will equalize the absorption rate. A pigmented penetrating resin sealer is recommended for use with latex paints.

The procedure for applying a latex paint to a fir plywood surface is as follows (Fig. 2):

STEPS 1–2   PREPARE THE WOOD SURFACE.

STEPS 3–4   APPLY A PENETRATING RESIN SEALER. SAND THE SURFACE LIGHTLY AND REMOVE THE DUST.

STEPS 5–6   APPLY A SECOND COAT OF A PENETRATING RESIN SEALER. SAND THE SURFACE LIGHTLY AND REMOVE THE DUST.

STEP 7   BRUSH ON A LATEX PAINT.

**Fig. 2. Procedure for painting fir plywood.**

1. Prepare the surface according to the suggestions offered in Chapter 7. It is essential that the surface be smooth and clean. Dirt, traces of glue, and other contaminants will combine with the finish and mar its appearance. Fill in all nail holes, dents and scratches, and sand smooth.

2. Remove any dust left by the sanding operation with a clean lint-free cloth or a tack rag.

3. Apply a penetrating resin sealer to the surface, and allow it sufficient time to sink into the wood and dry.
4. Sand the surface lightly with a fine grade of sandpaper, and remove all dust from the sanding operation with a clean lint-free cloth or a tack rag.
5. Apply a second coat of the penetrating resin sealer and allow sufficient time for it to thoroughly dry.
6. Sand the second sealer coat according to the instructions given in Step 4.
7. Brush on the latex paint.

## REPAIRING PAINT FINISHES

The best method for repairing a paint finish is to sand it down, remove the dust, and recover it with a fresh coat of paint. If there are scratches or dents on the surface, fill them in and sand them smooth (once again removing the dust left by the sanding operation). Cover the entire surface with a washcoat of shellac. This will act as a sealer over the original paint and whatever repairs may have been made, and provide a smooth, even base for the new coat of paint.

## PAINTING OVER OLDER FINISHES

A sealer coat is absolutely necessary when painting over non-paint types of finishes to prevent reactions due to a chemical incompatibility between the paint and the original finish. A washcoat of shellac will generally serve well as an all purpose sealer.

## PEASANT PAINTING

Peasant painting is a decorative technique developed among farm people as one of many activities followed to fill the long winter days. Essentially it consisted of painting rural motifs (barns, birds, flowers, etc.) on the surfaces of furniture (Fig. 3).

Today, peasant painting has developed in popularity to the point that it is now a full-fledged member of the arts-and-crafts

261

1. BORDERS

2. FLOWERS                           3. FRUIT

Fig. 3. Examples of some motifs used in peasant painting.

movement. It appears to be strongly oriented toward the Pennsylvania Dutch style.

Peasant painting is characterized by its limited use of colors, concentrating on the primary colors with black and white used for shading. Enamel paints are usually applied over an enamel base coat.

## BANDING AND STRIPING

Both banding and striping (Fig. 4) offer examples of two-tone color effects as methods of decorating furniture surfaces. Some make no distinction between the two, pointing to banding as simply a wider application of striping. In any event, the technique consists of applying bands or stripes across a finish for purposes of

262

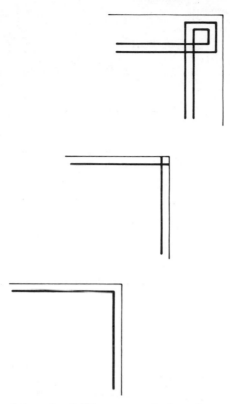

Fig. 4. Examples of different types of edge striping.

contrast and emphasis. The color of the bands or stripes is different from that of the finish. Most banding and striping is done over an enamel surface.

Striping requires a steady hand and steadier nerves. Very fine, very straight lines are required in this decorative technique. A fine pointed brush is a must. The brush strokes should be made toward the body, always in the same direction (Fig. 5).

## ENAMEL FINISHES

Enamels are often classified as paints. This may be due to the fact that enamel, like paint, is an opaque finish, and is used to

263

**Fig. 5. The proper use of a striping brush.**

cover wood surfaces that are too unattractive for a clear top coat. However, there are certain basic distinctions between enamels and paints that are important to know, because they may influence the decision concerning the selection of the finish.

Essentially, enamels may be regarded as finishes that belong to a broad classification of free flowing finishing materials that dry to a smooth, hard finish in a number of different sheens. They consist of color pigments ground in a suitable vehicle to which thinners and driers have been added. There are a number of different vehicles used in the production of enamels, including alkyd base and urethane catalytic base varnishes, lacquer, and oil.

When compared with paint, enamels will generally have the following characteristics:

1. Somewhat slower drying time,
2. More finely ground color pigments,
3. Higher gloss,
4. Tougher, more durable surface,
5. Higher cost.

## TYPES OF ENAMELS

There are so many different types of enamel available to the finisher one can readily understand why some confusion might exist over selecting the right one. For example, not all enamels are suitable for furniture finishes. Some are exclusively exterior enamel finishes or are designed for specific conditions (e.g. water resisting characteristics of marine or waterproof enamels). On the other hand, some gloss enamels can be used for both interior or exterior surfaces, and will provide an acceptable finish for furniture. The semi-gloss enamels (also know as eggshell enamels or satin finish enamels) are exclusively interior enamels, and are particularly suited for furniture surfaces. The point being made here is that you must be absolutely certain you are selecting the right enamel for the job. If you are not certain, then ask the store clerk for advice.

A final word of caution: do *not* mix enamels from different manufacturers even if they appear to be identical in color and type (e.g. both being "gloss enamels" or "eggshell enamels"). It is highly probable that differences in their chemical compositions will make them mutually incompatible. In other words, mixing them will produce a useless mess.

## ENAMEL THINNER

The manufacturer of the enamel will generally recommend a thinner and solvent. Turpentine, benzine, turpentine mixed with benzine, and acetone have all been used as thinners and solvents for different types of enamels. Remember: not every thinner is suitable for each enamel. The selection of a thinner and solvent is determined by the chemical composition of the enamel.

## ENAMEL UNDERCOATING

An undercoat is usually recommended when enameling large surface areas, because it will reduce the number of top coats required to finish the piece. The undercoat also serves as a sealer, protecting the enamel top coat from substances that might bleed into it. Finally, the undercoat provides a primer-type base to which the enamel top coat can adhere.

A number of different types of undercoats can be used with enamels, including latex paint, thinned shellac, or prepared undercoats. Undercoats are available in white or in colors tinted to match the enamel top coat. If the undercoat and top coat do not match, it is best the undercoat be lighter in shade.

265

Anywhere from one to three undercoats will be used on a wood surface. When they are completely dry, they should be *lightly* sanded with a fine grade of sandpaper. This will provide a better surface for the enamel top coats. Always remove all dust and other particles left by the sanding operation.

## ENAMEL FINISHING SCHEDULE (BRUSHING)

Brushing an enamel can be difficult. For that reason, additional attention has been given in this finishing schedule to using a brush. If at all possible, the beginner should use a spray enamel rather than attempting to enamel with a brush the first time.

The procedure for applying an enamel (with a brush) to a wood surface is as follows (Fig. 6):

**STEP 1**      PREPARE THE WOOD SURFACE.

**STEPS 2–4**   APPLY A SHELLAC WASHCOAT. LIGHTLY SAND THE SURFACE AND REMOVE THE DUST.

**STEPS 5–13**  PREPARE AND APPLY THE UNDERCOATS. LIGHTLY SAND EACH UNDERCOAT AND REMOVE THE DUST.

**STEP 14**     APPLY THE ENAMEL TOPCOAT.

**Fig. 6. Procedure for applying enamel.**

1. Prepare the wood surface according to the instructions suggested in Chapter 7. As with other finishes, it is very important that the surface be smooth and clean.
2. Apply a washcoat of shellac to seal the surface and raise the grain fibers.
3. Allow the washcoat sufficient time to thoroughly dry.

After it has dried, lightly sand the surface with a very fine grade of sandpaper.

4. Remove all dust and other particles left by the sanding operation with a clean lint-free cloth or a tack rag.

5. Mix the undercoat until it is uniform and smooth. The undercoat will either be white or tinted a color to match the enamel top coat. It is recommended that a colored undercoat be the same color or lighter than the top coat (never darker).

6. Pour part of the undercoat into a large jar or glass.

7. Dip the brush into the jar or glass, and work the enamel thoroughly into the bristles by wiping or pressing the brush against a piece of clean scrap wood.

8. When you are certain that the bristles in the lower one-third to one-half of the brush are thoroughly wet with enamel, dip the brush into the jar or glass and begin enameling the surface.

9. Brush the enamel onto the surface in the direction of the grain. Remove any excess with the tip of the brush. Do not attempt to brush the enamel smooth. Enamel will flow together on its own accord in an even, smooth coating before it dries.

10. When you have completed the undercoat, allow approximately 24 to 30 hours for it to dry.

11. As soon as the first undercoat has completely dried, *lightly* sand the surface with a very fine grade of sandpaper.

12. Remove any dust or other particles left by the sanding operation with a clean lint-free cloth or a tack rag.

13. A second or third coat of undercoating may be applied, but Steps 10 through 12 should be followed after each one.

14. The last coat (the top coat) is applied in the same manner as the undercoats (see particularly Steps 6 through 10). When mixing enamel, do not stir it too vigorously or you will cause bubbles to form.

15. Allow 24 hours for the top coat to dry. When you are

certain that it is dry, *rub* the surface with pumice stone and oil, or pumice stone and water. Always rub in the same direction as the grain with long, even strokes. Rub along the length of a section, rather than its width. Wipe off the excess pumice stone (and oil if it is used) with a clean lint-free cloth.

Close-grained woods are preferred for enameling. Open grained woods require extensive filling with a paste filler. If a filler is used, allow it time to set and then wipe away the excess with a piece of burlap. Lightly sand the surface with a fine grade of sandpaper and remove the dust. Clean the surface with a clean cloth dampened with denatured alcohol, benzine, or some other suitable solvent. These steps will precede Step 2 in the enamel finishing schedules described in this chapter.

## ENAMEL FINISHING SCHEDULE (SPRAYING)

Most enamel colors can be purchased in 16-oz. aerosol spray cans. These are lacquer-base enamels and are available in flat, semi-gloss, and gloss sheens.

The procedure for spraying enamel onto a wood surface is as follows:

1. Prepare the wood surface according to the instructions recommended in Chapter 7. As always, the surface must be smooth and clean before applying any of the finishing coats.
2. Brush on a washcoat of shellac, and allow it sufficient time to thoroughly dry. This will serve as a sealer over the bare wood, preventing the sap from bleeding through and ruining the top coat.
3. After the washcoat has completely dried, *lightly* sand it with a very fine grade of sandpaper. Take care not to sand through the washcoat.
4. Remove all dust and other particles left by the sanding operation with a clean lint-free cloth or a tack rag.
5. Spray the first coat onto the surface. Move the nozzle parallel to the surface and high enough so that no mist

forms during spraying (an indication that it is being held too high) or runs and sags develop on the finish (too low). Do not make swinging movements of the hand, because the arc formed by the movement will cause an uneven build up of the enamel.

6. Spray until the surface is completely covered with a smooth, even coat of enamel. There should be no uneven build up, runs or sags (all indications of improper spraying procedure or an excessive application of enamel).

7. Allow the first coat sufficient time to dry. Lacquer base spraying enamels will dry much more quickly than the brush-type.

8. The remaining coats of enamel will be applied in the same manner as described for brushing an enamel onto a surface. See Steps 11 through 15 of the finishing schedule for brushing. The drying time will be shorter for the lacquer base enamel. In addition, more coats of spray enamel will be required, because they are generally thinner than the brush-type.

## ENAMELING A FINISHED SURFACE

The two previously described finishing schedules dealt with spraying or brushing an enamel onto a bare wood surface. The finishing schedule for applying an enamel over an older finish is only slightly different during the initial steps. The procedure is as follows:

1. Lightly sand the old finish until it is smooth. It is not necessary to sand down to the bare wood.

2. Remove the dust or other particles left by the sanding operation with a clean lint-free cloth or a tack rag.

3. Apply a washcoat of shellac as a sealer. This will prevent the old finish from bleeding through into the enamel top coat.

4. Allow 2 to 3 hours for the washcoat to dry.

5. After the washcoat has completely dried, sand it lightly with a very fine grade of sandpaper.

269

6. Remove the dust or other particles left by the sanding operation with a clean lint-free cloth or a tack rag.
7. Apply the enamel undercoats and top coat in the same manner as described in the other enamel finishing schedules.

## Chapter 13

# Oil and Wax Finishes

Oil and wax finishes have been used for years to provide wood surfaces with durable protective coatings without obscuring the natural beauty of the wood. They are not characterized by a build up of coats as are other finishes, but many of them do require constant, periodic renewal. The types of oil and wax finishes that will be described in this chapter are:

1. Linseed oil finishes,
2. Penetrating (oil) finishes,
3. Wax finishes.

### PENETRATING FINISHES

*Penetrating finishes* (also variously referred to as *penetrating oil finishes, penetrating resin finishes, penetrating resin-oil finishes, sealer finishes,* and *penetrating sealer finishes*) consist primarily of either a resin-oil or wax-resin base to which a sealer stain has been added. Originally developed for use on floors, they are now finding widespread use in furniture finishing. Their new popularity as a furniture finish is due to a number of factors, including:

1. Ease of application,
2. Durability,
3. Beauty,
4. Ease of repair.

The major disadvantages of these finishes is that they lack depth and body, and are extremely difficult to remove.

Whether to use the resin-oil or wax-base finish is a matter of personal choice. You will always find finishers who swear to the advantages of one over the other. The major difference between the two is that a penetrating finish with a wax-base cannot be covered with another finish (e.g. a varnish or lacquer), because it will cause the topcoat to lift. However, it can be coated with one or more layers of a paste wax, and rubbed to a very pleasing sheen. The resin-oil finish, on the other hand, is essentially a very thin varnish. As such, it can be covered with a clear varnish topcoat and rubbed for a dull, satin, or a high gloss.

No particular skill is required for applying a penetrating finish. It is generally brushed or wiped onto the surface, allowed to penetrate for a period of time, and then the excess is wiped off. There are no brush marks to worry about, no runs, and no surface stickiness to trap dust, hair, and other contaminants.

This type of finish penetrates into the pores of the wood, and dries to form a solid, sub-surface layer *inside* the wood that resists fungus (the cause of dry rot) and insect damage. Because the penetrating finish waterproofs as it seals, it enables the wood to resist shrinkage and warping due to excess moisture absorption or loss.

A penetrating finish withstands most types of wear much better than other finishes. Minor scratches and dents cannot break through the surface color to expose the unfinished wood, because penetration has usually extended below this level. However, repairing is not very difficult. You need only to clean the surface, abrade it lightly with a fine grade of steel wool, and apply another coating of the penetrating finish.

Penetrating finishes are often recommended for hardwoods such as rosewood or teak which contain excessive amounts of natural oil. Even when kiln dried, these oils are still present in the wood and present a problem to the finisher if a lacquer, varnish, or shellac topcoat is applied. One method of eliminating the oil is to flood the surface with denatured alcohol. Let the wood dry naturally. Do not try to speed up the drying rate by placing the wood in the sun or by using artificial means. Apply two or three more coats of denatured alcohol, letting each coat dry before applying the next one. When you feel certain that the oil content of the wood has been reduced to an acceptable level, apply the penetrating finish according to the basic finishing schedule given in this chapter (see APPLYING A PENETRATING FINISH).

A penetrating finish should only be applied over a bare wood or a stain, but never over another finish. Even a surface that has been stripped will cause difficulties for a penetrating finish, because the wood pores will be clogged by the older finishing materials. Consequently, it will not be able to penetrate properly if it penetrates at all. As you can see, a filler is not necessary, because this type of finish penetrates the wood pores and functions as its own filler.

Penetrating finishes dry by evaporation. As a result, the finish on the surface dries before that portion which has penetrated into the wood pores. Because there is no way of knowing exactly when the sub-surface layer has dried completely, you must give it at least 3 days before applying certain types of waxes just to be on the safe side. Otherwise, the undried portions of the finish may combine with the wax and your work will be ruined. The more coatings of penetrating finish you use, the greater will be the possibility of this happening.

## APPLYING A PENETRATING FINISH

As was already mentioned, applying a penetrating finish is very easy, even for the beginner. Basically, it is a matter of applying the finish to the surface, allowing it sufficient time to penetrate, and then wiping off the excess. However, there are certain aspects of the application procedure that will enable you to do a much better job if you are aware of them before you attempt to apply a penetrating finish. For example, this type of finish requires no sanding in between coats. Although this decreases the amount of work you must do during the application of the finish, it means that you must make absolutely certain that you have properly prepared the surface during the wood preparation stages in the finishing schedule. The wood must be clean, smooth, and completely free of any defects before you apply the finish or the results will be unsatisfactory.

273

## Oil and Wax Finishes

The procedure for applying a penetrating finish is basically as follows (Fig. 1):

**STEP 1**        PREPARE THE WOOD SURFACE.

**STEP 2**        STAIN THE SURFACE WITH A STAIN COMPATIBLE WITH THE PENETRATING FINISH.

**STEP 3**        APPLY THE PENETRATING FINISH.

**STEP 4**        WIPE AWAY THE FINISH AT THE END OF THE "WETTING" PERIOD.

**STEPS 5–7**   APPLY EXTRA COATS OF PENETRATING FINISH.

**STEP 8**        APPLY A HARD PASTE WAX.

Fig. 1. Applying a penetrating finish.

1. Prepare the wood surface according to the instructions given in Chapter 7. Make absolutely certain that the wood surface is clean and smooth.
2. Stain the surface and allow 24 to 48 hours drying time. The stain must be compatible with the type of penetrating finish you are using. Read the manufacturer's instructions. They will generally recommend a compatible stain for use with the finish.
3. Apply a coat of penetrating finish with a brush or a clean lint-free cloth. Keep the surface wet for 25 to 30 minutes. This "wetting" period will differ in length depending upon which manufacturer's product you are using. The manufacturer will indicate the recommended length of time in the instructions. It is during the "wetting" period that the finish penetrates down into the pores of the wood.
4. At the end of the "wetting" period, wipe off the excess finish with a clean lint-free cloth. Let the surface dry for about 24 hours.

5. Apply a second coat of penetrating finish (see the instructions given in Steps 3 and 4 above).

6. Wipe off the excess finish with a clean lint-free cloth after it has been allowed to soak into the wood.

7. Continue to apply as many coats of the penetrating finish as the wood pores will absorb. Follow the instructions given in Steps 3 and 4.

8. Apply a hard paste wax to the surface with a pad of very fine steel wool, and rub with the grain. Complete the rubbing operation by polishing the surface with a soft clean lint-free cloth.

Applying a stain (Step 2) is optional. The color and grain pattern of some hardwoods is such that staining is not necessary.

Some finishers lightly abrade the final coat of the penetrating finish with a fine grade of steel wool. The purpose of this operation is to remove any rough spots and to create a uniform smoothness on the surface. Be sure to remove any steel wool residue with a clean lint-free cloth. The last coat of finish must be *completely* dry before you use the steel wool.

Do not try to cover the entire surface of a piece of furniture at one time. Apply the penetrating finish to a small section of the surface and move immediately to an adjacent one when the previous section is finished. A penetrating finish may be applied both against and with the grain. In this respect, it is similar to a filler.

## LINSEED OIL FINISHES

Linseed oil has been used for years as a penetrating finish and possesses many of the characteristics of the newer resin-oil and wax-resin base penetrating finishes. For example, it waterproofs the wood against moisture, resists minor scratching, denting, and other types of wear, and creates a hard, sub-surface layer in the wood. On the other hand, it is much more difficult to apply than the newer penetrating finishes. Moreover, the finish may become sticky if the weather turns hot and humid. Another objectionable feature of linseed oil finishes is the fact that, like wax finishes, they must be constantly renewed. Reapplication of the linseed oil must take place periodically.

Linseed oil is processed from crushed flaxseed and is available as *raw* linseed oil or *boiled* linseed oil. The former is produced by taking the oil by-product obtained from the crushed flaxseed and allowing it to season in the sun for a few years. The result is an oil finish that never completely dries, except for its outer film. The nondrying characteristics of the sub-layers of raw linseed oil make this a very flexible finish that is ideal for exterior surfaces. These exterior surfaces are subject to changing weather conditions that cause the wood to expand and contract. Unless the finish has a certain flexibility to it, it will crack under these conditions. Because of the nondrying characteristics of raw linseed oil, it is *not* recommended as a finish for furniture. However, many finishers have used it for this purpose, particularly after combining it with driers, or thinning it with turpentine or mineral spirits (which has a much more rapid drying rate than turpentine), or using boiled linseed oil coats after the use of raw linseed oil as the primary coat.

Boiled linseed oil has much better drying characteristics than raw linseed oil. This is brought about by the addition of driers (e.g. siccative drier, japan drier) or by boiling. The latter is the older method and can still be used by the finisher in the home workshop. If you *do* intend to boil the linseed oil, set the container of oil inside a pot filled with water. The heat should be applied to the water. Furthermore, I would recommend boiling the linseed oil in a garage or outside, but *not* in your house. Boiling linseed oil produces a distinctive and unpleasant odor.

Despite the fact that boiled linseed oil has far better drying characteristics than raw linseed oil, it is still somewhat tacky as a finish and will constantly trap dust particles on the surface.

## APPLYING A LINSEED OIL FINISH

The most common formula for a linseed oil finish is 2 parts boiled linseed oil mixed with 1 part turpentine. Mineral spirits can be substituted for the turpentine as a thinner. The procedure for applying a linseed oil finish is basically as follows (Fig. 2):

**STEP 1**    PREPARE THE WOOD SURFACE.

**STEP 2**    APPLY A PASTE FILLER TO OPEN
PORED WOOD.

**STEP 3–6**  APPLY TEN TO FIFTEEN COATS OF
LINSEED OIL. THE DRYING TIME
BECOMES PROGRESSIVELY LONGER
FOR EACH COAT OF LINSEED OIL
(SEE TEXT).

**Fig. 2. Applying a linseed oil finish.**

1. Prepare the wood surface according to the instructions given in Chapter 7. The surface must be sanded smooth, properly cleaned, and free of all dust. Although linseed oil does not normally raise the grain, it is best to guard against this possibiity by raising the grain during the wood preparation stage (Step 1) of the finishing schedule.

2. Apply a paste filler to open-pored woods to prevent excessive absorption of the linseed oil. See Chapter 7 for instructions concerning the correct application of a filler.

3. Take a clean cloth or brush and apply the linseed oil to a portion of the surface (always work on limited areas and do not try to cover the entire surface immediately). Rub the oil into the surface for about 15 minutes.

4. Let the linseed oil soak into the wood pores, and then wipe away the excess oil with a clean lint-free cloth.

5. Give the first coat of linseed oil at least 2 days to dry.

6. Apply 5 to 15 more coats of linseed oil in the same manner described in Steps 3 and 4 above. Give 2 days drying time between the first and second coats; 5 days between the second and third; and one month between subsequent coats.

277

The number of coats of linseed oil and the length of drying time between coats varies depending upon the finishing schedule and the preference of the finisher. However, regardless of the length of drying time between the coats of linseed oil required by your particular finishing schedule, *each coat must be absolutely dry* before applying the next. If you are in doubt, lengthen the drying period between coats. Remember also that drying periods should become longer as you progress through the finishing schedule.

## OTHER FORMULAS FOR LINSEED OIL FINISHES

Linseed oil finishes have been used for so many years that it is quite natural to find a great variety of formulas for their preparation. The 2-part boiled linseed oil and 1-part turpentine formula described in the preceding section is very common. Others differ by the type of thinner used, the mixing proportions between the linseed oil and the thinner, or by the use of raw linseed oil instead of boiled linseed oil. Some of the different types of formulas you may encounter are as follows:

1. One part boiled linseed oil and 1 part turpentine.
2. One part boiled linseed oil, 1 part turpentine, and 1 part spar varnish.
3. Three parts *raw* linseed oil and 1 part turpentine (first coat), followed by several coats of boiled linseed oil, followed by a coat of 1 part boiled linseed oil and 1 part japan drier.
4. Numerous unthinned coats of boiled linseed oil.

## WAX FINISHES

A wax finish should not be confused with wax finishing. The latter refers to the application of a polishing wax over a final finish to provide additional protection and to create a special pleasing luster. Some finishers prefer to use furniture polish instead of wax for the same purpose, although it is generally considered to be inferior. The merits of furniture polish and polishing wax are described in Chapter 14.

A wax finish is one in which a paste wax is applied over a sealer (thinned lacquer, varnish, or shellac), a stain, or a bare wood surface. The bare wood surface can be one from which an old finish has been removed or one that has never been finished.

Only a *paste* wax is recommended for a straight wax finish. The liquid and cream waxes should only be used for waxing a final finish. Staining waxes can also be used as straight wax finishes, but can only be applied over bare wood. They consist of wax to which a color stain has been added. Because the stain is already in the wax, there is no need to stain or seal the wood. An automotive paste wax will generally produce a very acceptable straight wax finish. Hard paste floor waxes are also good.

A wax finish does not penetrate the wood pores. Therefore, it can be applied over a wood surface from which an old finish has been removed. This is one advantage it has over linseed oil and other penetrating finishes. A wax finish possesses greater resistance to heat than linseed oil and never becomes sticky when it is humid or hot. On the other hand, it does not resist water moisture as well as linseed oil.

## APPLYING A WAX FINISH

A straight wax finish is a paste wax (e.g. an automotive paste wax) applied to the surface with a soft clean lint-free cloth. The procedure for applying a wax finish is as follows (Fig. 3):

1. Prepare the wood surface according to the instructions recommended in Chapter 7. The surface must be clean and uniformly smooth. When you are through preparing the surface, make certain that it is thoroughly clean and free of all dust.
2. Apply a sealer of thinned shellac, varnish, or lacquer to the surface, and give it enough time to completely dry.
3. After the sealer coat has thoroughly dried, lightly abrade it with a very fine grade of steel wool.
4. Remove all dust left by the steel wool with a tack rag or other suitable means.
5. Apply the paste wax with a clean lint-free cloth folded to

279

**STEP 1**      PREPARE THE WOOD SURFACE.

**STEPS 2–4**  APPLY A SEALER, LIGHTLY SAND
IT AFTER IT HAS DRIED AND
REMOVE ALL DUST.

**STEPS 5–9**  APPLY SEVERAL COATS
OF PASTE WAX.

Fig. 3. Applying a wax finish.

fit your hand. Rub the wax onto the surface with a circular movement. Do not apply too much wax at one time. This first coat should be thin and evenly distributed over the surface.

6. Allow the first wax coat sufficient time to dry. The manufacturer of the wax usually recommends how long this should be.
7. Rub the entire surface with a soft cloth. This will remove any excess wax.
8. When you are certain that all excess wax has been removed and that the remaining wax has been evenly distributed over the surface, polish it with a clean, hard cloth.
9. Apply 1 or 2 more coats of wax according to the instructions given in Steps 5 through 8.

The general rule for a good finish is to avoid using too much wax, because it only results in a buildup of excess wax in certain areas. Far better results can be achieved by applying 2 or 3 thin coats.

Most finishers prefer adding a wax finish over a sealer coat. This enables them to remove the finish much more easily (denatured alcohol or turpentine work well) and without the possibility of traces of the wax remaining in the pores of the wood. This condition, of course, results in the improper drying of any other finish that might be applied. Despite these difficulties, straight wax finishes are still sometimes applied directly to a bare wood surface, particularly in the case of very fine grained hardwoods.

# Chapter 14

# Rubbing, Waxing, and Polishing Finishes

Most furniture finishes are either waxed or polished as the final step in the finishing schedule. The purpose of these two procedures is to protect the surface while at the same time enhancing the beauty of the finish. Each has its advantages and disadvantages, and it will be these factors in relation to your needs that will influence your selection. Therefore, it is not a question of whether a polish is better *per se* than a wax (or vice versa), but rather which one is best suited for your needs.

Rubbing a finish is a different procedure altogether from polishing or waxing it, and should not be confused with the latter two. Rubbing a finish consists of polishing it with a very fine abrasive. (Fig. 1). It is essentially an abrading action designed to reduce the natural gloss of a shellac, varnish, or lacquer finish, while at the same time removing brush marks, runs, and dust and other particles from the finish. The result should be a uniformly smooth surface with a somewhat dull appearance. A high polish can be restored to the finish by a variety of rubbing techniques. The application of a suitable paste wax or polish is usually the final step.

Rubbing is also a finishing procedure that can be used after each of the intermediate coats of finish before the topcoat is applied. This is often the case with the better quality varnish finishes. Rubbing after each of the intermediate finishing coats is another way in which the rubbing procedure is distinguished from waxing and polishing. As was pointed out before, polishing and waxing are final steps *only* in the finishing schedule. Rubbing is very seldom a final step.

Fig. 1. Polish sanding to remove bubbles, brush marks, and trapped particles
in the finish.

## MATERIALS USED FOR RUBBING

Most of the materials used for rubbing a finish have already
been described in Chapter 2 (TOOLS AND MATERIALS). You
will probably find some new ones included in this section. In any
event, the various rubbing techniques will include the following
tools and materials:

1.  Pumice stone (FFF grade),
2.  Rottenstone,
3.  Steel wool (000),
4.  Sandpaper (6/0 - 9/0),
5.  Rubbing oil,
6.  Denatured alcohol,
7.  Rubbing felt,
8.  Naphtha.
9.  Clean cloths.

Although sandpaper is listed here, and can be used for rubbing the finish, it is not as satisfactory as other types of abrasives.

283

There is always the tendency to scratch through the finish. Steel wool is much preferred to sandpaper, but never in a grade coarser than 000. The finer the grade of steel wool used, the higher the sheen imparted to the finish.

Rottenstone will always follow the pumice stone in a rubbing schedule. The former is a finer abrasive and will produce a higher sheen.

A rubbing oil is the lubricant used with pumice stone or rottenstone. Raw linseed oil, paraffin oil, and mineral oil can all be used as rubbing oils. Water is frequently substituted for rubbing oils as a lubricant.

Rubbing is done with rubbing felt cut and folded to form a pad. Fold the felt so that it is at least one half inch thick. Some finishers feel they get better results by gluing the felt pad to a wood block. Another method is to rub the surface with the palm of the hand.

Naphtha is excellent for cleaning away the excess rubbing oil (or water) and abrasive residue. You should have clean cloths on hand to wipe this off the surface. If you are rubbing in between coats, you must make absolutely certain that you have cleaned all particles (abrasive powder, etc.) left by the rubbing operation. If you do not successfully do this, these particles will become trapped by subsequent coats of finishing materials.

## RUBBING FUNDAMENTALS

Rub in the direction of the grain as much as possible. This is especially true when using a block of wood to back up the rubbing pad. Remember that abrasives are being used and will tend to scratch the grain if rubbed across it. A toothbrush is recommended for rubbing carvings, moldings, and other portions of the surface too difficult to reach with a pad. A clean cloth dampened with a lubricant and sprinkled with a powdered abrasive is very useful for polishing turnings.

Rub the surface with movements that are straight and smooth. Apply a uniform pressure against the rubbing pad. In other words, do not bear down at the beginning or middle of your stroke and then let up at the end. Be careful not to skip spots or create highlights by improper rubbing.

This chapter contains descriptions of 8 different rubbing techniques used in the finishing schedule. These 8 techniques are:

1. Rubbing with pumice stone and water,
2. Rubbing with pumice stone and oil,
3. Rubbing with rottenstone and water,
4. Rubbing with rottenstone and oil,
5. Rubbing with sandpaper and water,
6. Rubbing with sandpaper and oil,
7. Rubbing with steel wool,
8. Spiriting off with alcohol.

## RUBBING WITH PUMICE STONE AND WATER

Rubbing a finish with pumice stone and water will generally result in a smooth, dull appearance. Some finishers prefer to use an FF grade of pumice stone first, and then proceed to the finer FFF grade during the final stages. Others use the FFF grade throughout the rubbing procedure. It is a matter of personal choice.

Carvings, moldings, borders, and other areas with difficult access should be rubbed first. A toothbrush is generally very helpful for these sections. The larger flat surfaces should be rubbed with a rubbing pad, and in such a way that all movements are in the direction of the grain.

It is sometimes a good idea to sift the pumice stone through a piece of cheesecloth before using it. This will eliminate any unusually large pieces of the powdered abrasive that might scratch the finish during the rubbing procedure.

The pumice stone is applied to the surface either by dipping a water (or oil) dampened rubbing pad into the powdered abrasive or by sprinkling the pumice stone across the finish as you rub.

*All* of the powdered abrasive must be removed from the surface once the rubbing procedure has been completed. Otherwise, the particles will mix with the next layer of finishing materials (e.g. another coat of varnish) or the wax.

285

## RUBBING WITH PUMICE STONE AND OIL

Rubbing a varnished surface with pumice stone and oil will produce a satin finish. The luster will be noticeably higher than that resulting from a pumice stone and water rubbing. Either an FF or FFF grade of pumice stone is used. A light mineral oil is recommended for the rubbing lubricant.

## RUBBING WITH ROTTENSTONE AND WATER

If the finish has already been rubbed with pumice stone and water, it can be followed with a rubbing of rottenstone and water. You should always use the same type of lubricant throughout the rubbing schedule. Rubbing the surface with rottenstone will eliminate any scratches left by the pumice stone rubbing, and will create a somewhat higher polish.

Rub the finish with the rottenstone and water not less than 24 hours after the previous rubbing (pumice stone and water) was completed. The rottenstone can be applied in the same manner as described for pumice stone. As with pumice stone, the rubbing must be done in the direction of the grain with smooth, straight, even strokes. All abrasive particles must be cleaned from the surface at the end of the rubbing operation. Any that remains will interfere with subsequent finishing materials.

## RUBBING WITH ROTTENSTONE AND OIL

Rubbing with rottenstone and oil should follow a rubbing with pumice stone and oil. Because oil rather than water is used as the lubricant, a much longer drying period is required between the completion of the pumice stone and oil procedure and the beginning of the one using rottenstone and oil (a drying period of 5 to 7 days is suggested).

## RUBBING WITH SANDPAPER AND WATER

Rubbing the finish with sandpaper and water will produce a dull surface that is somewhat smoother than the one produced by

286

rubbing with pumice stone. However, pumice stone is usually preferred to sandpaper during the preliminary stages in the rubbing schedule, because the latter shows a greater tendency to scratch the surface. Only a very fine (7/0 to 8/0) waterproof sandpaper should be used. Always rub with light, even, straight strokes in the direction of the grain.

## RUBBING WITH SANDPAPER AND OIL

Rubbing the finish with sandpaper and oil is not much different from the sandpaper and water technique except that less dust is involved when oil is used as the lubricant. There is also a tendency for the color of the wood to darken.

## RUBBING WITH STEEL WOOL

Steel wool can be used to rub the finish after it has been rubbed with sandpaper and water (or oil). The effect is much the same as switching to rottenstone after having rubbed the surface with pumice stone and a lubricant. Rubbing with steel wool results in a soft, satin sheen. *Always* rub with the grain, never across it. After the surface has been thoroughly cleaned of all steel wool residue and other possible contaminants, it may be waxed.

## THE SPIRITING-OFF TECHNIQUE

*Spiriting-off* is a finishing technique used to create a brilliant, high luster on a varnish finish *after* it has been rubbed. The materials required for this technique include:
1. Denatured alcohol,
2. A mineral oil base polish (no silicones),
3. Several clean lint-free cloths.

The spiriting off technique begins after the varnish finish has been polished with one of the several rubbing techniques described in this chapter. The steps involved are as follows:
1. Thoroughly clean the surface so that any traces of the powdered abrasive are removed.

287

2. Wipe the surface with a cleanser-polish. Remove any excess polish.

3. *Dampen* (do not soak) a cloth in denatured alcohol and wipe it lightly with circular movements across the surface. Do *not* allow it to come to rest on the finish or the alcohol may damage the finish. The alcohol will remove polishing oil and cause the surface to gleam with a brilliant, high luster.

## WAXES VERSUS POLISHES

This section is not intended to convert you to using either a wax or a polish. Both have certain advantages and disadvantages about which you should be aware. These will be described here in a very general way. There are so many waxing and polishing products on the market it would hardly be possible to do otherwise.

A wax will produce a thicker, more permanent coat than a polish. As a result, it provides better protection for furniture subject to heavy use. It exhibits a particularly strong resistance to alcohol and water. Finally, it has a tendency not to hold dust particles, which reduces the amount of dusting that has to be done.

Furniture polishes are very easy to apply, particularly those sold in aerosol spray cans. This is generally what the immaculately dressed housewife is using in those television commercials when she shows you how effortlessly she can make her furniture look as good as any wax can. And it *will* look as good (for a while). Unfortunately, dust, fingerprints, and smudges become very noticeable on any polished surface. Moreover, these surfaces require frequent dusting. This should not necessarily be regarded as a disadvantage, because no wood surface should be dry dusted. Many of your better furniture polishes are formulated to be cleaner-polishes.

A principal advantage of using a furniture polish is that it reduces the chances of certain finishing problems occurring. By sealing in the finish oils, a polish will often prevent cracking, crumbling, crazing, and related problems.

A final note: the addition of lemon to a furniture polish (or, for that matter, any other pleasing fragrance) will do absolutely *nothing* to improve its polishing characteristics. This is primarily an advertising gimmick.

## MATERIALS USED FOR WAXING AND POLISHING

Waxes and polishes are available as pastes, liquids, or sprays, and are sold under a wide variety of trade names. All manufacturers make highly confident claims about the effectiveness of their products. I would accept their claims with certain reservations. No waxing or polishing product is perfect. Be sure to carefully read the manufacturer's listing of ingredients contained in his product. A wax containing relatively high percentages of carnauba wax, for example, would indicate a fairly high quality, paste wax. High concentrations of paraffin, on the other hand, would indicate the opposite. Many finishers also avoid using waxes or polishes containing silicones, because they are sometimes difficult to remove when the finish is being stripped.

Waxes and polishes are generally regarded as two distinct categories of finishing materials, each having slightly different functions. Both waxes and polishes are designed to give the wood a special luster or glow, and are used to enhance the finish. However, another function of a furniture polish is to *clean* the surface. As you rub the polish onto the surface, it picks up dust and other contaminants without permitting them to grind into the finish (as dry dusting will do). When the excess polish is wiped from the surface, the dust and other contaminants are removed with it, leaving behind a thin film or polish. This film will temporarily give the finish a very pleasing appearance, but it must be frequently renewed. It cannot give the finish the durable protective coat that a wax can provide. This is the distinction between waxes and polishes.

Each wax that you purchase contains one or more waxes mixed together to form the base, a thinner, and certain other minor ingredients (e.g. coloring matter) as the manufacturer sees fit to add. The waxes used to form the base are usually one or more of the following:

1. Carnauba wax,
2. Candelilla wax,
3. Beeswax,
4. Paraffin wax.

These were listed in the order of the hardness of each wax. Silicones, though often considered to be polishes, are waxes by type and will be discussed at the end of this section.

*Carnauba wax* is the hardest paste wax used for polishing furniture finishes. It is also regarded by the experts as the best polishing wax.

An excellent polishing wax can be produced by shredding and mixing 1 part carnauba wax with 1 part beeswax or caresin wax (a beeswax substitute) and thinning the mixture to a good working consistency with pure turpentine.

Another formula for a carnauba base polishing wax is 1 part carnauba wax, 1 part paraffin, and 5 parts pure turpentine. The two waxes are shredded and mixed together, and then thinned to the proper working consistency by adding the turpentine. In this formula (as well as the previously described one), mineral spirits can be substituted for the turpentine as a thinner.

*Candelilla wax* is a hard paste wax derived from a plant grown in Mexico. It is not as hard as carnauba wax, having a melting point about 30° F lower than the latter. Its color ranges from yellow to brown. Candelilla wax is used in the same way as a carnauba wax.

*Beeswax* is not as hard as carnauba or candelilla wax, but it still possesses excellent polishing characteristics. It is available in either a yellow or white type, and is always thinned 50% or more with paraffin, pure turpentine, or other suitable means. Beeswax added to a paste rubbing wax or other types will tend to reduce the gloss and produce a dull appearance to the finish.

*Paraffin wax* is a white, translucent substance generally obtained from distillates of petroleum (coal, wood, and shale oil have been used). Paraffin wax is the basis for most commercial waxes used today. It is far softer than the other waxes mentioned so far. The more paraffin added to a paste wax, the greater will be the ease with which it can be worked. On the other hand, the wax will not be as hard as it could have been had it not been diluted by the addition of paraffin.

Although manufacturers often refer to *silicones* as "polishes" in their advertising, these types of finishing materials are actually more closely related to waxes. These silicone waxes are available in 16-oz. spray cans, and are most effectively used as dusting sprays. Some finishers do not like to use them, because they have experienced difficulty in removing finishes that had been sprayed with silicone waxes. There are paint and varnish removers now available that can overcome this difficulty.

Trying to list all the different formulas for furniture polishes would require a separate book. A majority of them appear to be oil-base polishes. That is to say, some sort of oil acts as their principal or base ingredient. The two oils used in furniture polishes are: (1) linseed oil, and (2) mineral oil. The former is restricted to its use in linseed oil polish. The latter, mineral oil, provides the major ingredient for almost every other kind of oil-base furniture polish. For example, lemon oil polish, cream or white polish, colored polish, and all so-called oil-base polishes use mineral oil as their basic ingredient. The cream or white polishes basically consist of mineral oil emulsified in water. It is a good polish, generally producing a very acceptable sheen (without that "wet" appearance). You can obtain similar results with the colored polishes which are produced by mixing dark brown aniline dye powder with mineral oil. The lemon oil polishes are simply mineral oils to which a lemon fragrance has been added.

## WAXING A FINISH

A new finish should be thoroughly dusted before applying a wax. Old finishes should be cleaned and any traces of old furniture wax or polish removed.

Use a section of heavy linen to make a wax rubbing pad. The linen can be folded to a suitable size, and used both to apply the wax and to polish the finish. Apply the wax with circular movements so that the rubbing movement goes both with and across the grain.

# Chapter 15

# Antiquing (Glazing) and Related Techniques

*Antiquing* (or *glazing*) (Fig. 1) are terms used interchangeably to describe a furniture finishing process that generally involves the application and removal of a glaze (a pigmented stain or thin wash). The purpose of this process is to create highlighting, shading, or other effects on the finish in order to suggest an aged appearance. This is a total process. That is, the entire surface of the piece of furniture is covered with the glaze.

Glazing is used to produce such well known finishes as "Pickled Finish," "Bone White Finish," and the various "Old World Finishes" (e.g. "French Provincial"). This chapter covers the various steps in the basic finishing schedule for antiquing (glazing).

## TOOLS AND MATERIALS

The contents of a typical antiquing kit (along with various tools needed) are shown in Fig. 2. You will notice that the tools needed includes a screwdriver and a pair of pliers for removing the hardware from the piece of furniture. The tack rag serves the same purpose as the lint-free cloth mentioned in the finishing schedule for antiquing. All of these tools and finishing materials can be purchased separately, and most of them are available at local paint and hardware stores.

## THE ANTIQUING (GLAZING) PROCEDURE

Antiquing (glazing) is probably one of the easiest finishing techniques for the beginner to use, because it does not require the

Fig. 1. Antiquing process.

extensive wood preparation steps found in the other finishes. Most antiquing kits contain a base coat finishing material that can be applied over varnish, paint, and other surfaces. The base coat functions as a sealer, preventing the older finish from bleeding through into the glaze coat.

Most antiquing procedures will consist of the following basic steps:

1. Prepare the surface by sanding it lightly with a very fine grade of sandpaper. The purpose is to create a smooth, uniform base for the finishing materials used in the antiquing process. All surface imperfections such as dents, gouges, and scratches should be patched with a suitable wood filler, and sanded smooth. (Fig. 3).

2. Remove all dust left by the sanding operation with a clean lint-free cloth.

293

# Antiquing (Glazing) and Related Techniques

GLAZE
SEALER

COLOR BASE
UNDERCOAT

COLOR
GLAZE

INSTRUCTION
BOOK

(A) Glazing kit.

SANDPAPER -- MEDIUM AND FINE

SANDING BLOCK

SCREWDRIVER AND PLIERS

MASKING TAPE

TACK RAG

DROP CLOTH OR
NEWSPAPER

CHEESE CLOTH,
TEXTURING
MATERIAL

PATCHING
PASTE

WIPE-UP RAGS

PAINT BRUSHES

(B) Tools generally used.

Courtesy Sherwin-Williams Co.

Fig. 2. Typical antiquing kit.

Fig. 3. Removing hardware and repairing dents and scratches with wood filler.

3. Brush on a base coat (undercoat) and allow it sufficient time to thoroughly dry. (Fig. 4).

Fig. 4. Applying the colored undercoat for the antique glaze.

4. When the base coat has dried, brush a coat of glaze onto the surface. (Fig. 5).

5. While the glaze is still wet, wipe it off with a folded piece

Courtesy Sherwin-Williams Co.

**Fig. 5. Applying the glaze.**

of cheesecloth before it has time to dry. The effect you create will depend on a number of factors including the colors you use and your wiping procedure. (Fig. 6).

6. A clear varnish topcoat or a wax can be applied over the antiquing glaze for additional protection, however this is optional. (Fig. 7).

Step 1 in the above described finishing schedule for antiquing should also include the removal and storage of all furniture hardware. Trying to mask these off so that the finishing materials can be applied around them is never completely successful. Some of the liquid always seems to find a way to get onto the metal.

Not only must the surface be sanded smooth, but all old wax, polish, dirt, grease, and other contaminants must be cleaned from the surface. If this is not done, the finishing material used in the antiquing process will not adhere properly. Lifting of the finish will most probably result. Do not use a cleaning preparation that will dissolve the old finish, or you will have to completely remove it (see the appropriate sections in Chapter 6 REPAIRING, RESTORING, AND STRIPPING). If the old finish is subject to

Courtesy *Sherwin-Williams* Co.

**Fig. 6. Wiping the glaze until the desired effect is achieved.**

Courtesy *Sherwin-Williams* Co.

**Fig. 7. Applying a clear finish, or sealer, over the antique glaze.**

297

severe lifting and other indications that it is no longer adhering properly to the surface, it will have to be removed for this reason also.

Topcoats are generally not required over an antique finish, although it is a good idea if the surface is expected to receive more than the average amount of wear. A satin sheen varnish or a wax will provide adequate protection under most conditions. Allow the glaze at least 4 days to dry before applying the topcoat.

Antiquing should never be done when the weather is excessively humid. Low temperatures (especially those below 50° F) will also have a harmful effect on the finish. Ideal conditions exist when the temperature ranges from 65° to 75° F, and the humidity is relatively low.

Removing the glaze from the surface can be done in a number of different ways, each with its own interesting effect. The two principal means of removing the glaze is with a pad of cheesecloth and a dry brush. The cheesecloth pad is used for wiping the larger (and generally flat) surface areas. A brush is used for carvings, trim, and other difficult to reach sections of the surface.

Wiping is done in long straight strokes always in the same direction. The pad of cheesecloth should be occasionally refolded to expose a clean, unsaturated surface. The brush is inserted into carvings and other recessed areas and dragged out, removing portions of the glaze. Clean the brush frequently with a suitable solvent or you will find that you are simply transferring glaze from one spot to another.

Never allow the glaze to dry completely before you start to wipe it. You simply cannot do anything with it once it is dry. The sooner you wipe it, the lighter the effect will be. Wipe from the center of an area out toward its edges, and try to create gradual shadings. Abrupt changes from light to dark indicate poor technique.

Apply the glaze over transfers (decalcomania), stripping, and other decorating techniques. Do not attempt to add them to the glaze. If varnish or lacquer are used as a protective topcoat, dull rub them or apply a polish. The former approach results in a more "antique" effect.

## ANTIQUING WITH GOLD

The white and gold finishes of much French Provincial furniture can be imitated by antiquing the surface with a gold enamel applied over a white enamel base coat. Other interesting effects can be obtained by using black, red, brown, or dark green as the base coat.

Apply the white enamel base coat (an "eggshell" or gloss enamel is recommended) in the same manner as described earlier in this chapter (see THE ANTIQUING PROCEDURE. Additional information on enameling is found in Chapter 12). Give the enamel sufficient time to thoroughly dry before proceeding any further. If the surface is glossy, lightly sand it with a very fine grade of sandpaper and remove the dust with a tack rag or clean cloth. Do not sand the base coat until you are certain it is dry.

The gold enamel can be applied by:

1.  Dry brushing,
2.  Spattering,
3.  Brushing and wiping.

In the dry brushing method, the brush is dipped into the enamel and wiped almost dry before it is applied. The tip of the brush is then gently dragged nearly parallel to the surface and manipulated with an irregular, flicking movement. Never apply any great amount of pressure or you will deposit concentrations of gold enamel. If properly applied, you will obtain an interesting streaked effect.

The base coat can also be spattered with gold by striking or flicking a brush dipped in enamel with a table knife or wood stick (a piece of wood dowel will do nicely). A toothbrush or small varnish brush can be used, but the latter should be cut shorter to make the bristles stiffer. You can also flick the brush with your finger if you do not mind messy fingers. The gold spatters will form irregular patterns on the surface, and this is exactly the effect you are seeking with this technique.

Gold enamel dries too quickly for the brushing and wiping method of application, so a substitute must be used. Try mixing gold bronzing powder with a clear antiquing liquid. The latter can be purchased from most paint supply stores that carry an-

299

tiquing kits and other finishing materials. You will probably have to experiment a bit until you succeed in obtaining a suitable mixture (see Chapter 16 GILDING AND BRONZING for suggestions). Brush the gold mixture onto the surface and wipe it off with a clean piece of cheesecloth.

If you want to apply a clear topcoat of varnish for additional protection, you must first seal the enamel with a washcoat of white shellac. Make certain that the washcoat has completely dried before applying the varnish.

## SHADING

The purpose of *shading* is to darken the edges of certain areas of the furniture. The contrast with the lighter areas gives the effect of the worn, faded surface one finds on old furniture. It differs from highlighting in that it generally involves the addition of a darker color tone to a lighter one, or applying the glaze more thickly on some areas than others. Highlighting is essentially the opposite procedure, except that in this case the color is lightened by wiping rather than by the addition of a lighter color (see HIGH-LIGHTING in this chapter). Some finishers also refer to this procedure (i.e. wiping the glaze to lighten the color) as shading, but are technically incorrect. The glaze is applied (most commonly by spraying) thinly in some spots, more thickly in others when shading. It is wiped away if you are highlighting the finish.

Shading can be done so that the lighter and darker color shades blend (i.e. are "feathered") into one another, or so that a somewhat more abrupt and contrastive transition occurs. The choice is yours to make.

## HIGHLIGHTING

*Highlighting* (Fig. 8) creates an aged, worn appearance by lightening or darkening portions of the surface so that other areas are accentuated (highlighted). The raised portions of carvings, moldings, or borders are most commonly highlighted by rubbing their surfaces lightly with a fine grade of sandpaper or steel wool.

SUGGESTED AREAS
FOR HIGHLIGHTING

**Fig. 8. Suggested areas for highlighting a chair or table leg.**

You must be careful not to remove too much of the finish or you may scratch through to the wood. Should this happen, you will have to strip the surface and refinish it.

A good highlighting technique will closely resemble the worn spots and other signs of wear that took years for the wood to acquire. Therefore, you must rub the surface in those areas that would have received wear under normal conditions. A haphazard removal of the finish must be avoided. Sometimes the corners or edges of a piece of furniture will be sanded with coarse sandpaper to give the appearance of wear. When the finish is applied, these artificially "worn" areas are highlighted.

Highlighting can also be accomplished chemically by darkening the recessed areas of carvings and moldings, or the edge of a border. A dark stain compatible with the previously applied finishing materials can be applied to the areas you want darkened. Wipe

301

the excess off before it dries (see GLAZING STAINS in this chapter). Another, though less commonly used chemical method of highlighting is wiping the surface with naphtha or a similar solvent.

## SPATTERING

*Spattering* (Fig. 9) is the technique of flicking specks of ink

Fig. 9. Spattering a glazed surface with specks of flat black paint.

or flat black paint against a glazed surface. Glaze of a different or darker color from the surface can also be used. A brush with the bristles cut off short or a toothbrush is barely dipped into the liquid to be spattered and flicked against the surface by moving a finger, knife blade, or wood dowel across the bristles. A wax or clear varnish can be applied as a protective topcoat.

## STIPPLING

*Stippling* produces a mottled effect on the surface. It can be created by blotting the glaze while it is still wet with a crumbled piece of paper, a sponge, or a cloth. After the glaze has thoroughly dried, cover the surface with a protective coat of wax or clear varnish.

## STRIPING

*Striping* is actually a painting technique (see Chapter 12), but is often used in conjuction with antiquing to add a special decorative touch. In antiquing, it generally consists of painting a gold or silver stripe along an edge for contrast. Other colors can also be used.

## MARBLEIZING

In *marbleizing*, the finish is given a marblelike decorative effect with a crumpled piece of paper or a brush. Although the paper technique is the easiest to use, it gives the poorest results and only faintly resembles a marble surface. It consists of wiping the still wet surface with short and long sweeping strokes. The paper must be dry or nearly dry, so it is recommended that you use a new piece of paper whenever the old one becomes too wet.

The brushing technique requires a certain degree of artistic talent, and takes considerably longer than using a piece of paper. Whereas the latter consisted of disturbing and removing portions of a wet finish, the brush technique involves spattering, dribbling, and blending other liquid finishing materials onto a completely dry finish. The procedure is as follows:

1. Sand the surface until it is completely smooth, and remove all traces of dust with a clean lint-free cloth or a tack rag. Any patching of surface defects should be done at this point.
2. Apply a base coat of white paint or enamel, and allow sufficient time for it to dry.

3. Select three or four colors (for example, those you would expect to find on a piece of marble). These will be referred to as color one, color two, and color three.
4. Dip your brush into the container of color one and dribble it across the surface in a random, irregular pattern.
5. Repeat the procedure with color two. Allow some of the second color to cross over the pattern made by the first one. It does not matter if the two mix (as a matter of fact, you will want them to do so).
6. Using a dry brush or a velvet pad with the pile facing outward, daub the wet surface until the two colors blend (where they overlap) or become indistinct.
7. Apply color three in the same manner as the first two (see Steps 4 through 6).
8. Dribble the white base coat across the surface in thin, random lines, but do *not* daub it as you did the others. This will create a sharply contrastive vein effect against the indistinct, blended background of the three original colors. See Fig. 10.

Marbleizing can also be used on gold leaf after the varnish top coat has thoroughly dried. Use the finishing schedule for marbleizing described above, but omit Steps 1 and 2. The surface had already been prepared before the gold leaf was applied. Furthermore, a base coat of paint or enamel would cover the gold leaf and hide it from view. Immediately after Step 6, in the marbleizing finishing schedule, you might try splattering benzine mixed with boiled linseed oil onto the surface. Turpentine can also be used. This results in blending many of the colors.

## DISTRESSING

*Distressing* refers to the marking of furniture in such a way as to create an antique effect. Marking can be done in any one of the three following ways:

1. Physically scratching, gouging, or denting the wood,
2. Placing random marks on the filler, sealer, or between *finishing* coats with a black or dark brown crayon.

1. FIRST COLOR

2. SECOND COLOR

3. THIRD COLOR

4. WHITE BASE COAT LINES

Fig. 10. Marbelizing a wood surface.

3. Spattering the filler, sealer, or intermediate finishing coats with a dark color.

## WOOD GRAINING

*Wood graining* refers to the creating of simulated grain patterns in a glaze applied over the surface. The purpose of graining is to make a wood with an uninteresting grain appear more attractive. This technique is designed to achieve a special decorative effect, not to create an exact reproduction of a wood grain.

Complete wood graining kits are available through local and

305

mail-order suppliers of wood finishing materials, but the same tools and materials can be found in many home workshops. You will need two brushes to apply the base coat and glaze, a flat base coat, enough glaze for two coats, a tool device for graining, and a clear topcoat. A brush, whisk broom, or steel comb can be used in place of the graining found in the commercial kits.

The steps in the wood graining procedure are as follows:

1. Prepare the surface by sanding until it is completely smooth.
2. Remove the dust left by the sanding operation with a tack rag or a clean lint-free cloth.
3. Apply a base coat of flat paint or enamel, and allow it sufficient time to thoroughly dry.
4. Sand the surface lightly with a very fine grade of sandpaper.
5. Clean off all the dust left by the sanding operation.
6. Quickly brush a coat of glaze over the entire surface.
7. Before the glaze has a chance to dry, draw the graining tool across the surface from one end to the other in parallel, overlapping rows. The simulated grain lines must be continuous and unbroken. The grain lines may slant, weave, or wiggle. They should not be drawn in a straight line across the surface, because this is rarely natural. Draw the graining tool so that the lines move around knots in the wood.
8. Allow the glaze sufficient time to thoroughly dry.
9. Apply a topcoat of clear varnish or wax to protect the wood graining.

The bristles or teeth of a typical wood graining tool are flexible. By putting pressure on the tool, you can cause the simulated grain lines to have the same irregular spacing as the natural ones.

Varnish can be used as both the base coat and the glaze (see Steps 3 and 6) instead of the ones described above. The varnish base coat should be a lighter color or shade than the glaze. If you are more interested in a decorative effect that imitating wood grain, try experimenting with colors not natural to wood such as gold, silver, bronze, or bright red.

## GLAZING STAINS

Highlighting a finish is often done with a *glazing stain*. These are secondary or additive stains. In other words, they are added to the surface for decorative purposes, and not for such primary functions as filling, sealing, or staining (see SHADING STAINS).

Glazing stains may be applied by either brushing or spraying, and generally require about 24 hours to dry. Faster drying glazing stains are available, but these are usually not of the same quality as the slower drying oil-base types.

A cloth, camel's hair brush, or other suitable blending device can be used to remove the glazing stain before it dries. The brush is recommended for the slower drying glazing stains.

## SHADING STAINS

Shading stains are used principally to equalize the color of previously stained furniture. These are primary stains that have a definite and important function in finishing schedules that require their use. However, shading stains can also be used to create a highlighted effect, which gives them a secondary or decorative function as well.

The composition of a shading stain is equivalent to that of a thinned colored lacquer. As a result, it is characterized by a very rapid drying time and fast setting characteristics. It should be applied by spraying.

Shading stains are usually applied directly over pigment stain, non-grain raising stain, or lacquer sealer. Applying these stains over the sealer is the most common method used, especially in the furniture industry. Its one major disadvantage is that chipping or other forms of impact may cause part of the finish to be removed, carrying with it some of the color. This can be avoided by applying the shading stain directly over the base stain rather than the sealer.

# Chapter 16

# Gilding and Bronzing

*Gilding* and *bronzing* are special decorating techniques in-volving the application of metal in extremely thin sheets or powder to the finish. Gilding is the older of the two techniques, dating to as early as the Egyptian Pharoahs. The use of bronzing powders is a comparatively recent development and has largely replaced gilding. The former is easier to apply, but lacks the durability of gilding.

## TOOLS AND MATERIALS

Many of the tools and materials used in gilding and bronzing have already been described in other chapters. However, there are a few new ones that are used specifically for these two decorating techniques. A brief description of their nature and use will be covered in this section.

A home workshop completely equipped to do any type of gilding or bronzing should have the following tools and supplies:

1. Sharp scissors or a knife for cutting the metal leaf.
2. Metal leaf or bronzing powder in the desired color.
3. Agate burnisher or velvet pad for burnishing (polishing) the gilded surface.
4. A sealer (shellac washcoat or a sanding sealer) to cover a wood surface.
5. Gold size to serve as a base for the metal leaf (a clear coat of varnish will be adequate).
6. Red or black acrylic paint to serve as a contrast for the gilding.

7. A camel's hair brush to smooth wrinkles out of the metal leaf.
8. Suitable brushes for applying the various finishing materials (sealer, size, etc.). (See Chapter 2 TOOLS AND MATERIALS).
9. A gilder's brush (or tip) for picking up the gold leaf. A thin piece of cardboard also works well.

## GILDING

*Gilding* is the technique of applying leaf metals (extremely thin sheets of metal) to the finish for a special decorative effect

Fig. 1. Examples of metal leaf.

(Fig. 1). Gold leaf or metal leaf made to imitate gold (particularly in contrast with a red or black finish) was, for a long time, a popular favorite, but others such as silver leaf and aluminum leaf were also used. Because of the popularity of gold as a color, gilding is frequently referred to as *gold leafing*.

Gilding can be applied to varnish, lacquer, paint, or enamel

309

finishes. It can also be applied *under* varnish. Gilding can be used as the final step in the finishing schedule, or it can be used to decorate previously finished furniture. In the latter case, all wax and polish must be removed from the surface before the gilding procedure begins. Otherwise, the metal leaf will not adhere well to the surface.

Gold leaf is sold in books containing 25 leaves to the book. Each leaf is tissue thin, and about 4 inches square in size. Sheets of tissue paper are placed between each gold leaf to provide easier handling. Gold leaf is also sold in ribbons or rolls for use as borders.

## GILDING (GOLD LEAFING) PROCEDURE

Gilding (gold leafing) may be applied to either plaster of paris (usually the "carved wood" border on many ornate picture frames), a bare wood surface, or a finish (e.g. paint, enamel, varnish, or lacquer).

As was already mentioned, gold leafing is an older decorating technique than bronzing and dates back to at least the Ancient Egyptian period in history. It is far more durable than bronzing (we still have excellent examples of this technique taken from Egyptian tombs), but it takes much longer to apply. Because of this and a mistaken belief that it requires great skill, most people avoid gold leafing and choose bronzing.

Gilding may be applied to either plaster of paris or the wood surface. In either case, the surface will have to be properly prepared so that it will serve as a suitable base for the finishing materials and gold leaf. The procedure for preparing plaster and wood surfaces for gilding is as follows (Fig. 2):

1. A wood surface should be prepared according to the instructions suggested in Chapter 7. Plaster of paris moldings should be inspected for damage and repaired before proceeding any further (see REPAIRING MOLD-INGS in this chapter).

2. Seal the wood surface with a washcoat of shellac, and allow it sufficient time to dry.

| | |
|---|---|
| **STEP 1** | PREPARE THE WOOD SURFACE SO THAT IT IS SMOOTH AND EVEN. |
| **STEP 2** | BRUSH ON A WASHCOAT SEALER (LIGHTLY SAND AND REMOVE DUST IN STEP 3 AND 4). |
| **STEP 5** | BRUSH ON A COAT OF RED ACRYLIC PAINT. |
| **STEP 6** | BRUSH ON A COAT OF THIN VARNISH (= GOLD SIZE). |
| **STEPS 7–12** | APPLY GOLD LEAF |

**Fig. 2. The gold leafing procedure.**

3. Lightly sand the undercoat with a very fine sandpaper.
4. Remove all dust left by the sanding operation with a tack rag or a clean lint-free cloth.
5. Apply a coat of red acrylic paint over the shellac washcoat, and allow it sufficient time to thoroughly dry.
6. Brush on a thinned coat of varnish. Follow the manufacturer's recommendations for thinning or read the appropriate sections in Chapter 10. Mineral spirits can be used in a 1:1 formula. The surface is now ready for application of the gold leaf.
7. Before the varnish dries completely and while it is still tacky, apply the gold leaf to the surface. Press the gold leaf down and smooth out wrinkles with a soft camel's hair brush or ball of cotton.
8. Apply the next gold leaf so that there is a slight overlap (⅛ to ¼ inch) with the first one. Smooth the second leaf down so that your movements are always in the direction of the first one (Fig. 3). This eliminates the problem of tearing up the edge of a leaf.
9. Breaks, holes, or tears in the gold leaf can be repaired with

311

1. SLIP A THIN PIECE OF CARDBOARD UNDER THE METAL LEAF AND REMOVE IT FROM THE BOOK.

2. POSITION THE METAL LEAF.

3. SLIP OUT THE CARDBOARD.

SLIGHT OVERLAP

4. PLACE THE NEXT LEAF SO THAT IT SLIGHTLY OVERLAPS THE ONE BEFORE.

**Fig. 3. Applying the gold (or metal) leaf.**

10. Let the gilding dry for 24 to 48 hours. You will want to be absolutely certain that the surface is completely dry, or the gold leaf will not adhere properly.

11. After the surface has thoroughly dried, lightly smooth the gilded areas with a ball of cotton. This will break off all loose and ragged ends.

12. Polish (burnish) the gilding by rubbing it lightly with an

agate burnisher or a velvet pad. Burnish only the high points of the moldings.

There are several suitable variations of this finishing schedule that you might like to consider. For example, a flat enamel (also red) can be substituted for the acrylic paint in Step 5. A black enamel or acrylic paint will also give an interesting effect. Some finishers like to use two or three undercoats of gesso (a mixture of glue or size, white zinc, and gypsum) over the shellac washcoat. Gesso was originally developed as a sealer for French and Italian furniture of the 18th and early 19th centuries, and was usually made by mixing glue and plaster (or whiting). Gesso can be purchased in most local paint supply stores. Each gesso coat is sanded and all the dust removed before the next coat of finishing materials is applied. The gesso coat, properly sanded, gives an extremely smooth surface for the rest of the finishing materials. An abbreviated finishing schedule in which gesso undercoats are used is as follows:

1. Wood preparation,
2. Shellac washcoat,
3. First gesso undercoat,
4. Light sanding,
5. Removal of dust,
6. Second gesso coat,
7. Light sanding,
8. Removal of dust,
9. Continue with Steps 5 through 12 of the basic finishing schedule for gilding.

A sanding sealer can be substituted for the shellac washcoat in Step 2 of the finishing schedule. This would make a gesso undercoating unnecessary since a sanding sealer will also produce a smooth and uniform surface when properly sanded. The consistency of an acrylic paint is such that you could probably do away with any type of sealing step. Consequently, some finishers try to reduce the application time by working with an acrylic paint and no sealer. This would eliminate Steps 2 through 4 of the finishing schedule for gilding.

The varnish added to the surface in Step 6 is referred to as *size* or *gold size*. The size need not be limited to varnish. Shellac, lacquer, glue and water, and others have also been used with varying degrees of success. The important thing to remember is that whatever size used *must* be chemically compatible with the topcoat should you decide to apply one. Gold leaf does not need to be protected, but some of the other metals may tarnish slightly. Spraying the surface with a light topcoat of shellac, lacquer, or clear varnish should give adequate protection.

## REPAIRING MOLDINGS

Many times the carvings on gilt picture or mirror frames are made of plaster of paris. If they are broken, they can be repaired by molding a replacement piece from one of the carvings on a different corner. Liquid latex-base molding compounds can be used to make the mold and is available in most paint and hardware stores.

The procedure for repairing plaster moldings is as follows:

1. Clean the surface of the break so that no dirt, grease, or other contaminants will prevent the glue from sticking properly.
2. Coat the carvings you wish to use as a replacement piece with latex. Coat it thickly with two to three coats. Allow enough time for the latex to completely dry.
3. Remove the latex mold, place it in a supporting box (containing dirt or sand), and adjust it. That is to say, push it into the dirt or sand so that the mold will retain its shape when the plaster of paris is poured into it. Wet plaster can also be used in the box. It should be allowed to dry before it is used as a support for the mold.
4. Pour the plaster into the mold and allow it sufficient time to dry.
5. Remove the mold, and fit the replacement piece to the broken carving. Some trimming may be necessary.
6. Glue the replacement piece in position and fill any cracks with a suitable filler material.

7. Finish the new surface in the same manner as the rest of the surface (see GILDING PROCEDURE or BRONZING PROCEDURE in this chapter).

## BRONZING

*Bronzing* (or *powder gilding*) is the process of covering, or overlaying, a surface with a metal powder. The bronzing powders are available in a much greater variety of colors than gold leaf which gives it a certain advantage over the latter. However, the bronzing powder does not hold its color as well and is subject to fading after a period of time.

The bronzing powder may be rolled onto a surface after a coating of bronzing liquid has been applied, or it may be mixed with the bronzing liquid before application and the solution then brushed onto the surface. Both methods give good results. The manufacturer's instructions should suggest an appropriate formula for mixing the bronzing powder and bronzing liquid.

Bronzing powder is made by grinding metal leaf into a powder form. The grinding is done in several grades ranging from fine to coarse. Bronzing liquids are of several types, depending largely upon the type of topcoat that will be used. For example, a lacquer-base bronzing liquid is designed specifically for use with a clear lacquer topcoat. If the bronzing liquid is chemically incompatible with the topcoat, it will cause it to dissolve and lift.

## BRONZING PROCEDURE

The procedure for bronzing is similar to the one described for gilding (gold leafing) in the initial stages of the finishing schedule. As a convenience to the reader and for purposes of review they will be repeated here.

The procedure for bronzing a surface is as follows (Fig. 4):

1. Read the instructions for preparing a wood surface suggested in Chapter 7. If you are dealing with molding, examine them for damage. Methods for repairing damaged

315

**STEP 1**      PREPARE THE WOOD SURFACE—
                SO THAT IT IS SMOOTH AND EVEN.

**STEP 2**      BRUSH ON A WASHCOAT SEALER
                ( LIGHTLY SAND AND REMOVE
                DUST IN STEPS 3 AND 4).

**STEP 5**      APPLY A COAT OF BRONZING LIQUID.

**STEPS 6–7**    APPLY BRONZE POWDER.

**STEP 8**      APPLY CLEAR FINISH (OPTIONAL).

**Fig. 4. The bronzing procedure.**

    moldings are covered in this chapter (see REPAIRING MOLDINGS).

2. Seal the surface with a washcoat of shellac, and allow it sufficient time to thoroughly dry. A sanding sealer may be used instead, if you wish.
3. Sand the sealer coat lightly with a fine grade of sandpaper. Always sand in the direction of the grain.
4. Remove the dust left by the sanding operation with a tack rag or a clean lint-free cloth.
5. Apply a coat of bronzing liquid (varnish with a japan drier added) to the surface. This serves the same purpose as does gold size in the gold leafing procedure (i.e. the sticky surface to which the bronzing powder adheres). A thinned coat of varnish, shellac, or lacquer will serve as an excellent substitute for the bronzing liquid.
6. Before the bronzing liquid or clear finish completely dries and while it is still tacky, apply the bronzing powder to the surface. This is commonly and most effectively done by wrapping a piece of velvet (the pile facing out) around the finger, and using this as the "brush". The finger is dipped into the bronzing powder and gently tapped onto the surface.

316

7. Allow the bronzing liquid or clear finish sufficient time to thoroughly dry before attempting to remove any excess powder. This can easily be done by placing a vacuum hose near (but *not* touching) the bronzed surface.

8. The bronzed surface may be coated with a clear finish varnish, shellac, or lacquer) or left uncoated.

Step 6 can be eliminated by mixing the bronzing powder with the bronzing liquid or clear finish prior to applying it. This is done on a one to one basis, and the resulting mixture is then thinned to brushing consistency with an appropriate solvent (e.g. denatured alcohol for shellac, turpentine for varnish, and lacquer thinner for lacquer).

## STENCILING WITH BRONZING POWDER

Stenciled designs can also be added to finishes with bronzing powders. This technique is somewhat more complicated than stenciling with paint, but should offer no difficulty if the instructions are carefully followed.

The procedure for stenciling with bronzing powder is as follows:

1. Follow Steps 1 through 5 in the finishing schedule for bronzing (see BRONZING PROCEDURE in this chapter).

2. Apply the stencil to the tacky surface. Gently press the stencil down until all the edges of the design are tight against the surface.

3. Apply the bronzing powder with a piece of velvet (see Step 6 in the basic finishing schedule for bronzing).

4. Work inward from the edges of the stencil. The greatest concentration of bronzing powder should be along the outer edges of the stencil design; the smallest toward the center point. This shading effect creates the appearance of depth.

5. The bronzing powder is applied either with a circular move-ment or in the natural direction of the design.

6. After having allowed the bronzing liquid 24 hours to dry, remove any excess bronzing powder by first vacuuming (do not let the nozzle touch the surface) and then rinsing

with lukewarm water. Another method is to press the surface lightly with a damp cloth.

7. Remove the stencil, and apply a clear finish compatible with the underlying finishing materials.

## IMITATION GOLD COATINGS

Metallic colored enamels and lacquers in various shades of bronze and gold can be brushed or sprayed onto the surface. Both the enamel and lacquer must be stirred constantly to prevent the metallic colored pigments from settling to the bottom of the can. If you are using a spray can, shake the can often to keep the nozzle clean.

The surface must be properly prepared and sealed before applying the enamel or lacquer. The procedures are described in Chapter 11 (LACQUER FINISHES) and Chapter 12 (PAINT AND ENAMEL FINISHES).

## SPECIAL EFFECTS

The finishing schedules for gilding (gold leafing) described earlier in this chapter may be extended with several more steps to give an interesting antiquing effect. The gilding finishing schedule ended with the burnishing (polishing) of the gold leaf (see Step 12). This can be extended as follows:

1. Cover the entire surface (including the gold leaf) with a coat of white enamel. A white water or oil-base paint may also be used.

2. Before the coat has dried, take a soft, clean, lint-free cloth and wipe the enamel (or paint) from the high points of the gilding.

3. Allow sufficient time for the surface to completely dry.

4. Apply a glaze (raw umber mixed with varnish) to the entire surface. Wipe away portions of the glaze to obtain a shaded effect.

5. After the glaze is completely dry, smooth it with a very fine steel wool.

6. Apply a wax and rub the surface gently with a clean, lint-free cloth.

Gold leaf (as well as silver and other types of metal leaf) may be antiqued or given a marbleizing effect. For more information, read the appropriate sections in Chapter 15 (ANTIQUING AND RELATED TECHNIQUES).

# Chapter 17

# Decorating Furniture

A variety of techniques for decorating furniture have been developed over the years. Those that will be considered in this chapter are primarily the type that involve adding or attaching a decorating material to the surface of the finish. Antiquing and related finishing procedures (distressing, marbleizing, wood graining, etc.) have already been examined in Chapter 15. The use of gold coloring to decorate furniture has also been described in a separate chapter (Chapter 16. GILDING AND BRONZING).

This chapter concerns itself with a description of the following furniture decorating techniques:

1. Decoupage,
2. Flocking,
3. Decorating with fabric,
4. Decorating with wallpaper,
5. Stenciling,
6. Using decalcomania transfers,
7. Attaching relief carvings.

All of these furniture decorating techniques involve the addition of some sort of decorative material to the finish. Some, such as decoupage and flocking, require a slight modification of the finish.

## DECOUPAGE

Decoupage is the decorative process of pasting or gluing pictures, fabrics, photographs, or, for that matter, any suitable flat material to a base (in this case the surface of the furniture) and covering it with a clear finish. It is easy, enjoyable, and fully satisfying.

Decoupage is a decorating technique that dates from the late seventeenth and early eighteenth centuries. It represents the attempts of European cabinetmakers to imitate the beautiful lacquer furniture being imported at that time from Japan and China. Although originating in Italy, it quickly spread to France, Germany, England and other European countries in which it resulted in creating unique forms and styles. Its great popularity in eighteenth

Fig. 1. A decoupage print sold in arts and crafts stores.

century France earned it its name: *decoupage* (a noun derived from the French verb *decouper* "to cut out, cut up").

The subjects and designs are practically limitless and are found everywhere in your daily life. For example, magazines provide excellent colored illustrations for decoupage subjects. Other excellent sources are postcards and greeting cards. Arts and crafts stores also carry prints suitable for decoupage (Fig. 1). Perhaps the only real limitations is the size of the design. The size should be such that it is "in scale" to the surface area for which it is intended. That is to say, it should not be so out of proportion that it destroys the balance of the overall appearance.

## DECOUPAGE MATERIALS

The materials required for decoupage are as follows:

1. The illustrations or materials (photographs, sketches, pictures, fabrics, etc.) to be done with decoupage.
2. Two pairs of small scissors for trimming the illustration or material. One pair should be straight, the other pair curved.
3. Tweezers for handling small objects.
4. A lint-free soft cloth or tack rag for removing the dust and residue of any sanding operations from the surface.
5. A supply of very fine to fine sandpaper is recommended for the surface preparation.
6. A sealer. This will be a thinned version of the topcoat, or a thinned shellac (a shellac sealer can be used under most lacquers and varnishes).
7. Glue or paste for attaching the design to the surface.
8. An undercoating. These are usually paints or enamels and provide a flat, opaque background to the design.
9. A clear topcoat.

A word of caution: the sealer, undercoating, and topcoat *must all be compatible with one another.* Remember that the various manufacturers use different formulas for the production of their materials. Moreover, certain finishing materials are by their very nature incompatible with others. The results of combining incompatible finishing materials are very discouraging. Sometimes the topcoat will never completely dry, retaining a permanent tacky condition. Another effect is for the sealer or undercoating to bleed through into the topcoat causing the finish to lift or bulge. The only solution to the problem is the time consuming one of completely stripping off the finish and starting all over. It would be better to select the finishing materials with care and avoid this type of problem altogether. If you have any doubts, follow the manufacturer's recommendations.

Decoupage materials are very easily obtained almost anywhere in the United States. If local retail outlets do not carry them, there are a number of mail-order houses that do. One of the most complete lines of decoupage supplies is offered by Patricia Nimocks, Inc., 12200 Shelbyville Road, Middletown, Kentucky 40043. A catalog is available on request. I might also add that Patricia Nimocks is considered by many to be the contemporary dean of the decoupage decorative technique. For those who wish to pursue this subject in greater depth I would recommend reading her very informative book *Decoupage* (Charles Scribner's Sons, 1968).

Every kind of material necessary for decoupage is commercially available. This includes not only the basic finishing materials, prints, illustrations and other items, but also small pieces of furniture (magazine racks, boxes, small tables, etc.) in an unfinished condition.

## THE DECOUPAGE PROCEDURE

The procedure for applying a decoupage design to a wood surface is as follows (Fig. 2):

1. Sand the surface with a fine grade of sandpaper (6/0). The surface must be smooth and clean. Remove all dust resulting from the sanding with a tack rag or other appriate means.

2. Apply a sealer over the old finish. The type of sealer you use will depend upon the type of topcoat already on the surface. If you applied the original topcoat and you still have the finishing materials, the manufacturer will most

323

Courtesy Deft, Inc.

Fig. 2. The decoupage procedure.

likely have suggested a suitable sealer in the instructions.
If you did not apply the original topcoat, it would be wise
to test a small portion of it (preferably on the bottom or
some other area not usually in view). A sealer of thinned
shellac will probably be your best bet. A shellac sealer
can be applied over paint, wax, and many other types of
surfaces without causing the old topcoat to lift and combine with the newer finishing materials.

3.  Allow the sealer coat enough time to thoroughly dry.
Sand it lightly with a fine grade of sandpaper (6/0),
removing all dust resulting from the sanding. Apply the

desired undercoating. Remember that it must be compatible chemically with the sealer and topcoat you have selected. Allow the undercoating enough time to thoroughly dry.

5. Choose a suitable design and trim it to the desired size. Careless cutting will detract from the final overall appearance so a certain amount of care must be taken with this step. The beginner should not expect to obtain excellent results on the first attempt. Cutting is much more difficult than it looks, and requires some degree of practice.

6. Apply water paste or white glue to the back of the design and to the area which it will cover. The paste or glue should be diluted so that lumps will not form between the surface and the design.

7. Press the design onto the surface and smooth out all wrinkles and any excess paste or glue. Wipe away the excess paste or glue with a damp cloth, and allow sufficient time for it to completely dry. Both water paste and white glue clean up very easily.

8. A clear lacquer or varnish or the specially prepared coatings provided with decoupage kits can now be applied to the entire surface area as the topcoat. The number of coatings applied will depend upon the desired effect. For example, a varnish topcoat could have as many as 15 to 20 coats. Allow each coat sufficient time to dry. After having applied the first nine or ten coats, wet sand the surface with a fine grade of waterproof sandpaper.

9. Apply the remaining coats, allowing each to thoroughly dry before applying the next one. The maximum number of topcoats one should use is really an individual decision. However, the minimum number is governed by the amount of topcoat required to cover the design without any noticeable transition between it and the surrounding area. After each coat has dried, test it lightly by running your finger across the surface. When the surface is smooth and even, you have reached the minimum number of topcoats.

10. As soon as the final coat has dried, it should be lightly, but thoroughly, rubbed with a fine grade of sandpaper. This will be a wet rubbing and is designed to produce a uniformly smooth surface that imparts a soft, satiny glow. A fine grade of steel wool or pumice and rottenstone (oil may be used as a lubricant instead of water) may be substituted for the sandpaper.

11. Remove any residue left by Step 10, make certain that the surface is completely dry, and apply several coats of a paste wax. Polish the surface with a soft lint-free cloth.

Some finishers prefer to sand after each topcoat application rather than once after nine or ten have been applied (see Step 8 above). This will take longer, but it will probably increase the smoothness of the surface. Surface uniformity and smoothness are the primary reasons for sanding. Take particular care not to sand through the topcoat and damage the illustration or object used in the decoupage. Always sand lightly and work slowly. Haste not only makes waste in this case, it also causes disasters.

If there is any printing on the reverse side of an illustration to be used in decoupage, it should be sealed so that it will not bleed through the illustration. A diluted solution of white glue is ideal for this purpose. Make certain that the glue sealer has dried before proceeding to the next step. The same results can be obtained by lightly spraying the surface with clear lacquer. This also reduces the tendency of the paper to wrinkle.

The coloring on the surface of the illustration or object used in the decoupage can also breed through into the topcoat. This, too, may be prevented by sealing the surface. A clear lacquer spray or a thin washcoat of thinned shellac is recommended for this purpose (subject always, of course, to the chemical compatibility with the topcoat as well as the coloring composition of the illustration or object being covered.

## FLOCKING

Flocking (Fig. 3) is a procedure for creating a soft, felt-like surface by spraying material fibers onto a background coating of

Fig. 3. Process of flocking.

enamel, lacquer, varnish, or water-soluble glue. It was originally a novelty finish, but it has become so widely used that it is now regarded as one of the standard finishing procedures. Not only is it employed for its decorative effect, but also quite commonly for such utilitarian uses as drawer linings, table tops, and similar items.

All the equipment and supplies necessary for preparing the surface up to (but not including) the application of the flock are the same as those listed for other finishing processes. However, two items unique to flocking are the sprayer and the supply of flock fibers.

327

The sprayer is a simple hand-operated insecticide sprayer that can be purchased at any hardware store, garden supply store, or nursery. *Never* use a sprayer that has already been used to spray an insecticide. They are so relatively inexpensive that it is simply not worth the trouble worrying about whether or not you got the sprayer clean enough to use in the flocking operation. Special flock spraying guns (both powered and hand-operated) are avaliable from the manufacturers of flocking supplies, but these do not do the job any better than the simple insecticide sprayer.

Flock is commercially available in many different types of fibers (e.g. wool, cotton, rayon, etc.) and fiber colors (Fig. 4). Fiber sizes range up to ¼ inch in length, and are produced so that all fibers are of the same length in a specific size. By selecting a particular type and length of fiber, various materials can be

Fig. 4. Flocking material.

Courtesy Craft Master Corp.

simulated. For example, cotton flock will produce a finish having the appearance of suede, and rayon flock produces the texture and characteristics of velvet or velour.

Flocking is a relatively easy decorative technique for the beginner to learn, and the results can be quite satisfying.

The steps in the flocking procedure are as follows:

1. Prepare the surface according to the instructions given in Chapter 7. As is always the case, the surface must be clean and smooth.

2. Seal the surface. The sealer selected should be compatible with the flock undercoating. This is particularly true if lacquer is selected for the undercoating. The safest procedure is to follow the manufacturer's recommendations.

3. Apply the undercoating. This can be done by brushing or spraying, although the latter method is especially recommended for lacquer. Generally the manufacturer of the flocking material will recommend his own undercoating. If enamels, varnishes, or lacquers are used, they should be thinned before application.

4. Allow the undercoating to dry until it is tacky to the touch.

5. Spray the flocking material onto the tacky surface. Try to cover the surface with a uniform layer of flock. Avoid leaving thin spots.

6. Allow the surface about 24 hours to become completely dry. Blow or shake off the excess flock. Vacuuming is also recommended so long as the nozzle of the hose or attachment (the brush type) does not touch the surface. Do *not* brush off the excess flock. Brushing could result in removing part of the flock attached to the finish.

Flock designs (flowers, symbols, etc.) can be created by using a stencil. The stencil should be cut from oiled stencil paper. When using the stencil, take particular care not to allow any of the undercoating for the flock to get under the edges of the stencil.

## FABRIC FINISHES

Fabrics are also used for decorative finishes. They are cut to fit panels and other surface areas of furniture. Because of the relative thickness of a piece of fabric, it is best to use it on a portion of the surface bordered by a raised trim. In this respect, pieces of colored burlap provide an interesting decorative effect on a child's dresser or playroom furniture.

Fabric can be attached with white glue or paste. Coat both the back of the fabric and the area to which it is to be attached. Press down on the fabric and smooth from the center out toward the edges until all the excess glue or paste is squeezed out at the edges. Wipe away the excess paste with a damp, clean cloth.

## WALLPAPER FINISHES

Wallpaper can be used in the same way as fabrics to decorate the larger surface areas of furniture. Wallpapers come in an almost unlimited variety of designs, colors, and textures, so the finisher is provided with a great deal of latitude in selection.

The same white glues or pastes used to attach fabrics can also be used for wallpaper. The method of attachment is also the same. Coat both the back of the wallpaper and the area of the surface to which it is to be attached with the glue or paste. Position the wallpaper, cover it with a piece of transparent plastic to protect it from fingerprints, and press out the excess glue by smoothing from the center out toward the edges. Wipe away the excess glue or paste with a clean, damp cloth.

## STENCILING

*Stenciling* is a decorating technique in which designs are added to surfaces by means of pre-cut patterns (stencils). Stenciling can be done with paint or with bronzing powders. Both techniques use the same kind of stencil.

A *stencil* is a pattern (design, letters, or numbers) cut into a sheet of stencil paper (although other materials can be used) which is affixed to the surface of a piece of furniture. The cut-out areas of the stencil expose the surface that is to be decorated.

Stenciling with paint requires a special brush. The brush strokes are almost vertical, using an up and down motion. The paint is applied in a direction away from the edges of the stencil and toward the center. This prevents paint from working up under the edges of the stencil and marring the outline of the design.

Instead of using paint, you might want to try applying flock material to the open areas of the stencil (see FLOCKING in this chapter).

The stencil should be stiffened with a thin coat of shellac (even if you are using stencil paper). Particular care must be taken when attaching the stencil to the surface of the furniture. Every edge of the stencil must be tight against the surface or paint will seep through.

The stencil can be affixed to the surface with tape or by pressing it into the tacky surface of a coat of varnish. Complicated designs have narrow ties between sections that "float" free within major cut-out areas. These can be painted out after the stencil paper is removed from the surface.

Another method of stenciling is to make a separate stencil for each part of a design. A variation is to mark out certain portions of the design in order to add other colors. Both these methods take considerable time and patience. A fine sable brush is used for touching up the stencil.

## DECALCOMANIA TRANSFERS AND DECALS

*Decalcomania transfers* (decals) are colorful designs and pictures that can be affixed to a surface for an additional decorative touch.

These decals consist of a specially coated paper which is covered with a clear varnish or lacquer. A design or picture is superimposed over this clear finish. This is done by painting, hand drawing, or printing.

The decal is first soaked in warm water until the varnish or lacquer film (with the design or picture imprinted on its surface) frees itself from the paper backing. It is then placed on the surface to be decorated.

It is becoming increasingly difficult to find good decals in stores. Some of the smaller arts and crafts stores may still carry

331

them, but they are no longer as popular as they once were. However, for those who are interested in decorating furniture with decals, it is now possible to make decals from any kind of illustration (magazine pictures, greeting cards, calendars, etc.) with a special transfer process in kit form. These kits are marketed under the trade name *Decal-it,* and consist essentially of the three following chemicals:

1. A transfer emulsion,
2. A waterbase glaze,
3. A clear acrylic varnish.

The illustration is coated with the transfer emulsion and

Fig. 5. Coating the picture with the transfer emulsion.

allowed to set for at least 6 hours (Fig. 5). The illustration is then soaked in water until the paper can be pulled from the back of the decal illustration (Fig. 6). The back of the decal illustra-

Fig. 6. Removing the paper after soaking in water.

tion is coated with the transfer emulsion, allowed to dry, and mounted on the wood surface. It is then coated with the waterbase glaze and the clear acrylic varnish.

## ATTACHING RELIEF CARVINGS

Another method of decorating furniture is by attaching relief carvings and applying a finish that matches the rest of the surface

Fig. 7. Examples of wood carvings.

(or one that creates a contrast between the carving and the background). Fig. 7 illustrates some typical examples of relief carvings. They are available unfinished through mail-order firms specializing in wood finishing materials, and many local retail outlets.

# Index

# INDEX

342

# AUDEL BOOKS *practical reading for profit*

## APPLIANCES

### Air Conditioning (23159)

Domestic, commercial, and automobile air conditioning fully explained in easily-understood language. Troubleshooting charts aid in making diagnosis and repair of system troubles.

### Commercial Refrigeration (23195)

**Installation, operation, and repair of commercial refrigeration systems.** Included are ice-making plants, locker plants, grocery and supermarket refrigerated display cases, etc. Trouble charts aid in the diagnosis and repair of defective systems.

### Air Conditioning and Refrigeration Library—2 Vols. (23196)

### Home Appliance Servicing (23016)

**A practical "How-To-Do-It" book for electric & gas servicemen, mechanics & dealers.** Covers principles, servicing and repairing of home appliances. Tells how to locate troubles, make repairs, reassemble and connect, wiring diagrams and testing methods. Tells how to fix electric refrigerators, washers, ranges, toasters, ironers, broilers, dryers, vacuum sweepers, fans, and other appliances.

### Home Refrigeration and Air Conditioning (23133)

Covers basic principles, servicing, operation, and repair of modern household refrigerators and air conditioners. Automotive air conditioners are also included. Troubleshooting charts aid in trouble diagnosis. **A gold mine of essential facts for engineers, servicemen, and users.**

### Oil Burners (23151)

Provides complete information on all types of oil burners and associated equipment. Discusses burners—blowers—ignition transformers—electrodes—nozzles—fuel pumps—filters—controls. Installation and maintenance are stressed. Troubleshooting charts permit rapid diagnosis of system troubles and possible remedies to correct them.

## AUTOMOTIVE

### Automobile Guide (23192)

**New revised edition.** Practical reference for auto mechanics, servicemen, trainees, and owners. Explains theory, construction, and servicing of modern domestic motorcars. FEATURES: All parts of an automobile—engines—pistons—rings—connecting rods—crankshafts—valves—cams—timing—cooling systems—Fuel-feed systems—carbureators — automatic choke — transmissions — clutches — universals — propeller shafts—dierentials—rear axles—running gear—brakes—wheel alignment—steering gear—tires—lubrication—ignition systems—generators and alternators—starters—lighting systems—batteries—air conditioning—cruise controls—emission control systems.

### Auto Engine Tune-up (23181)

**New revised edition.** This popular how-to-do-it guide shows exactly how to tune your car engine for extra power, gas economy, and fewer costly repairs. New emission-control systems are explained along with the proper methods for correcting faults and making adjustments to keep these systems in top operating condition.

### Automotive Library—2 Vols. (23198)

## Diesel Engine Manual  (23199)

A practical treatise on the theory, operation and maintenance of modern Diesel engines. Explains Diesel principles—valves—timing—fuel pumps—pistons and rings—cylinders—lubrication—cooling system—fuel oil—engine indicator—governors—engine reversing—answers on operation—calculations. AN IMPORTANT GUIDE FOR ENGINEERS, OPERATORS. STUDENTS.

## Foreign Auto Repair Manual  (23078)

Contains complete, service and repair data for the most popular imported makes, including Fiat, Hillman Minx, M.G., Opel, Peugot, Renault, SAAB, Simca, Volkswagen, and Volvo. Introductory chapters provide complete data on operation and maintenance of fuel and ignition systems.

## Gas Engine Manual  (23061)

A completely practical book covering the construction, operation and repair of all types of modern gas engines. Part I covers gas-engine principles; engine parts; auxiliaries; timing methods; ignition systems. Part II covers troubleshootng, adjustment and repairs.

## Truck & Tractor Guide  (23020)

A shop companion for truck mechanics and drivers—shop foremen—garagemen—maintenance men—helpers—owners—troubleshooters—fleet maintenance men—bus mechanics and drivers—farm tractor operators and mechanics. Covers gas and diesel motor principles—construction—operation—miantenance—repair—service operations —troubleshooting—engine tune-up—carburetor adjusting—ignition tuning—brakes—service of all parts.—1001 FACTS AT YOUR FINGER TIPS.

# BUILDING AND MAINTENANCE

## Answers on Blueprint Reading  (23041)

Covers all types of blueprint reading for mechanics and builders. The man who can read blueprints is in line for a better job. This book gives you the secret language, step by step in easy stages. NO OTHER TRADE BOOK LIKE IT

## Builders Encyclopedia  (23178)

A book of terms used by members of the building and construction trade. A valuable book for the carpenter, plumber, electrician, steel erector, bridge builder, general contractor, architect and others in the building and construction industry.

## Building Construction and Design  (23180)

A completely revised and rewritten version of Audel's **Architects and Builders Guide.** New illustrations and extended coverage of material makes this treatment of the subject more valuable than ever. Anyone connected in any way with the building industry will profit from the information contained in this book.

## Building Maintenance  (23140)

A comprehensive book on the practical aspects of building maintenance. Chapters are included on: painting and decorating; plumbing and pipe fitting; carpentry; calking and glazing; concrete and masonry; roofing; sheet metal; electrical maintenance; air conditioning and refrigeration; insect and rodent control; heating maintenance management; cutodial practices: A BOOK FOR BUILDING OWNERS, MANAGERS, AND MAINTENANCE PERSONNEL.

## Grounds Maintenance  (23186)

A comprehensive guide for the homeowner, industrial, municipal, and estate grounds-keepers. Information on proper care of annual and perennial flowers; various house plants; greenhouse design and construction; insect and rodent control; complete lawn care; shrubs and trees; and maintenance of walks, roads, and traffic areas. Various types of maintenance equipment are also discussed.

## Building- and Grounds-Maintenance Library—
## 2 Vols. (23197)

## Carpenters & Builders Library—4 Vols. (23169)

**A practical illustrated trade assistant on modern construction for carpenters, builders, and all woodworkers.** Explains in practical, concise language and illustrations all the principles, advances and short cuts based on modern practice. How to calculate various jobs.

Vol. 1—(23170)—Tools, steel square, saw filing, joinery, cabinets.
Vol. 2—(23171)—Mathematics, plans, specifications, estimates.
Vol. 3—(23172)—House and roof framing, laying out, foundations.
Vol. 4—(23173)—Doors, windows, stairs, millwork, painting.

## Carpentry and Building (23142)

**Answers to the problems encountered in today's building trades.** The actual questions asked of an architect by carpenters and builders are answered in this book. No apprentice or journeyman carpenter should be without the help this book can offer.

## Do-It-Yourself Encyclopedia (23207)

**An all-in-one home repair and project guide for all do-it-yourselfers.** Packed with step-by-step plans, thousands of photos, helpful charts. A really authentic, truly monumental, home-repair and home-project guide.

## Home Workshop & Tool Handy Book (23208)

**The most modern, up-to-date manual ever designed for home craftsmen and do-it-yourselfers.** Tells how to set up your own home workshop, (basement, garage, or spare room), all about the various hand and power tools (when, where, and how to use them, etc.). Covers both wood- and metal-working principles and practices. An all-in-one workshop guide for handy men, professionals and students.

## Plumbers and Pipe Fitters Library—3 Vols. (23155)

A practical illustrated trade assistant and reference for master plumbers, journeyman and apprentice pipe fitters, gas fitters and helpers, builders, contractors, and engineers. Explains in simple language, illustrations, diagrams, charts, graphs and pictures, the principles of modern plumbing and pipe-fitting practices.

Vol. 1—(23152)—Materials, tools, calculations.
Vol. 2—(23153)—Drainage, fittings, fixtures.
Vol. 3—(23154)—Installation, heating, welding

## Masons and Builders Library—2 Vols. (23185)

**A practical illustrated trade assistant on modern construction for bricklayers, stonemasons, cement workers, plasterers, and tile setters.** Explains in clear language and with detailed illustrations all the principles, advances, and shortcuts based on modern practice—including how to figure and calculate various jobs.

Vol. 1—(23182)—Concrete, Block, Tile, Terrazzo.
Vol. 2—(23183)—Bricklaying, Plastering, Rock Masonry, Clay Tile.

## Upholstering (23189)

**Upholstering is explained for the average householder and apprentice upholsterer in this Audel text.** Selection of coverings, stuffings, springs, and other upholstering material is made simple. From repairing and regluing of the bare frame, to the final sewing or tacking, for antiques and most modern pieces, this book gives complete and clearly written instructions and numerous illustrations.

## Questions and Answers for Plumbers Examinations   (23206)

Many questions are answered as to types of fixtures to use, size of pipe to install, design of systems, size and location of septic tank systems, and procedures used in installing material. Subjects such as traps, cleanouts, drainage, vents, water supply and distribution, sewage treatment, plastic pipe, steam and hot water fittings, just to name a few.

## ELECTRICITY-ELECTRONICS

### Wiring Diagrams for Light & Power   (23028)

Electricians, wiremen, linemen, plant superintendents, construction engineers, electrical contractors, and students will find these diagrams a valuable source of practical help. Each diagram is complete and self-explaining. A PRACTICAL HANDY BOOK OF ELECTRICAL HOOK-UPS.

### Electric Motors   (23150)

Covers the construction, theory of operation, connection, control, maintenance, and troubleshooting of all types of electric motors. A HANDY GUIDE FOR ELECTRICIANS AND ALL ELECTRICAL WORKERS.

### Practical Electricity   (23160)

This updated version is a ready reference book, giving complete instruction and practical information on the rules and laws of electricity—maintenance of electrical machinery—AC and DC motors—wiring diagrams—lighting—house and power wiring —meter and instrument connections—transformer connectors—circuit breakers— power stations—automatic substations. THE KEY TO A PRACTICAL UNDERSTANDING OF ELECTRICITY.

### House Wiring—2nd Edition   (23210)

Answers many questions in plain simple language concerning all phases of house wiring. A ready reference book with over 100 illustrations and concise interpretations of many rulings contained in the National Electrical Code. Electrical contractors, wiremen, and electricians will find this book invaluable as a tool in the electrical field

### Guide to the 1971 National Electric Code   (23193)

**This important and informative book is now revised to conform to the 1971 National Electrical Code.** Offers an interpretation and simplification of the rulings contained in the Code. Electrical contractors, wiremen, and electricians will find this book invaluable for a more complete understanding of the NEC.

### Questions and Answers for Electricians Examinations   (23200)

**Newly revised to conform to the 1971 National Electrical Code.** A practical book to help you prepare for all grades of electricians examinations. A helpful review of fundamental principles underlying each question and answer needed to prepare you to solve any new or similar problem. Covers the NEC; questions and answers for license tests; Ohm's law with applied examples, hook-ups for motors, lighting, and instruments. A COMPLETE REVIEW FOR ALL ELECTRICAL WORKERS.

### Electrical Library—6 Vols.   (23194)

### Electric Generating Systems   (23179)

Answers many questions concerning the selection, installation, operation, and maintenance of engine-driven electric generating systems for emergency, standby, and away-from-the-power-line applications. Private homes, hospitals, radio and television stations, and pleasure boats are only a few of the installations that owners either desire or require for primary power or for standby use in case of commercial power failure. THE MOST COMPREHENSIVE COVERAGE OF THIS SUBJECT TO BE FOUND TODAY.

## Electrical Power Calculations    (23050)

**275 TYPICAL PROBLEMS WORKED OUT.** Presents and explains the mathematical formulas and the fundamental electrical laws for all the everday, practical problems in both AC and DC electricity. EVERY ELECTRICAL WORKER AND STUDENT NEEDS THIS MODERN MATHEMATICAL TOOL.

## Electronic Security Systems    (23205)

**Protect your home and business.** A basic and practical text written for the electrician, electronic technician, security director and do-it-yourself householder or businessman. Such subjects as sensors and encoders, indicators and alarms, electrical control and alarm circuits, security communications, closed circuit television, and security system installations are covered.

## New Electric Library

**For engineers, electricians, electrical workers, mechanics and students.** Presenting in simple, concise form the fundamental principles, rules and applications of applied electricity. Fully illustrated with diagrams and sketches, also calculations and tables for ready reference. Based on the best knowledge and experience of applied electricity.

Vol.   1 (23031)—Electricity, magnetism, armature winding, repairs.

Vol.   3 (23033)—Electrical testing instruments, storage battery construction and repairs.

Vol.   4 (23034)—Alternating current principles and diagrams, power factor, alternators, transformers.

Vol.   8 (23038)—Railways, signals, elevators.

Vol.   9 (23039)—Radio, telephone, telegraph, television, motion pictures.

Vol. 10 (23040)—Refrigeration, illumination, welding, X-ray, modern electrical appliances.

## ENGINEERS-MECHANICS-MACHINISTS
## Machinists Library    (23174)

**Covers modern machine-shop practice.** Tells how to set up and operate lathes, screw and milling machines, shapers, drill presses and all other machine tools. A complete reference library. A SHOP COMPANION THAT ANSWERS YOUR QUESTIONS.

Vol. 1—(23175)—Basic Machine Shop.
Vol. 2—(23176)—Machine Shop.
Vol. 3—(23177)—Toolmakers Handy Book

## Millwrights and Mechanics Guide— 2nd Edition    (23201)

**Practical information on plant installation, operation, and maintenance for millwrights, mechanics, maintenance men, erectors, riggers, foremen, inspectors, and superintendents.** Partial contents: • Drawing and Sketching • Machinery Installation • Power-Transmission Equipment • Couplings • Packing and Seals • Bearings • Structural Steel • Mechanical Fasteners • Pipe Fittings and Valves • Carpentry • Sheet-Metal Work • Blacksmithing • Rigging • Electricity • Welding • Mathematics and much more.

## Practical Guide to Mechanics    (23102)

**A convenient reference book valuable for its practical and concise explanations of the applicable laws of physics.** Presents all the basics of mechanics in everyday language, illustrated with practical examples of their applications in various fields.

## Questions & Answers for Engineers and Firemans Examinations  (23053)

**An aid for stationary, marine, diesel & hoisting engineers' examinations for all grades of licenses.** A new concise review explaining in detail the principles, facts and figures of practical engineering. Questions & Answers.

## Welders Guide—2nd Edition  (23202)

**New revised edition.** Covers principles of electric, oxyacetylene, thermit, unionmelt welding for sheet metal; spot and pipe welds; pressure vessels; aluminum, copper brass, bronze, plastics, and other metals; airplane work; surface hardening and hard facing; cutting brazing; underwater welding; eye protection. EVERY WELDER SHOULD OWN THIS GUIDE.

# FLUID POWER

## Practical Guide to Fluid Power  (23136)

**An essential book for the owner, operator, supervisor, or maintenance man concerned with hydraulic or pneumatic equipment.** A complete coverage of modern design, application, and repair of fluid power devices. Fully illustrated.

## Pumps  (23167)

**A detailed book on all types of pumps** from the old-fashioned kitchen variety to the most modern types. Covers construction, application, installation, and troubleshooting.

# MATHEMATICS

## Practical Mathematics for Everyone—2 Vols.  (23112)

**A concise and reliable guide to the understanding of practical mathematics.** People from all walks of life, young and old alike, will find the information contained in these two books just what they have been looking for. The mathematics discussed is for the everyday problems that arise in every household and business.
Vol. 1—(23110)—Basic Mathematics.
Vol. 2—(23111)—Financial Mathematics.

# OUTBOARD MOTORS

## Outboard Motors & Boating  (23168)

Provides the information necessary to adjust, repair, and maintain all types of outboard motors. Valuable information concerning boating rules and regulations is also included.

# RADIO-TELEVISION-AUDIO

## Handbook of Commercial Sound Installations  (23126)

**A practical complete guide to planning commercial systems,** selecting the most suitable equipment, and following through with the most proficient servicing methods. For technicians and the professional and businessman interested in installing a sound system.

## Practical Guide to Auto Radio Repair  (23128)

**A complete servicing guide for all types of auto radios,** including hybrid, all-transistor, and FM . . . PLUS removal instructions for all late model radios. Fully illustrated.

## Practical Guide to Servicing Electronic Organs  (23132)

**Detailed, illustrated discussions of the operation and servicing of electronic organs.** Including models by Allen, Baldwin, Conn, Hammond, Kinsman, Lowrey, Magnavox, Thomas, and Wurlitzer.

## Radioman's Guide    (23163)

**Audel best-seller,** containing the latest information on radio and electronics from the basics through transistors. Covers radio fundamentals—Ohm's law—physics of sound as related to radio—radio-wave transmission—test equipment—power supplies—resistors, inductors, and capacitors—transformers—vacuum tubes—transistors—speakers—antennas—troubleshooting. A complete guide and a perfect preliminary to the study of television servicing.

## Television Service Manual    (23162)

**Includes the latest designs and information.** Thoroughly covers television with transmitter theory, antenna designs, receiver circuit operation and the picture tube. Provides the practical information necessary for accurate diagnosis and repair of both black-and-white and color television receivers. A MUST BOOK FOR ANYONE IN TELEVISION.

## Radio-TV Library—2 Vol.    (23161)

SHEET METAL

## Sheet Metal Workers Handy Book    (23046)

**Containing practical information and important facts and figures.** Easy to understand. Fundamentals of sheet metal layout work. Clearly written in everyday language. Ready reference index.